AF766817

The Limits of Law and Development

The book examines the well-established field of 'law and development' and asks whether the concept of development and discourses on law and development have outlived their usefulness.

The contributors ask whether instead of these amorphous and contested concepts we should focus upon social injustices such as patriarchy, impoverishment, human rights violations, the exploitation of indigenous peoples, and global heating? If we abandoned the idea of development, would we end up adopting another, equally problematic term to replace a concept which, for all its flaws, serves as a commonly understood shorthand? The contributors analyse the links between conventional academic approaches to law and development, neoliberal governance and activism through historical and contemporary case studies.

The book will be of interest to students and scholars of development, international law, international economic law, governance and politics and international relations.

Sam Adelman and **Abdul Paliwala** are respectively Reader and Emeritus Professor of Law at the University of Warwick and have been involved in the internationally renowned programme on International Development Law and Human Rights since its inception in 1981 and in the founding of the global Law and Development Research Network (LDRN).

Part of the
LAW, DEVELOPMENT AND GLOBALIZATION
series

series editors
Julio Faundez, *University of Warwick, UK*
Adriaan Bedner, *University of Leiden, The Netherlands*

for information about the series and details of previous and forthcoming titles, see https://www.routledge.com/law/series/CAV30

A GlassHouse book

The Limits of Law and Development

Neoliberalism, Governance and Social Justice

Edited by Sam Adelman
and Abdul Paliwala

Routledge
Taylor & Francis Group
a GlassHouse Book
London and New York

The Limits of Law and Development
Neoliberalism, Governance and Social Justice
Edited by Sam Adelman and Abdul Paliwala

First published 2021
by Routledge
2 Park Square, Milton Park, Abingdon, Oxon OX14 4RN

and by Routledge
605 Third Avenue, New York, NY 10017

First issued in paperback 2022

Routledge is an imprint of the Taylor & Francis Group, an informa business

A Glasshouse book

© 2021 selection and editorial matter, Sam Adelman and Abdul Paliwala; individual chapters, the contributors

The right Sam Adelman and Abdul Paliwala to be identified as the authors of the editorial material, and of the authors for their individual chapters, has been asserted in accordance with sections 77 and 78 of the Copyright, Designs and Patents Act 1988.

All rights reserved. No part of this book may be reprinted or reproduced or utilised in any form or by any electronic, mechanical, or other means, now known or hereafter invented, including photocopying and recording, or in any information storage or retrieval system, without permission in writing from the publishers.

Trademark notice: Product or corporate names may be trademarks or registered trademarks, and are used only for identification and explanation without intent to infringe.

Publisher's Note
The publisher has gone to great lengths to ensure the quality of this reprint but points out that some imperfections in the original copies may be apparent.

British Library Cataloguing-in-Publication Data
A catalogue record for this book is available from the British Library
Library of Congress Cataloging-in-Publication Data
Names: Adelman, Sam, editor. | Paliwala, Abdul, editor.
Title: The limits of law and development: neoliberalism, governance and social justice/edited by Sam Adelman and Abdul Paliwala.
Description: Abingdon, Oxon; New York, NY: Routledge, 2020. | "A Glasshouse book" | Includes bibliographical references and index.
Identifiers: LCCN 2020011017 (print) | LCCN 2020011018 (ebook) | ISBN 9781138300354 (hardback) | ISBN 9780203733561 (ebook)
Subjects: LCSH: Law and economic development. | Sociological jurisprudence.
Classification: LCC K3820 .L558 2020 (print) | LCC K3820 (ebook) | DDC 340/.115–dc23
LC record available at https://lccn.loc.gov/2020011017
LC ebook record available at https://lccn.loc.gov/2020011018

ISBN: 978-1-138-30035-4 (hbk)
ISBN: 978-0-367-52800-3 (pbk)
ISBN: 978-0-203-73356-1 (ebk)

DOI: 10.4324/9780203733561

Typeset in Galliard
by MPS Limited, Dehradun

This book is dedicated to the memory of

Dwijen Rangnekar
(17 April 1965–30 October 2015)

and

Peter Fitzpatrick
(1 November 1941–20 September 2020)

Colleagues, comrades, friends and fighters for social justice

Contents

List of contributors

Sam Adelman teaches law and development, human rights and climate change at the University of Warwick. He was a student leader and a social justice activist during the struggle against apartheid in South Africa. He co-edited *Law and Crisis in the Third World* (1993) with Abdul Paliwala. His recent publications cover issues including climate change, climate justice, international environmental law, human rights and development. He is co-authoring a book on climate justice in the Anthropocene with Upendra Baxi. He is a research associate at Nelson Mandela University in South Africa and a visiting fellow at the University of Rosario in Colombia.

Upendra Baxi is Emeritus Professor of Law at the University of Warwick and honorary Professor at the National Law University of India (Bangalore). He has been Vice-Chancellor of the University of Delhi and University of South Gujarat. His global contribution to human rights and social justice has been recognised worldwide through lecturing and honorary awards. In India his contributions have been recognised through the prestigious national Padmashree award. During his long academic career he taught on the LLM in International Development Law and Human Rights at Warwick Law School. He was one of the four global scholars selected for William Twining's tribute to global South Scholarship in *Human Rights, Southern Voices* (2009). As an activist he has struggled for the rights of the people affected by the Bhopal disaster and for constitutionalism in India and throughout the world. His prodigious academic works include *The Future of Human Rights* (1999/2013) and *Human Rights in a Posthuman World: Critical Essays* (2007).

Radha D'Souza is Professor of International Law, Development and Conflict Studies at the University of Westminster. She previously taught law at the University of Waikato in New Zealand, and development studies, sociology and human geography at the University of Auckland. She practised law in the High Court of Mumbai in the areas of labour rights, constitutional and administrative law, public interest litigation and human rights. She worked with labour movements and democratic rights movements as an organiser and as activist lawyer. She has worked with social justice movements in the Asia-Pacific region to focus attention on the effects of international economic policies on developing countries. Her many publications include *What's Wrong with Rights? Social Movements Law and Liberal Imaginations* (2018) and *The Surveillance State: A Composition in Four Movements* (2018).

Julio Faundez is Emeritus Professor of Law at the University of Warwick where he was co-founder and main directive force of the International Economic Law programme. His main research interests are international economic law and law and development. He has written extensively on law and democracy, legal and judicial reform and has evaluated legal reform projects for the World Bank, the Department for International Development in the UK and the Inter-American Development Bank. He is editor of the book series *Law, Development and Globalization* (Routledge) and a founding editor of *The Hague Journal on the Rule of Law*.

Tomaso Ferrando is Research Professor at the University of Antwerp Law School (Law and Development Research Group) and the Institute of Development Policy. His current work is in three main research areas: the role of law in building and dismantling socially and environmentally just food systems, the construction and implications of the green bonds market, and the distributive impact of law in global value chains. He is a member of the Legal Committee of the Global Legal Action Network (GLAN), where he co-directs the section on land rights and transnational investments and is part of the Extraterritorial Obligation Consortium (ETO).

Peter Fitzpatrick died on 20 September 2020. At the time he was Honorary Professor of Law at the University of Kent and a Fellow of the Oñati International Institute for the Sociology of Law, following a distinguished academic career at the Universities of Belfast, Papua New Guinea, Kent and London, as well as teaching by invitation at universities worldwide. He was a long-term friend of Warwick's Law in Development programmes. He has been a prolific publisher of works on legal philosophy, law and social theory, law and racism, and imperialism – his best-known being *The Mythology of Modern Law* and *Modernism and the Grounds of Law*. Outside academia he has been in an international legal practice, and worked in the Prime Minister's Office in Papua New Guinea for several years.

Jennifer Lander is Lecturer in Law at De Montfort University in Leicester, where she teaches constitutional law. Her research focuses on the political and legal dynamics of national development in a globalising economy, with particular interest in understanding new patterns of state formation in frontier economies like Mongolia. She received her PhD in Law from the University of Warwick in 2017 and has a background in development studies and international relations. Prior to taking up her lectureship at De Montfort, she held an Early Career Fellowship at the Institute of Advanced Study at

Warwick. She has conducted research in Mongolia since 2012, focusing on the way that social conflict in the mining sector has catalysed significant changes in national governance. She has published a monograph on *Transnational Law and State Transformation: The Case of Extractive Development in Mongolia* (2019).

Abdul Paliwala is emeritus professor of law at the University of Warwick where he was involved in the founding and teaching of the Law in Development LLM (renamed International Development Law and Human Rights) since 1981. He previously taught at the Queen's University of Belfast, the University of Dar es Salaam and the University of Papua New Guinea, where he also worked as the Secretary of the Law Reform Commission. He was Director of the CTI Law Technology Centre for UK Law Schools, the Law Courseware Consortium, the UK Centre for Legal Education and the Electronic Law Journals Project that published the *Journal of Information Law and Technology* and *Law Social Justice and Global Development.* His work on law and development includes *Law and Crisis in the Third World* (co-edited with Sam Adelman) (1993) and *Law's Ethical Global and Theoretical Concerns: Essays in Honour of William Twining* (co-edited with Upendra Baxi and Christopher McCrudden) (2015).

Sol Picciotto is Emeritus professor, Lancaster University (UK), Senior Adviser, Tax Justice Network, visiting professor at the Centre for Law, Regulation and Governance of the Global Economy (GLOBE) at Warwick University, and senior fellow at the International Centre for Tax and Development. He has formerly taught at the University of Dar es Salaam and the School of Law, University of Warwick, where he co-founded the International Economic Law programme. His many works include *International Business Taxation: A Study of the Internationalization of Business Regulation* (1992) and *Regulating Global Corporate Capitalism* (2011) and International tax, regulatory arbitrage and the growth of transnational corporations, *Transnational Corporations* 25(3), 27–53 (2018).

Issa G. Shivji is acknowledged as a pre-eminent African scholar on human rights, social justice and development. He is currently director of the Nyerere Resource Centre, Tanzania Commission for Science and Technology. He was formerly Professor of Law, University of Dar es Salaam (1971–2006) and Mwalimu Nyerere University Professor of Pan-African Studies, University of Dar es Salaam (2008–2013). As Visiting Professor at the University of Warwick for two years, he made a substantial contribution to the Law in Development (International Development Law and Human Rights) programmes. He was Chair of the Tanzanian Commission of Inquiry into Land Matters 1994. His many publications include *The Concept of Human Rights in Africa* (1989), *Where is Uhuru? Reflections on the Struggle for Democracy in Africa* (2009), *Let the People Speak* (2009) and *Poems for the Penniless* (2019).

William Twining was Quain Professor of Jurisprudence at University College London from 1983 until 1996. He became Emeritus in 2004. He has taught in Khartoum, Dar-es-Salaam, Belfast and Warwick and at several leading American law schools. At the start of his career William taught for seven years in Sudan and Tanzania. At Warwick and elsewhere, as a prominent member of the Law in Context movement, he has contributed and published widely on jurisprudence, legal method, legal education and legal intellectual history. His *Southern Voices* project culminating in *Human Rights: Southern Voices* (2009) has promoted global awareness of global South legal scholarship. His other major recent works include *General Jurisprudence* (2009) and *Jurist in Context: A Memoir* (2019).

Preface

The two of us have taught and written about law and development in the LLM in Law in Development (formerly International Development Law and Human Rights) at Warwick Law School since the 1980s, in conjunction with many of the contributors to this volume. Our research has always been characterised by interdisciplinarity, reflecting the Law School's pioneering role in teaching law in context. This approach led us to consider the political, economic, social and cultural aspects of development and the related concept of law and development, concepts that we have consistently problematised along with the contributors to this volume. During our collaboration we have seen development metamorphose from modernisation as westernisation, through development as freedom and capabilities and the human-focused discourses that emerged from them, to neoliberal globalisation and latterly to the dominant contemporary framing as sustainable development. We have watched as the spaces of development have changed with the disappearance of the First, Second, and Third Worlds following the collapse of the Soviet Union and the emergence of the global North and South. With the neoliberal globalisation in the last quarter of the twentieth century – accompanied by the conditionalities of the IMF and the World Bank, the explosion of free but unfair trade under the aegis of the WTO, and 'good' governance and the rule of law – it became apparent that this topography of development was increasingly problematic because the existence of pockets of the 'South' found in Northern ghettoes and pockets of the 'North' in gated communities in the South blurred conventional territorially bounded conceptions of development. This prompted us to organise an international symposium to discuss changing conceptions of development and its relationship with law.

The idea that led to the symposium that resulted in this book and its forthcoming companion came from Dwijen Rangnekar, a dearly missed colleague to whom this book is dedicated, together with Peter Fitzpatrick, a long-term friend of the Law in Development programme who died shortly before publication. Participants in the symposium entitled *Beyond Development? New Imaginaries of Law and Social Justice* that took place at Warwick University in April 2016 were invited to consider whether development and law and development had outlived their usefulness; if so, what might replace them? Would it not be better to abandon such amorphous and contested concepts and focus instead on specific social injustices such as patriarchy, impoverishment, rights violations, the exploitation of indigenous peoples, global heating, etc. as many scholars have done? If we eschewed development, would we end up adopting another, equally problematic term to replace a concept which, for all its flaws, serves as a commonly understood shorthand? The contributions to this volume contain critiques that address these questions by going beyond orthodox law and development thinking. The contributors are part of an international community of scholars that created, perpetuated and enriched the distinctive approach to law and development typified at Warwick Law School. We have also learned much from our students, whose knowledge of the global South has enhanced our teaching and research. They include Sahar Shah, whose contribution to the production of this volume is greatly appreciated.

Sam Adelman and Abdul Paliwala

Introduction

Sam Adelman and Abdul Paliwala

Development

After the Second World War, development was promoted as the means whereby what was then referred to as the Third World could achieve economic growth, reduce poverty and promote social justice. In principle, development is a process of social change designed to improve the wellbeing of people. In practice, it has regularly manifested itself as underdevelopment or maldevelopment so that its scope and rationale have been vigorously contested. As Björn Hettne observes (1995: 29), it is 'one of the oldest and most powerful of all Western ideas' and is closely associated with growth and progress from backwardness to modernity and an almost teleological process of modernisation (Rostow, 1999). As Westernisation, it was designed to incorporate developing countries into global capitalism; in the Soviet model, it was the path to socialism. Ecological sustainability was not a priority in either paradigm. In the 1970s and 1980s, dependency and world systems theorists cogently argued that the development of the West depended upon long histories of colonialism and imperialism that incorporated what was then called the Third World into the global political-economy on unequal terms. Walter Rodney famously argued that Europe 'underdeveloped' Africa in pursuit of raw materials and profits, creating structural inequalities that persist to the present day (Rodney, 1972). Such arguments reflected the significant anti-development or postdevelopment backlash that emerged in the last quarter of the 20th century. For example, Arturo Escobar deployed Michel Foucault's concept of power to argue that development is a power–knowledge nexus ostensibly designed to save the victims of underdevelopment from themselves while protecting the interests of the superpowers during the Cold War (Escobar, 2011). Developmentalism became an almost evangelical ideology of salvation through industrialisation, modernisation and integration into the global political economy through the exploitation and trade of natural resources (Escobar, 2011; Esteva 1992). It was a process that Wolfgang Sachs described as intrinsically and inexorably destructive of the environment and, we might add, a process that intensifies the risks to vulnerable communities (Sachs, 1992).

Hettne writes that 'Development is a contested concept, which implies that it has meant different things from one historical situation to another and from one actor to another' (2009: 1). One of the major criticisms levelled against the concept is that it has seldom been 'owned' by those subjected to it and too often been imposed on populations through violent forms of neocolonialism and imperialism that repeatedly resulted in chronic socio-political, economic and environmental crises. Gustavo Esteva argues that 'The metaphor of development gave global hegemony to a purely Western genealogy of history, robbing peoples of different cultures of the opportunity to define the forms of their social life.' It is a concept that cannot 'delink itself from the words with which it was formed – growth, evolution, maturation', and has become totemic – a magic solution to the problems that confront us. But for many people 'this positive meaning of the word "development" ... is a reminder of what they are not ... To escape from it, they need to be enslaved to others' experiences and dreams' (Esteva 1992: 9, 10). To the objects of development in the global South, it has always been a Eurocentric, technocratic, depoliticising concept.

In response to persistent criticism, the dominant idea of development metamorphosed under the aegis of the World Bank, the International Monetary Fund (IMF) and the World Trade Organization (WTO) into human centred development (influenced by Amartya Sen's conception of development as freedom) and latterly as sustainable development. However, economic growth has remained central.[1] The emergence of neoliberalism in the early 1980s marked a crucial turning point. Hitherto, development had generally been understood as a state-driven process; afterwards, the so-called Washington Consensus promoted dogmatic market fundamentalism that demanded privatisation, deregulation, free trade in pursuit of endless economic growth, the sanctity of private property and protection of contractual and investor rights.[2] Eduardo Gudynas's (2011) argument that the classical Western idea of development has been declared dead several times in the last decades but persists in a zombie form applies equally to the neoliberal ideology that infects sustainable development. There is a significant difference between alternative development and alternatives to development. Whereas the former envisages development in a different form, the latter rejects the concept of development as irredeemable.

1 Amartya Sen (2013) attempted to shift the focus of development from growth to freedom and human capacities.

2 Williamson (1993). See Baxi's (2012) analysis of the emergence of trade-related, market-friendly human rights.

Neoclassical (especially neoliberal) economists view economic growth as essential and inevitable. Wellbeing is clearly linked to economic activity, but it is quality rather than the quantity that is crucial. As Kate Raworth (2017) observes, nothing in nature grows forever;[3] uncontrollable growth is cancerous. We are confronted with the conundrum of whether it is possible to promote the wellbeing of the Earth system and all species under a mode of production predicated upon growth – a fetishism which cannot countenance non-capitalist economic activity or commons governance (Hamilton, 2003: 184).

In Latin America, alternatives *to* development have emerged based upon Andean cosmovisions such as *buen vivir* (roughly translated as living well). Many indigenous knowledges have no concept similar to the Western idea of development. *Buen vivir* takes several forms but all seek to dissolve the society–nature dualism in eurocentric rationality, to overturn the notion that human beings are the only source of values, and to move beyond modernity's obsessions with growth and progress. It:

> moves away from the prevalence of instrumental and manipulative rationality. It rejects the modern stance that almost everything should be dominated and controlled, either persons or Nature, so as to become a means to our ends. Furthermore, the Buen Vivir does not endorse the classical understanding of a unidirectional linear progression of history, following a precise path, as several directions are possible.
>
> (Gudynas, 2011: 445)

Buen vivir is intrinsically pluralistic and rejects the hierarchies and dualisms that characterise Western philosophy but has nevertheless evolved to incorporate aspects of Western thinking where they are not antithetical, such as Western science. Its salience to sustainability flows from the conviction that wellbeing is only possible within a community in harmony with nature, symbolised by the centrality in its axiology of *Pachamama* (Mother Earth), the source of life. *Buen vivir* 'calls for a "biocentric" understanding of life in which Nature has rights of its own and an intrinsic significance regardless of its value for human life' (Ramirez, 2010: 24). As such, it provides a coherent critique of modernity and hegemonic theories of development that rejects the reduction of human identity to a *homo economicus* defined by material consumption. It has a strong communitarian ethos that promotes substantive participatory democracy and progressive visions of social, environmental and climate justice (Acosta, 2010; Acosta and Gudynas, 2011). *Buen vivir* has been incorporated into the constitutions of

3 Raworth rehearses the overwhelming arguments against using GDP as the primary measure of development, not least because of the danger this poses to the Earth system. She advocates a form of economics that addresses impoverishment within planetary limits.

Ecuador (2008) and Bolivia (2009), albeit in contradictory ways.[4] Concepts such as *Buen Vivir* are replicated in other global South cultures such as the Maori in Aotearoa/NewZealand, Ubuntu in South Africa and India (see Chapter 5, this volume). Above all, it promotes a conception of what sustainable development might mean that is markedly different to mainstream Western understandings.

Ramírez-Cendrero (2018) distinguishes between 'pure' postdevelopmental proposals such as *buen vivir* (living well or good living) and those based on the rights of nature, identifies possible spaces for an alternative to capitalist development, and clarifies the differences between alternatives to development and alternatives to capitalism. He is sceptical that postdevelopment models can transcend capitalism, although he recognises that 'post-developmentalist criticism has contributed decisively to the awareness of the physical and environmental limits of capitalism's production and consumption patterns … and the risks of neo-extractivism associated with new development strategies in some Latin American countries as merely new forms of capitalist modernization' (Ramírez-Cendrero, 2018: 15).

China's communist-capitalism constitutes an alternative to North-driven neoliberal globalisation. China's economic growth and poverty reduction is unprecedented and it has become one of the strongest players in economic development with its Belt and Road initiative with an apparent emphasis on non-intervention in domestic affairs (see Chapter 1, this volume). Nevertheless, the denial of human rights and disregard of the rule of law suggest the rise of a different oppressive imperium. As the Chinese proverb has it, be careful what you wish for, as it may come true.

Law and development

Like development discourse, the sub-field of law and development, which has closely tracked the trajectories and power dynamics of economic development, has also been the subject of critique, fragmentation and self-reflection ever since David Trubek and Marc Galanter's (1974) seminal article.[5] As we indicate in the next chapter, each phase of the development discourse, beginning with the colonial 'civilising mission' has had its concomitant in the law and development literature. The underlying theme throughout has been the instrumental one of law as the institution which can produce civilisation or development. This is

4 The Ecuadorian Constitution guarantees the rights of *buen vivir* (articles 12–34) and grants rights to nature (articles 71–4). *Constitución Política de la República del Ecuador*, 20 October 2008. In Bolivia, *buen vivir* informs the 2009 Constitution, which does not grant rights to nature. However, *Pachamama* is protected under the Law of the Rights of Mother Earth (Law 071 of the Plurinational State) passed by the Plurinational Legislative Assembly on 21 December 2010.

5 David Trubek helped to define the sub-field and continues to influence it (Trubek and Santos, 2006).

sustained by an epistemological negation or subordination of concepts of law and justice and legal institutions such as customary and religious laws.[6] The naïve belief that the adoption of modern Northern legal institutions such as property and contract accompanied by judicial processes and the rule of law would seamlessly facilitate economic development continues to pervade law and development policies and practices, particularly those under the aegis of the IMF and the World Bank through structural adjustment programmes, good governance conditionalities, poverty relief strategies, human-centred development based upon the capabilities approach and sustainable development.

Nevertheless, the place of law in development strategies has fluctuated from time to time. The recognition of failure of emphasis on the instrumental role of law led to a more subdued attention to law in the period of structural adjustment even while neoliberal legal reforms continued. Renewed emphasis was placed on law in the 1990s in the new law and development movement on the assumption that the failures of the structural adjustment programmes were not a consequence of wrong economics and politics, but an absence of good governance (Rittich, 2004; Tamanaha, 2011). Legal institutions became central to good governance aided by a shift to Douglass North's New Institutional Economics and there has been a great deal of investment in law and justice including both substantive law reforms, reforms of courts and judiciaries and some effort on improved access to justice (Trubek and Santos, 2006; Faundez, 2014). Yet, unlike the first generation reforms which focused on the state as the engine for development, the new law and development was more concerned with integration into the neoliberal global economy (Faundez, 2014). This time, law and justice had to be measured by indicators (Paliwala and Kamchedzera, 2013). The enormous effort of the new law and development has again resulted in failure (Tamanaha, 2011). Yet, the approach to law and justice has not been uniform in those promoting the new law and development. At the World Bank, lawyers, apparently influenced by Senian capabilities approach, saw law as important in itself, whereas the economists considered it as an instrumental adjunct to their neoliberal strategy. The economists seem to have won! (Faundez, 2010; Sarfaty, 2009).

Nevertheless, whatever the internecine politics of the International Financial Institutions, the underlying issue remains one of an overall neoliberal thrust, with lip-service to countenance alternative epistemologies and the relevant local context. More significantly, the new law and development does not merely represent a shift towards neoliberal economics, but becomes an intrinsic part of

6 It was not until 2006 that the World Bank started paying attention to customary and religious laws (World Bank, 2006; Chirayath et al., 2005). While recent statements of the Bank on Justice Reform do give attention to customary and religious laws, it is clear that this has a subordinate status normally confined to access to justice: https://www.worldbank.org/en/topic/governance/brief/justice-rights-and-public-safety.

new forms of governance. The very nature of the shift towards good governance, poverty relief, human and sustainable development and the accompanying indicatorology result in the transformation of the nature of governance (including law) into intrusive disciplinary forms serving what Pope Francis aptly described as 'unseen Empires' (Chapter 4, this volume). The question we have to answer is not 'does law matter for development?' But 'what law, what form of law, whose law and for whose (in)justice?' The inevitable result of continually wrong question and answers is that countries and peoples in the global South remain locked into global economic, legal and political structures which promote the interests of global capital and facilitate corruption, inequality and environmental degradation.

Contributions to this volume

The contributions to this volume, divided into three parts, contain critiques from a variety of perspectives that address the above questions in the quest to go beyond orthodox law and development thinking. Part I, Theoretical Perspectives on Development and Law, explores the notions of development and law and development. Part II, The Academy and Social Activism, addresses the role of the academy in law and development and in particular, the ignorance of global South perspectives as well as the relationship between the academy and activism. Part II, Global Governance and Justice, addresses issues in the development of global governance and considers case studies on the impact of new forms of governance on local communities.

Part I consists of four chapters which trace the way in which the conceptual frameworks of development and law and development have failed to produce social justice in the global South and whether the alternatives such as post-development or alternatives to development provide any answers. Chapter 1, entitled 'Beyond Law and Development?', discusses the history of law and development and its becalment in a world in which the failed tenets of neoliberalism continue, zombie-like, to underpin mainstream, hegemonic conceptions such as sustainable development. The chapter suggests the need for new imaginaries inspired by subaltern global South and feminist perspectives based on alternative conceptual frameworks of relationality, care, commons and new economics to meet contemporary challenges in a world beset by rising authoritarian populism, nationalism, xenophobia and democratic and legitimacy deficits. Addressing enduring global injustices requires more than the recycling of stale ideas such as the recent resurrection of a general theory of law and development that ignores the history of the field (Lee, 2019).

In Chapter 2, 'Ameliorating Human Futures through Class Divided Postdevelopment?', Upendra Baxi discusses the same issue from a different tangent in questioning both ideas of postdevelopment and beyond development. Do they continue to be dependent discourses, dependent on the very idea of development they are supposed to go beyond and replace? Would they like human and sustainable development, end up being colonised by the dominant powers as new 'discursive objects of governance' or DOGS? He suggests that while development and postdevelopment have focused on the destruction and violence caused by practices of development, there has been an absence of understanding why this 'evil' happens. For him one must abandon all hopes of going 'beyond development' if approaches to understanding contradictions and evil are not worked out.

Chapter 3, 'Beyond Development: Towards Sustainability and Climate Justice in the Anthropocene' by Sam Adelman, critiques sustainable development for fostering the dangerous delusion that endless growth is possible on a finite planet while protecting the environment and achieving social justice through poverty eradication. Adelman discusses the harms and injustices caused by anthropogenic global heating that undermine the conditions for all forms of economic development and threaten the livelihoods of current and future generations. What is needed, he argues, is an alternative approach because sustainable development replicates the defects intrinsic to the idea of development.

All three chapters raise the issue of the colonisation of meaning. Progressive social justice demands, whether for development as raised first by Sun Yat-Sen and Haile Selassie (McVety, 2018: 21, 25), following on to notions of human and sustainable development and even postdevelopment, are anaesthetised into conformity with global powers. It is the complexity of global power and the need for an epistemological decolonisation, for new intercultural communication, which forms the kernel of Chapter 4, 'In Search of Nothing: "Unseen Empires" and the Law Beyond Development', by Peter Fitzpatrick. 'Unseen empires' was used evocatively by Pope Francis to highlight the transformation of the nature of imperium, thus demanding resistance to 'uniform systems of economic power'. Fitzpatrick endows the unseen with elusive visibility through the lens of Michel Foucault's concept of governmentality – an approach equally applicable to 'development.' For Fitzpatrick, new modes of governance 'seek to orient developing nations consensually yet they do so more intrusively, more intimately, than the modes typical of the prior and more 'formal' imperialisms'. He argues that law (and thus law and development) is essential to the operational efficacy of this governmentality, which he terms the law implicate. Yet the law bears a complex relation to the governmentality of development. While it is intrinsic to governmentality, it can also be 'outside' it, and thus capable of transforming the nature of governmentality, giving some hope for those engaged with epistemological decolonisation.

In Part II, the three chapters challenge academics in relation to their roles in law and development. The academics involved in law and development orthodoxy operate as teachers, researchers and consultants. As teachers, they reproduce students as 'model missionaries and mongers' (Braithwaite and Drahos, 2000); as researchers they are observers and analysers; and as consultants the policy makers and foot soldiers of law and development projects. However, the three papers explore a transgressive role both as critics of epistemology and as activist practitioners of alternatives to the orthodoxy. The call by Fitzpatrick for epistemological decolonisation is taken up in Chapter 5, 'Southern Voices: Extending a Project', by William Twining and Abdul Paliwala. The chapter is a product of numerous conversations between Twining and Paliwala about the submerging of Southern voices in legal scholarship arising from neocolonial and imperial practices that subordinate the global South to Northern epistemologies, especially in relation to human rights and social justice. For Twining this calls for the deparochialisation of Northern legal scholarship by including Southern perspectives, whereas for Paliwala the primary objective is to develop de/anti-colonial perspectives through Southern voices. Southern voices challenge the hegemony of international law or provide through gender, indigenous, subaltern, or peoples' struggles radical new epistemologies such as *buen vivir*. Twining's original Southern Voices project provided a template for the ways in which the voice of prominent Southern legal and human rights scholars could provide epistemological challenges to the Northern orthodoxy (Twining, 2009). The chapter considers how this project can be extended today both in terms of its scope and its gaze.

In Chapter 6 Issa G. Shivji focuses on the ways in which popular epistemologies and activist struggles could inform the thinking of Southern intellectuals. He criticises how academics as law teachers, researchers and consultants, however well-meaning, can become enmeshed in promoting law and development orthodoxies. In 'Practice Teaches Paradigm: Reflections on Radical and Liberal Law Perspectives', Shivji uses his personal experiences as a prominent Southern intellectual to reflect upon the relationship between radical scholarship and activist practice. Drawing upon his involvement in developing radical legal education in the University of Dar es Salaam Law Faculty, work as an activist legal practitioner, and as chairman of the 1994 Tanzanian Presidential Commission of Inquiry into Land Matters – one of the most comprehensive analyses of land in sub-Saharan Africa –he suggests that radical lawyers engaging with legal paradigms and theories of law and development have much to learn from the masses. Shivji argues that fighting legal battles under adverse conditions in Tanzania provided more instructive and humbling lessons for (petit) bourgeois law and development academics than lectures and seminars. Similarly, active engagement with ordinary people throughout Tanzania by the Land Commission resulted in profound critiques of bourgeois approaches to land and law and development issues.

In Chapter 7 Sol Picciotto reflects on his experiences as an academic and activist in 'Academia, Activism and the New Global Governance'. Whereas Shivji's gaze is on the Southern intellectual, Picciotto is concerned with academics as activists working with global NGOs challenging the transformation of global governance into disciplinary unseen empires which have fundamentally affected the relationship between peoples, states and global corporate capital in favour of the latter. He discusses the relationship between research on the one hand and academic engagement with policy and politics on the other by reflecting on his work on international economic law during the past half-century, starting with his formative experiences in postcolonial Africa. Picciotto analyses the importance of the interaction between theory and practice, and the need to maintain academic independence and a research perspective based on reflexive methodology and immanent critique. He emphasises the need for critical engagement by scholars of international economic law to address corporatist public–private governance structures controlled by small elites. Picciotto emphasises the importance of expertise in dealing with complex problems that risk accusations of technocracy. This is especially important in the global South where research and policy formation tend to be dominated by global corporate interests, global governance institutions and powerful states.

Picciotto and Fitzpatrick's focus on transformations in global governance is elaborated in Part III, Global Governance and Justice. Two historical chapters by Julio Faundez and Radha D'Souza about how the construction of the new global governance has disadvantaged developing countries are followed by Chapter 10 by Tomaso Ferrando and Chapter 11 by Jennifer Lander, which provide case studies of the operation of the global at the local level. Chapter 8 by Julio Faundez, 'Between Bandung and Doha: International Economic Law and Developing Countries', examines the legal and political dilemmas that confronted developing countries during the Cold War and compares them to the position they are in today. He describes the legacies of the Bandung Conference and UN resolutions on the New International Economic Order as examples of the ways in which developing countries have influenced the development of international law. His analysis of the legal framework of neoliberal economic globalisation is followed by identification of the main factors responsible for the demise of the Bandung spirit. For Faundez, the legal strategies employed by developed countries deepen neoliberal globalisation and lead to divisive consequences of global economic integration for many developing countries.

Whereas Faundez deals with the postcolonial, Radha D'Souza in Chapter 9, 'International Law and Development: From "Company Raj" to Global Governance via Indirect Rule', locates the roots of contemporary problems in the colonial itself. She contends that principles of colonial governance developed by the British Empire – specifically ideas of indirect rule which promoted notions of a hierarchy of sovereignties – are reproduced in the contemporary structures of global governance in which the formal equality of states coexists with the institutionalisation of unequal relations of economic, political and ideological power between former colonial powers and colonised nations in ways that redound to the benefit of global corporate capital.

Chapter 10, 'Multiple Enclosures through Land Concessions: Water, Fiscal Resources and Police Power', by Tomaso Ferrando, explores the impact on the ground of new forms of governance which provide the overwhelming power for corporate actors in developing countries. He argues that human rights, domestic law and transnational advocacy are wrongly portrayed as remedies for widespread illegality in the global South through the displacement of local populations.

Ferrando's analysis is based upon ten land concession agreements that lead him to argue for the importance of critical engagement with law, sovereignty and legality as tools that produce the injustices of dispossession through the enclosure of large tracts of land in the global South. These agreements create new legal frameworks that crystallise the inequality of the state-market-community power dynamics and enable global enclosures of land, the transfer of power and control over access to water, indulgent taxation regimes and a shift from public/communal to private policing.

The final chapter, 'Community Development Agreements and the State's Extractive Strategy in Mongolia: Participatory Governance or Governance Participation?', by Jennifer Lander, analyses 'accountability' in the governance of the Mongolian mining sector through Community Development Agreements. She argues that CDAs are part of a broader 'toolkit' of global social and environmental governance, which has developed alongside the expansion of global protections for foreign investment. Resistance to mining projects by local communities led the World Bank to encourage the Mongolian government to stimulate investment into the minerals economy and to 'remedy' conflict-prone relationships between communities, local authorities and mining companies. Lander focuses on the ways in which this phenomenon functions within the juridical-political structure of the Mongolian state and its objective of subordinating resistance to extractive development. The analysis incisively points to a new governmentality of complex relationships between global agencies, corporate capital and national and local government structures which operate to undermine local resistance.

The book's title 'The Limits of Law and Development' invited the contributors to question and challenge existing development discourses. We believe that the result has been not so much the invention of new ways to achieve 'development' but effective decentring of the concepts of law and development through their location within particular historical and contemporary global power hierarchies. Although the authors vary in their approaches, they establish that it may be as important to consider the nature of governance and governmentality and the manner in which they promote injustices as opposed to fostering development. How does one respond to these injustices? This is alluded to in various chapters, but we intend to explore this in further detail in our forthcoming work.

References

Acosta, A. and Gudynas, E., 2011. La renovacion de la critica al desarrollo y el buen vivircomo alternativa. *Utopia y Praxis Latinoamericana, 16* (*53*): 71–83.

Acosta, A., 2010. El Buen (con) Vivir, una utopia por (re)construir: Alcances de la Constitucion de Montecristi. *OBETS. Revista de Ciencias Sociales, 6* (*1*): 35–67.

Baxi, U., 2012. *The Future of Human Rights.* Oxford University Press.

Braithwaite, J. and Drahos, P., 2000. *Global Business Regulation.* Cambridge University Press.

Chirayath, L., Sage, C. and Woolcock, M., 2005. *Customary Law and Policy Reform: Engaging with the Plurality of Justice Systems*. Background Paper for the World Development Report. https://www.burmalibrary.org/sites/burmalibrary.org/files/obl/docs23/World_Bank-2005-Customary_Law-engaging.pdf.

Escobar, A., 2011. *Encountering Development: The Making and Unmaking of the Third World*. Princeton University Press.

Esteva, G., 1992. Development. In Sachs, W. (ed.), *The Development Dictionary; A Guide to Knowledge as Power*. Zed Books, pp. 6–25.

Faundez, J., 2010. Rule of Law or Washington Consensus: The Evolution of the World Bank's Approach to Legal and Judicial Reform. In Perry-Kesaris, A. (ed.), *Law in the Pursuit of Development*. Routledge.

Faundez, J., 2014. *Douglass North's Theory of Institutions: Lessons for Law and Development*. Research Paper No. 2014/13. University of Warwick School of Law.

Frank, A., 2004. The Development of Underdevelopment. In Wheeler, M. and Beatley, T. (eds), *The Sustainable Urban Development Reader*. Routledge.

Gudynas, E. 2011. Buen Vivir: Today's Tomorrow. *Development*, *54* (*4*): 441.

Hamilton, C., 2003. *Growth Fetish*. Allen & Unwin.

Hettne, B., 1995. *Development Theory and the Three Worlds: Towards an International Political Economy of Development*. Longman.

Lee, Y-S., 2019. *Law and Development: Theory and Practice*. Routledge.

McVety, A., 2018. Wealth and Nations: The Origins of International Development Assistance. In Macekura, S. and Manela, E. (eds), *The Development Century: A Global History*. Cambridge University Press.

Paliwala, A. and Kamchedzera, G., 2013. Justice Indicatorology: A New Theatre for Justice? *Law Social Justice and Global Development 2013* (*2*). https://warwick.ac.uk/fac/soc/law/elj/lgd/2013_2/paliwala_kamchedzera.

Ramírez, R., 2010. La transición ecuatoriana hacía el buen vivir. In León, I. (ed.), *Sumak Kawsay/Buen vivir y cambios civilizatorios*. FEDAEPS, p. 24.

Ramírez-Cendrero, J., 2018. Limits and Contradictions of Post-Developmentalism as a Heterodox Approach to Capitalist Development. *Capitalism Nature Socialism*, *29* (*4*): 68–87.

Raworth, K., 2017. *Doughnut Economics: Seven Ways to Think Like a 21st-Century Economist*. Random House.

Rittich, K., 2004. The Future of Law and Development: Second Generation Reforms and the Incorporation of the Social. *Michigan Journal of International Law*, *26* (*1*): 199–243.

Rodney, W., 1972. *How Europe Underdeveloped Africa*. Bogle-L'Ouverture.

Rostow, W., 1999. *The Stages of Economic Growth: A Non-Communist Manifesto*. Cambridge University Press.

Sachs, W., 1992. Environment. In Sachs, W. (ed.), *The Development Dictionary; A Guide to Knowledge as Power*. Zed Books, pp. 26–52.

Sarfaty, G., 2009. Measuring Justice: Internal Conflict over the World Bank's Empirical Approach to Human Rights. In Clarke, K. and Goodale, M. (eds), *Mirrors of Justice: Law and Power in the Post-Cold War Era*. Cambridge University Press.

Sen, A. 2013. *Development as Freedom*. Oxford University Press.

Tamanaha, B., 2011. The Primacy of Society and the Failures of Law and Development, *Cornell International Law Journal, 44* (2): Article 1. https://scholarship.law.cornell.edu/cilj/vol44/iss2/1.

Trubek, D. and Galanter, M., 1974. Scholars in Self-Estrangement: Some Reflections on the Crisis in Law and Development Studies in the United States. *Wisconsin Law Review, 4*: 1062–1103.

Trubek, D. and Santos, A. (eds), 2006. *The New Law and Economic Development: A Critical Appraisal.* Cambridge University Press.

Twining, W. (ed.), 2009. *Human Rights, Southern Voices: Francis Deng, Abdullahi An-Na'im, Yash Ghai and Upendra Baxi.* Cambridge University Press.

Williamson, J., 1993. Democracy and the Washington Consensus. *World Development, 21 (8)*, 1329–1336.

World Bank, 2006. *World Development Report 2006: Equity and Development.* World Bank.

Part I

Theoretical perspectives on development and law

Chapter 1

Beyond law and development?

Sam Adelman and Abdul Paliwala

Introduction

'Or alternatively, is it the case that development really did die, but there was no funeral and no burial ... and from the rotting corpse all kinds of pests are currently crawling?' (Esteva et al., 2013: vi) We live in a period of multiple crises. Promises to alleviate poverty – for example in the Millennium Development Goals – remain distant while the gap between rich and poor within and between states continues to widen (Brian, 2015; Pogge, 2002). The postwar liberal international order based upon human rights, democracy and the rule of law is under sustained attack from authoritarian, nationalist and populist regimes in the global North and South.[1] Digitalisation is abused to implement surveillance societies by states and social media companies, while automation and artificial intelligence (AI) threaten millions of jobs worldwide (Lyon, 2001; Morozov, 2012; Zuboff, 2019; Ragnedda, 2017). Ecological destruction, global heating and biodiversity loss in the Sixth Great Extinction pose existential threats to all species (Kolbert, 2014; Chapter 3, this volume). These trends call into question the relevance of existing discourses on *law and development*[2] in the context of these crises. The title of this volume and its forthcoming companion imply a need to move beyond law and development, not least because of the profound challenges posed in the Anthropocene (Chapter 3, this volume). Law and development discourses have been subjected to thoroughgoing critiques since they emerged in conjunction after the Second World War – most notably in David Trubek and Marc Galanter's anguished 'Scholars in Self-Estrangement' (1974). Progressive critiques have focused on the depredations of growth,

1 The clearest statement is Vladimir Putin's dismissal of liberalism (Barber, L. and Foy, H. Vladimir Putin: Liberalism Has 'Outlived Its Purpose'. *Financial Times.* Available online at: https://www.ft.com/content/2880c762-98c2-11e9-8cfb-30c211dcd229 (accessed 15 July 2019)). Putin favours 'managed democracy' along the lines of Viktor Orbán's 'illiberal democracy'. Presidents Bolsonaro and Trump display similar neo-fascist tendencies.

2 We use 'law and development' to signify both development and law and development as appropriate.

extraction, industrialisation and modernisation and the ways in which the Bretton Woods financial and economic institutions have sought to ameliorate the negative impacts of development through 'human' and 'sustainable' development, and the capabilities approach. These shifts have persistently failed to address the structural inequalities in the global framework resulting from colonisation of development by the development industry: the international financial institutions (IFIs)[3] and other global development institutions, non-governmental development organisations, aid agencies, transnational corporations, private lenders, and global markets (Korten, 2015). Progressive critics have challenged the idea of development itself and called for alternatives such as postdevelopment or alternatives *to* development.

This chapter considers the underlying problems in successive hegemonic development discourses and critically examines alternative forms *of* and alternatives *to* development and postdevelopment. We suggest that law and development concepts and discourses – orthodox, reformist or critical – create a risk of shifting our gaze away from concrete social injustices because they are preoccupied with models of development, institutions and economic and political factors such as growth and governance. For this reason, we argue that new imaginaries that focus on harms and injustices are required.

Four key themes

Any new imaginary must engage with the interconnected, underlying concerns that have characterised successive dominant development discourses. First, there is a need to confront the historical political, economic and discursive domination of the global North forged under colonialism and imperialism. Despite the emergence of formally equal sovereign states following decolonisation, Northern domination was perpetuated through its control of international political and economic institutions and global markets (Hoogvelt, 2001) until coming under challenge from rising powers such as China and India towards the end of the 20th century. Second, there is a need to overturn teleological Eurocentric ideas of progress, the concomitant notion that Western modernity prefigures the future of the global South, and the fetishisation of economic growth at the expense of ecological sustainability. Third, private property and possessive individualism exercise a powerful hold on development discourses and legal systems across the globe despite challenges from relational feminist and subaltern perspectives in the global South. Fourth, we need to explain and challenge the continuing hegemony of neoliberal globalisation since the last quarter of the 20th century despite the destruction it has wrought in North and South. Neoliberalism is symbolised by *homo economicus:* the putative profit-seeking, efficiency-maximising rational actor whose counterparts are the abstract legal subject (apotheosised in the

3 Primarily the IMF and the World Bank.

corporate form) and the Anthropos capable of altering the geology of the planet. All these factors are under challenge, but they continue to frame development discourses incapable of resolving the multiple overlapping crises confronting humanity.

Northern domination

Colonisation denied sovereignty and self-determination in order to facilitate exploitation, expropriation and oppression. The conferment of formal sovereignty under postcolonialism was accompanied by different forms of subordination to Western hegemonic states, global markets and the international economic institutions, and the dogmas of neoliberal globalisation (Quijano, 2007; Anghie, 2005). Development discourses usually prescribe how states ought to develop while brushing over enduring constraints arising from their colonial or imperial histories. 'Sovereign' postcolonial states were made responsible for their development on terms dictated by the global North through skewed international law and the changing conditionalities of the WTO, IMF, the World Bank and a myriad other institutions controlled by the North. The ostensibly participatory language of the World Bank's erstwhile Poverty Reduction Strategy Papers and its current Country Partnership Frameworks or the OECD Paris Declaration on Aid Effectiveness (2005) camouflage their intimate disciplinary and biopolitical controls (Tan, 2011). Yet the very complexity of these disciplinary demands makes them practically difficult to implement and may enable authoritarian illiberal and corrupt regimes to obviate them (Craig and Porter, 2006: 158). McCourt's (2018) study of Sri Lanka and Cote d'Ivoire suggests that only lip-service is paid to countries' priorities. Furthermore, the IFI's fear of poor governance is used to limit state power by promoting direct engagement by civil society organisations in governance mechanisms (Eichenauer and Reinsberg, 2017). A different but equally problematic idea of development underpins China's development aid and its Belt and Road strategy. While it constitutes an enormously impressive counterbalance to Northern aid approaches, especially in not requiring conditionalities, it subordinates human rights and the rule of law and provides a template for authoritarian regimes from Zimbabwe to Sudan and Myanmar (Biukovic, 2014; Naim, 2007; Strange et al., 2017).

Growth, progress, modernity and ecological catastrophe

Development conceived as progress through economic growth became a Western doxa when development was discovered after the Second World War and viewed as the only way to reduce poverty and promote social justice and nation-building (Escobar, 1995/2012: 24). Hegemonic ideas of progress and modernisation underpinned extractive, growth-driven development, which was extremely uneven and heedless of the negative impacts of environmental degradation on the material conditions required for all economic activity (Sachs, 2010; Raworth, 2017; Chapter 3, this volume). These flaws are replicated in the contemporary manifestation of developmental hegemony, the oxymoronic concept of sustainable development and the Sustainable Development Goals in 2015 (Adelman, 2018). As we argue below, the so-called Global Goals are old wine in new, green, neoliberal bottles when radical transformation is required to avert ecological catastrophe.

Individualism versus relationality

From colonialism to neoliberalism, Western developmentalism has privileged possessive individualism in the form of the rational economic man or entrepreneur (Duffield, 2008). It has drawn negative contrasts with traditionalism, communitarianism, collectivism and socialism, which ineluctably lead to economic failure and explain the relative success of Northern countries (Inglehart and Oyserman, 2004). Furthermore, it emphasised connected notions of rigid rights of property and contract. In contrast, neoliberal dominance has been attacked by discourses inspired by gender justice, subalternism and indigenous cultural values which emphasise the ethics of relationality, interdependence and care (Held, 2006; Gudynas, 2013; Tronto, 1993). Relationality places emphasis on fluid shaping and re-shaping of human practices through reciprocal relations between and among individuals and groups rather than through rigid rights and identities (Bourdieu and Wacquant, 1992: 224–35). Care adds an ethical dimension to relationality by suggesting that people inter-relate with one another, and their environment in a complex 'caring' life-sustaining web to live as well as possible (Tronto, 2013: 103). A further dimension is added to this by group rights and activities in which durable cooperative institutions are organised and governed by the resource users themselves (Ostrom, 1990).

The contradictions intrinsic to development were reflected in the protection by Britain of women in the Raj against practices such as suttee immolation while entrenching patriarchal domination (Loomba, 1993). Since the 1980s, development initiatives have emphasised women's rights but remain two-faced. Women's rights and participation in society, politics and the economy are promoted but their anchoring in neoliberal ideology means that there is no overall reduction in gender injustices. Southern women have opposed simple transplantations of Northern liberal feminism in asserting that the intersection between global and local patriarchal relations produces distinct forms of oppression in the global South. This chimes with feminist critiques of individualist socio-economic relations at the expense of alternative ethics of relationality and care (Robinson, 2011; Stewart, 2011).

A further challenge to Northern law and development discourses is directed at its wilful ignorance, orientalisation and misrepresentation of Southern subaltern voices characterised by Boaventura de Sousa Santos (2007) as 'abyssal thinking' and by Walter Mignolo (2012: ix) as 'monoculture of the mind'. Enrique Dussel

(2003: 47) calls for a 'philosophy of liberation' as a counter-discourse, 'a critical philosophy born in the periphery (from the perspective of victims, the excluded), which has the intention of being relevant on a global scale'.

Peter Fitzpatrick (1992) exposed the othering of non-European laws and customs through denial, denigration and the invention of the uncivilised, indolent native that underpinned the myth of civilised modern Western law, paradoxically through the denial of law to the savage, particularly property law, enabling European colonisers to expropriate their lands while placing the right to property at the centre of international law (Anghie, 2005). Law and development discourses have perpetuated these Northern epistemologies by insisting that the South must adopt Western institutions of law and justice as preconditions for development. Repeated failures have led to declarations of death of Northern development approaches, which nevertheless persist in zombie forms (Gudynas, 2013; Tamanaha, 2011).

In the colonies, the unfettered export of grain led to disasters such as the 16 million deaths in successive famines in India between 1875 and 1914 (Collingham, 2017). In the immediate postcolonial period, the shift from European colonialism to US imperialism and the strategic requirements of the Cold War combined to usher in the contemporary era of development. Initially, the main thrust was the reconstruction of war-ravaged Europe, followed by aid and investment flows to the erstwhile Third World to promote modernisation and industrialisation in the teeth of opposition from neoliberals such as Hayek who opposed import-substitution in favour of the neocolonial export-orientation of agricultural and mineral commodities by plantation owners and traditional producers (Plehwe, 2015). By the end of the 1970s neoliberalism had become the primary means of furthering Northern business and geo-strategic interests (ibid). The global South was forced to accede to market discipline and global regulation under the aegis of WTO, the IMF, and the conditionalities of structural adjustment programmes and subsequently ostensibly voluntary Poverty Reduction Strategies and new Country Partnership Frameworks imposed by the IFIs. Braithwaite and Drahos (2000: 585) characterised global and local agents of neoliberalism as model missionaries, mercenaries, mongers, misers and modernisers. These have been prevalent in the technocratic 'Rule of Experts' (Mitchell, 2002) by economists, lawyers and social scientists. Neoliberalism is encouraged through training programmes and other inducements designed to normalise competitive individualism and market fundamentalism. Just as colonialism adapted to local conditions, neoliberalism has been sufficiently flexible to encapsulate developmental discourses ranging from structural adjustment to notions of good governance inspired by new institutional economics and supposedly participatory anti-poverty strategies (North, 1995; Faundez, 2014). Neoliberalism colonises concepts such as human and sustainable development, 'development as freedom' and appropriates human rights through trade-related, market friendly human rights (Baxi, 2006/2012). Its antipathy to state-driven development has even infected non-statist modes of governance such as community-based self-reliance through which people are constructed as market actors and responsibilised for sustainable development and resilience to the linked threats of poverty and global heating (Duffield, 2008: 69).

Avatars of development and law

Colonialism: the civilising mission[4]

British colonialism shifted from mercantilism to free trade with the repeal of the corn laws in 1846. Britain had maintained significant control of its colonies through the violence of slavery, indentured labour and migration within the empire. Slavery underpinned sugar production, Indians were encouraged to export cotton but prevented from exporting cloth, and Africans were encouraged to grow maize rather than traditional foodstuffs to serve British interests (Collingham, 2017). Imperial aims were cloaked under the civilising mission of colonialism and modernisation (Rist, 2008). As Victor Hugo put it, 'Go forward, the nations! Grasp this land! Take it! From whom? From no one' (ibid.: 51). Imperial avarice 'grabbed hold of places and living people' as its civilising mission 'exerted its sway over minds in the name of universalism and humanity' (ibid.: 67). They imposed cultural change and an inferior cultural identity incapable of producing the *homo economicus* of neoliberalism (Jones, 1960). They also disrupted relations by emphasising male economic dominance and patriarchy (Stewart, 2011).

The emergence of law and development

The idea of national development goes back at least as far as demands by Sun Yat-sen in China in 1919 and Haile Selassie in Ethiopia in 1923 for development assistance to the global South (McVety, 2018: 21, 25). However, in typical Eurocentric fashion, the transition from the civilising mission to development with the US's postwar domination is often attributed to President Truman's 1949 speech outlining 'a bold new program for making the benefits of our scientific advances and industrial progress available for the improvement and growth of underdeveloped areas'.[5] Whereas Keynesianism in the form of the Marshall Plan was deemed acceptable for Europe, the Third World was subjected to the disciplinary mechanisms of the Bretton Woods institutions (Woods, 2006; Duffield, 2008). The Cold War gave the Third World limited room for manoeuvre and little incentive to promote democratic institutions as East and

4 This section focuses on British colonialism. For a broader analysis, see Rist, 2008.

5 Truman, H.S. *Inaugural Address*. 20 January 1949. Available online at: http://www.trumanlibrary.org/whistlestop/50r_archive/inaugural20jan1949.htm (accessed 10 May 2019)). Esteva (2010).

West favoured military juntas, civilian dictatorships and one-party states in a series of proxy conflicts. Northern postcolonial discourses promoted modernisation as the best strategy for economic growth along the lines of Rostow's Stages of Growth (1960).[6] Postcolonial states were encouraged to abandon 'backward traditions' and embrace entrepreneurial institutions for capital accumulation stimulated by foreign aid. The unfavourable outcomes that resulted led to critiques such as dependency theory and calls for a New International Economic Order.

The North's discovery of development was accompanied by the invention of technocratic sub-disciplines such as development economics and law and development which commonly argued that ending traditionalism required the replacement of colonially constructed customary law by modern Northern institutions, especially private property, freedom of contract and investor rights. The gap between law's putative aims, between law in statutes and law in action created authoritarian regimes and debased manifestations of rule of law under colonialism, and its inability to seamlessly modernise resulted in anguished analyses of its defects (Trubek and Galanter, 1974). Law and development were attacked from the left by dependency theorists and besieged from the right by neoliberalism, the latter prompting the emergence of a second law and development movement (Rittich, 2004).

Dependency theory

In the 1960s, mainstream development policies prioritised import substitution as the optimal path to industrialisation; import substitution was ironically blamed for the financial and debt crises of the 1970s even though Latin American output grew at an annual rate of 5.3 per cent during the decade and 2.2 per cent afterwards (Palma, 2003).[7] Dependency theorists argued that core metropolitan states systematically exploited peripheral countries for cheap labour and raw materials through the 'development of underdevelopment' (Cardoso and Faletto, 1979; Love, 1990).[8] They demonstrated how the incorporation of the Third World into the global political-economy took place on structurally unequal terms that endure to the present day in the tautological processes of developmentalism whose main aim is development detached from human wellbeing (Escobar, 1995/2012; Esteva, 2010). Walter Rodney (1972) famously described how Europe underdeveloped Africa. Dependency theory critiqued the

6 Soviet and Chinese strategies promoted state-centric development in this period with mixed results (Clarkson, 1978).

7 From the 1980s onwards, neoliberalism was based upon the new dogma of export-oriented growth apparently exemplified by the emergence of the Tiger economies in Asia.

8 World System theory also critiqued relationships of dependency between the core and the periphery but discerned a greater degree of dynamism and room for manoeuvre in the latter. A prominent example is Wallerstein, 2004.

underlying epistemological dependence of what later became the global South on Northern rationalities and called for a New International Economic Order to rebalance the global economy. Postcolonialism was accompanied by demands from former colonies for permanent sovereignty over natural resources, the right to self-determination and, more recently, the right to development.

Dependency theory led to a critique of legal instrumentalism and challenged the idea that successful development required the transplantation of Western law. It focused on the political economy of law and the ways in which Western legal institutions such as contract, property and investor rights perpetuated inequality and underdevelopment. Ghai et al. rejected existing law and development approaches in favour of political-economy analysis of 'law, legal institutions and processes in their social, economic and political context' (1987: xii). Such analyses described the ease with which transnational corporations avoided state attempts to control them (Bierstecker, 1987; Korten, 2015).

The Washington Consensus

The rise of neoliberalism undermined the influence of Keynesian approaches and dependency critiques as failures of development were attributed to the central role of inefficient states. The left considered the state to be over reliant on international capital while the right saw the main problem of development as collusion between the state and rent-seeking local elites (Toye, 2004: 31). Neoliberalism's proponents argued that law should be used to construct domestic markets and smooth the integration of developing countries into the global economy through reform of trade, taxation, intellectual property and financial flows (Chimni, 2004: 7).

The victory of the right was reflected in the so-called Washington Consensus and its demands for small states, privatisation, liberalisation and deregulation. The role of the state should be limited to the maintenance of law and order and the provision of health and education. The Washington Consensus moved through avatars ranging from structural adjustment to poverty reduction strategies rooted in market fundamentalism (Faundez, 2010; 2014). In reality, the state remained as essential as it had been in all forms of development throughout history, a truth rediscovered by the Bretton Woods institutions following the explosion of the global economy by finance capital in 2008.

Structural adjustment conditionalities weakened the bargaining position of Southern states in fora such as the WTO (Tan, 2011). Although the Multilateral Agreement on Investment was aborted in 1998 following widescale protests around the world, the countries of the global South were compelled to open their economies to foreign investment through bilateral investment treaties and other measures (Braithwaite and Drahos, 2000; Dezalay and Garth, 2002). Structural adjustment generated equally widespread resistance throughout the global South as the World Bank's spurious claims of success were exposed by growing poverty and inequality (World Bank 1994a; cf. Lall, 1995).

International financial institutions viewed the problems of structural adjustment primarily as the consequence of governance failures, a shift that coincided with a renewed focus on institutions and governance in New Institutional Economics (North, 1995; Faundez, 2014).[9] The result was an instrumental emphasis on law and legal institutions as the bases for good governance (World Bank, 1994b; IMF, 1997; Faundez, 2010; 2014).

The underlying aims of internal economic liberalisation and opening the South to global trade and markets required the creation of institutions to facilitate capital accumulation, the eradication of corruption and the rule of law. Good governance appeared to require human rights and democracy even as it seemed to be good for global capital and local elites rather than those subject to conditionalities, national debt and market discipline. In an analysis of Article 10 of the World Bank's charter, which prohibits interference in domestic politics, Ibrahim Shihata argued that the Bank considered human rights, particularly socio-economic rights, only when they affected unfettered economic activity (Shihata, 2000; Schlemmer-Shulte, 2001) and continued to lend to countries with weak human rights records. The result was a mushrooming of law and development projects on judicial and legal reform, corruption, land reform, and tax and economic legislation (Rittich, 2004; Tamanaha, 2011). In parallel with the IFIs, Northern aid agencies promoted human rights and constitutional reforms towards multi-party democracy. This brought new acknowledgements of failure and questioning of law and development by some believers in the project (Tamanaha, 2011).

The failure of neoliberal strategies led to a new focus on poverty and on local state and civil society participation in development that camouflaged the intensive disciplinary relationship between global institutions and developing countries. While global capitalism continued to be strengthened through the creation of domestic institutions such as stock markets, there has been renewed emphasis on incorporating the poor into the formal economy. For example, vast sums have fruitlessly been spent on land titling in attempts to commodify peasants' property to enable them to raise capital (De Soto, 2000; cf. Cousins et al., 2005).[10]

Human development

The relentless focus on growth in mainstream development discourses led critics towards a model that prioritised human development. The most well-known example is Amartya Sen's iconic formulation of *Development as Freedom* and his

9 North is one of several Nobel economics laureates whose malign influence on development has been substantial. Others include Hayek and Friedman.

10 Seemingly benevolent strategies such as microcredit systems have also come under criticism (Roodman, 2011).

promotion of human capabilities to be and do what people have reasons to value. Increasing individual capabilities requires political freedoms, economic and social opportunities, transparency, and protective security (Sen, 1999). Sen's approach was extended in Martha Nussbaum's (2000) work on flourishing and resonated with Mahbubul Haq's (1996) work on human development. The product of these interventions was the creation of the UN Human Development Index (HDI)[11] and subsequently the Millennium Development Goals (MDGs) in 2000.[12] The HDI has been supplemented by other indicators of democracy, the rule of law and transparency (Paliwala and Kamchedzera, 2013). Sen's work is an important corrective to economic simplicities which seeped into law and development theory. In particular, he is critical of the economic theorists' misunderstandings of law and the simplicities of 'law and economics'. He also critiques the transcendentalism of Rawls and others in their universal approach to social justice. His critique of rational choice theory that people may make their choices because of their 'commitment' rather than personal advantage comes close to an acknowledgement of relationality (Sen, 2009). Nevertheless, he is limited by his embedment in orthodox economics even when he looks out to the disciplines of law and ethics (Tully, 2013). He acknowledges that markets are imperfect, fail and need regulation, but fails to analyse the structures of colonialism, imperialism and contemporary global capitalism which generate contemporary social injustices (Chimni, 2008). Equally significantly, there is an absence of sociological/anthropological dimension which would have enriched his otherwise enticing analysis (Tully, 2013). His work is an antidote to authoritarian statism, yet he is constrained within the limits of formal liberal democratic forms (Sen, 2011: 129).

While there was a greater emphasis on constitutional change, the rule of law and access to justice during the early 1990s, neoliberalism entrenched contract, property and investment rights as countries in the global South were integrated into a global economy defined by free trade under the aegis of the WTO. Rittich (2004: 243) problematises the dissonance between human development, the MDGs and the neoliberal conception of economic efficiency as 'speculative at best and suspect at worst'. This dissonance was reflected in conflicting positions taken at the World Bank between lawyers promoting good governance and neoliberal economists. The result was clear ascendancy of the latter with human development approaches being reduced to instrumental and indicatorological devices amenable to economists (Faundez, 2010;

11 The HDI ranks countries' development on three criteria of longevity (life expectancy), knowledge (education) and standard of living, but while departing from growth fetishism, it does not reflect Sen's emphasis on political, social, transparency and security. UNDP. 'About Human Development'. Available online at: http://hdr.undp.org/en/humandev (accessed 19 May 2019)).

12 Further information about the Goals is available online at: https://www.un.org/millenniumgoals (accessed 3 June 2019)).

Sarfaty, 2009). An even harsher critique suggests that the hypocritical colonial civilising mission which justified colonial plunder is substituted by the new rule of law 'that justifies looting to the paradoxical point of being itself illegal' (Mattei and Nader, 2008: 3).

Sustainable development

Almost all economic activity is environmentally destructive to a greater or lesser extent, but development models rooted in ideas of teleological progress, modernisation and endless growth have produced widespread ecological degradation and undermined the material conditions for any type of development in the Anthropocene (Sachs, 2010; Chapter 3, this volume). Sustainable development was introduced to mainstream development discourses with the Brundtland Commission's report to the 1987 World Conference on Environment and Development (WCED, 1987); as ecological catastrophe has unfolded it has become the dominant conception of development.

The adoption by the UN General Assembly of the Sustainable Development Goals (SDGs) as replacement for the MDGs in 2015 promises to reconcile endless growth, environmental protection and social justice, but the so-called Global Goals are old development wine in new greenwashed neoliberal bottles because they are designed to preclude the radical transformation required to stave off ecological catastrophe (Hickel, 2015; Carant, 2016). The Anthropocene forces us to rethink development and sustainability on a planetary scale (UNRISD, 2016; cf. McNeill, 2014; Colville, 2016; Chapter 2 and Chapter 3, this volume),[13] but planetary thinking is retarded by the persistence of sovereign-centric Westphalian rationality that prioritises collusion between states and global capital.

The SDGs contain 17 goals and 169 targets that envisage a win-win relationship between green capitalism and the environment (Gupta and Vegelin, 2016: 440; Adelman, 2018). Net responsibility for sustainability has been broadened to all countries, but it is voluntary for both governments and corporate actors. There are significant implications for law and development. For example, Goal 4 (gender inequality), Goal 10 (reducing inequality) and Goal 16 (promoting inclusive society and institutions) call for access to justice, good governance and constitutionalism.[14] This approach replicates the flaws of existing approaches to law and development which are unlikely to be remedied

13 Welcome to the Anthropocene. Available online at: http://www.anthropocene.info/great-acceleration.php (accessed 15 May 2019)).

14 Goal 16 has been translated by the UN India Office as requiring 'good governance' measure including ending violence, exploitation and corruption, promoting the rule of law and access to justice, combating corruption and promoting participation and transparency (India-UNDAF, 2018).

by the holistic approach of the SDGs in the absence of enforcement mechanisms and adequate funding. The SDGs are undermined by the contradictory belief that it is possible to grow our way to sustainability. Political ecologists have called for alternative models of development based upon degrowth (Hickel, 2019) or steady state economics (Daly, 2019) or alternatives to development such as *buen vivir* (Kothari et al., 2014; Adelman, 2018; Chapter 3, this volume; Chapter 5, this volume). In contrast, Aaron Bastani's (2019) luxury communist manifesto suggests that the underlying issue is not growth or degrowth but the need to transcend the unjust structures of neoliberal capitalism.

The developmental state

The rapid growth of the East Asian 'Tigers' and China in the second half of the 20th century challenged liberal and neoliberal notions of economic development. Whereas neoliberal ideology emphasised the role of markets and a small state, the East Asian approach was predicated upon the central role of the developmental state and industrial strategies as drivers of development (Chang, 1994; Wade, 1990/2004; Haggard, 2018). In contrast to the new institutionalists, the character of the state and its bureaucracy, close regulation of business and labour, and the provision of education, health and housing, often by authoritarian governments, mattered more than civil and political market and property rights, checks on the executive, and the rule of law (Haggard, 2018). East Asian development was *sui generis*, context specific and adroit in responding to changing global and local circumstances, for example in relation to globalisation and free trade. Social change led to greater openness and democratisation in countries such as South Korea while China's unprecedented economic growth occurred under the direction of an authoritarian state. These different paths beg the question of whether they are models that are replicable elsewhere in the global South or the result of cultures, traditions and specific local circumstances (World Bank, 1993), although Ha-Joon Chang argues that Confucianism can and has been successfully adapted to promote development (Chang, 2003: 119; Stiglitz, 2001).

For Lee (2017), East Asia's success signifies the failure of the Washington Consensus. He suggests that these models of development may require authoritarian rule, legal frameworks suitable for corporate entities such as South Korea's Chaebol, the suppression of labour, and the promotion of savings rather than democracy and the rule of law. Imported laws must be adapted to fit local conditions; the role of law and development is to ensure a culture of regulatory compliance and enhance the capacity and political will to implement laws and policies. Lee's approach does not rely on an abstract universal set of institutions characteristic of North-based law and development initiatives, and he criticises the capability approach's failure to consider local circumstances and historical priorities. He is less critical of the ends justifies the means mentality that underpins East Asian approaches and their emphasis on authoritarianism. For Lee,

Senian capabilities and free markets must initially be subordinated to rapid economic growth to provide the space for the latter to prevail.

Lee's analysis is too crude. While developmental state theorists acknowledged that most East Asian states grew rapidly under authoritarian rule, their underlying focus was on the nature of industrial policies and the efficiency of bureaucracy and its relationships with local businesses (Chang, 2003; Haggard, 2018). Industrial policies in countries such as Japan, South Korea and Taiwan have been accompanied by land, educational, technology and health reforms (Haggard, 2018). Unlike Lee, who considers that neoliberalism may replace active state involvement after achievement of rapid growth, the active state involvement in promoting industrial and trade policy continues in development states (Wade, 2018). A key underlying issue for the global South is therefore how to transcend the imbalances of power between the global South and North including the Northern dominance of global institutions. Although the IFIs paid lip-service to the role of the state at the behest of China and Japan, they generally refused to acknowledge an active role for industrial policy (Wade, 2018), and their principles of law and development continued to favour the domination of Northern-based transnational corporations (Duffield, 2008; Wade, 2018; Korten, 2015).

Postdevelopment and alternatives to development

The idea of development is criticised by postdevelopment theorists as a hegemonic project 'to remake the world in America's image' (Esteva et al., 2013: 3; Klein and Morreo, 2019). Does the 'post' prefix challenge the practices of development or the concept itself (Chapter 2, this volume)? The literature suggests both on the basis that theory and practice are inextricable (Escobar, 1995/2012, 2016; Esteva, 2010; Sachs, 2010). The idea of postdevelopment highlights a radical disenchantment with exploitative, extractive and environmentally destructive development models based upon endless growth and market fundamentalism. It is a much-needed critique that clearly adumbrates the failings of development but is less clear about what should replace it and how to escape the development/postdevelopment binary. Furthermore, while postdevelopment approaches correctly emphasise the cleavages between Northern and Southern perspectives, there is relative ignoring of the injustices perpetrated by global South actors against each other.

In contrast, there is a growing argument for alternatives to the intrinsically flawed idea of development. The central problem is compound cumulative growth as the central ideology of developmentalism, a major cause of the climate crisis and ecological destruction. Amongst the alternatives promoted are degrowth and steady-state economics (Hickel, 2019; Daly, 2019). Esteva, Babones and Babcicky's 'radical manifesto' (Esteva et al., 2013) argues that overconsumption by the global North leads to environmental destruction and impoverishment, for which development aid is a sticking plaster: 'If rich people in the North want to help poor people in the global South, they can best do so by taking less rather than giving more' (Esteva et al., 2013: 93). Some of the most coherent alternatives to development are based upon Andean cosmovisions underpinned by onto-espistemologies diametrically opposed to possessive individualism, communitarianism and harmonious relationships between humans and nature (Kothari et al., 2014; Gudynas, 2013; Chapter 5, this volume; Chapter 3, this volume). Conceptions such as *buen vivir* do not recognise the notion of linear progress from underdevelopment to development. Instead the holistic focus is on relationality between humans, other species and the environment. There is an

> emphasis on pluriculturalism and co-existence between communities, inseparability of all life's elements (material, social, spiritual), opposition to the concept of perpetual accumulation, return to use values and movement even beyond the concept of value. *Buen vivir*, in short, proposes a civilizational change.
>
> (Kothari et al., 2014: 367)

The Indian based ideas of Ecological Swaraj link with ideas such as *buen vivir* in their emphasis on the rights of the earth, respect for other species, social justice and equity, and the involvement of every person in decision making (Kothari et al., 2014: 368).

There is a need for exploration of relevant legal strategies to link with development strategies required by these alternative approaches. The Constitutions of Ecuador and Bolivia already give some recognition to these cosmovisions (Chapter 5, this volume). Broader legal translation of these alternatives require radical transformations of trade, investment and debt laws to protect against ecological destruction, institutional change and a paradigm shift in legal theory to overturn the ways in which legal systems naturalise credit, debt, interest and rent, all of which require endless compound growth (Chapter 3, this volume). Legal cultures must undergo fundamental change to tilt the balance away from contract, property and other trade-related, market friendly human rights (Baxi, 2006/2012) towards human and ecological wellbeing, and away from individualism towards relationality, collective and environmental rights.

The end of law and development?

Yet, orthodox approaches to law and development are existentially threatened from different directions. China's developmental model and its Belt and Road strategy challenges Northern domination of aid while subordinating human rights and the rule of law and offering an authoritarian template for regimes from Zimbabwe to Sudan and Myanmar (Brautigam, 2011; Naim, 2007; Strange et al., 2017; Gehring et al., 2018). Chinese aid does not come with the conditionalities of Northern states and the IFIs, but its focus is no less imperialist than Northern models. Gehring et al.'s (2018) study suggests that while such an approach does not promote internal civil conflicts, it clearly facilitates oppression by authoritarian rulers (Gehring et al., 2018). Rule by law is the authoritarian alternative to the rule of law.

Trump's America first strategy threatens the liberal international order over which the US presided following the Second World War (Koh, 2017; Crane and Maguire, 2017). The soft power that cloaked the violence of US and European imperialism is being replaced in the case of US by climate denial, protectionism, racism, and indifference to corruption, inequality, human rights violations, authoritarian rule and general lack of concern about the global South apart from restricting migration and promoting US trade interests.

Dominant global powers increasingly use bilateral trade and investment agreements as vehicles to bypass a multilateral international order in which the global South had relatively more leeway (Morosini and Sanchez Badin, 2017). The neo-imperial geostrategies unfold in the midst of linked global economic and environmental crises which promote authoritarian rule, magnify impoverishment and inequality, drive forced migration to escape exclusion and oppression, and create new geographies of global social injustices in which the global North and South exist cheek by jowl in Johannesburg, Mumbai and New Orleans.

Digital technologies herald further disruptions that deepen authoritarianism and surveillance capitalism while reducing employment and increasing the numbers of people for which capitalism has no need. As Bridle (2018: 116) suggests, AI robotics are 'reducing workers to meat algorithms, useful only for their ability to move and follow orders, makes them easier to hire, fire and abuse'. The global digital divide is reconfigured by AI, robotics and a small number of global digital monopolies apparently able to escape democratic regulation and sovereign jurisdiction, at least in the North (Morozov, 2012; Paliwala, 2013). Whereas development initiatives have sought to ameliorate the global digital divide (WSIS, 2005; Paliwala, 2007), digitalisation threatens to exacerbate existing injustices (Ragnedda, 2017).

New imaginaries: beyond development to social justice

Development and law have not eliminated impoverishment and gender, ethnic and other forms of discrimination that deepen other injustices. Development theory has failed to overturn the dominance of neoliberal, extractive, growth-driven development that drives the climate and environmental crises. The postwar rhetoric of development as modernity and progress camouflaged the entrenchment of underdevelopment and injustice in much of the global South, which intensified with neoliberalism. It failed to eliminate injustices because it was rooted in injustice. One of the lessons of scholars in self-estrangement is that law does not provide simple, unproblematic nostrums for the depredations of development because it is not designed to do so. The form of law that underpins 'good' governance privileges individualism and private property. Katharina Pistor (2019) suggests a very broad range of legal instruments and practices as the Code of Capital which sustains neoliberal capitalism, a code which needs to be deconstructed in the interest of justice. Law is therefore important, not least as a site of struggle for global and local equality and justice. International environmental law may be full of soft norms and principles that are difficult to enforce such as the precautionary approach and polluter pays principle, but histories of struggle suggest we should take it seriously as a strategy against injustice.

Modifiers such as 'human', 'alternative', 'sustainable' development or 'capabilities' have sought to attenuate the underlying logic of mainstream Northern models but paid insufficient attention to the structural causes of underdevelopment, inequality and injustice, enabling states and international development institutions to express fealty to these less hard-edged discourses. Similarly, the postdevelopment critique, which is locked in the binary discourse of under/development, does not adequately address local causes of injustice or proffer an alternative imaginary.

The causes of injustice are multiple and overlapping. For example, global heating undermines developmental gains and deepens poverty, which weakens resilience to climate, political, economic and social crises. Overarching development discourses which insist that the true path to development lies through export-oriented trade, good governance or other dogmas have too often treated social injustices as unfortunate by-products. A new imaginary based upon a bottom up approach that seeks to deal with specific harms and injustices may be more productive because it highlights the quotidian realities of human suffering arising from war, racism, patriarchy, migration, economic stresses, digitalisation and the climate crisis. Caouette and Kapoor (2016) demonstrate how these realities lead to struggles by peasants, farmworkers, migrant women and indigenous peoples against neoliberal globalisation, the powerful and the very idea of development, an issue explored in greater detail in the forthcoming companion volume to this work. As we write, events in Chile, Hong Kong and elsewhere confirm the potency of resistance. These instances highlight the importance of continuous collective struggle by social movements that engage locally and also transcend Westphalian boundaries (Rajagopal, 2005; Sarangi, 2002; Caouette and Kapoor, 2016).

Moving beyond development demands a paradigm change that overturns economic orthodoxies. The climate crisis cannot be solved by its main cause: capitalism, even reformed, green capitalism, not least because it is unlikely that greenhouse gas emissions can be completely decoupled from economic activity (Hickel and Kallis, 2019). The existential threat confronting us requires a fundamental transformation in production and consumption. Maja Göpel (2016) proposes decoupling production from unsustainable and uncaring approaches to humans, nature and animals and decoupling satisfaction of human needs from the obsession with growth in a manner that subordinates economic needs to human and environmental interests in ways that human development approaches have failed to do. Kate Raworth's 'doughnut economics' goes further is seeking to keep humanity within planetary boundaries while meeting human needs. The doughnut represents the:

> regenerative and distributive economy which constitutes the just and safe space for humanity' as the basis for good management of the global household. The inner hole border constitutes the social constraints such as the human needs for food, energy, health, housing, education, income and work, gender justice, social equity, peace and justice which cannot be transcended. Beyond the outer ring is the ecological ceiling such as atmospheric, oceanic and land surface pollution, water resource depletion and climate change.
>
> (Raworth, 2017: 44)

Raworth seeks to escape the shackles of neoclassical economics and growth but her holistic vision views the SDGs as exemplars of a new economics (ibid.: 45) rather than rebundled green capitalism.

In conclusion, we need to reassess the utility of the concepts of 'development' and 'law and development' to the tasks of promoting human and planetary wellbeing in the Anthropocene because it is not possible to decolonise the idea of development. New imaginaries of law and development as law in global (in)justice offer ways to urgently construct sustainable economies underpinned by legal systems that provide solutions to the excrescences of mal-development in collective, holistic, harmonious and relational discourses.

References

Adelman, S., 2018. The Sustainable Development Goals, Anthropocentrism and Neoliberalism. In French, D. and Kotze, L. (eds), *Sustainable Development Goals: Law, Theory and Implementation*. Monograph Books, p. 15.

Anghie, A., 2005. *Imperialism, Sovereignty and the Making of International Law*. Cambridge University Press.

Bastani, A., 2019. *Fully Automated Luxury Communism: A Manifesto*. Verso.

Baxi, U., 2006/2012. *The Future of Human Rights*. Oxford University Press.

Bhupinder, C., 2008. The Sen Conception of Development and Contemporary International Law Discourse: Some Parallels. *The Law and Development Review*, *1* (*1*): 3–22.

Bierstecker, T., 1987. Transnational Corporations and the Neutralization of Legislation. In Ghai, Y., Luckham, R. and Snyder, F. (eds), *The Political Economy of Law: A Third World Reader*. Oxford University Press.

Biukovic, L., 2014. Is There Policy Space for Human Rights Linkages in China's Trade and Investment Network? In Drache, D. and Jacobs, L. (eds), *Linking Global Trade and Human Rights; New Policy Space in Hard Economic Times*. Cambridge University Press, pp. 274–299.

Bourdieu, P. and Wacquant, L., 1992. *Invitation to a Reflexive Sociology.* University of Chicago Press.
Braithwaite, J. and Drahos, P., 2000. *Global Business Regulation.* Cambridge University Press.
Brautigam, D., 2011. Chinese Development Aid in Africa. In Golley, J. and Song, L. (eds), *Rising China: Global Challenges and Opportunities.* ANU ePress, chapter 13.
Brian, K., 2015. *The Gap between Rich and Poor.* OECD.
Caouette, D. and Kapoor D. (eds), 2016. *Beyond Colonialism, Development and Globalisation.* Zed Books.
Carant, J., 2016. Unheard Voices: A Critical Discourse Analysis of the Millennium Development Goals' Evolution into the Sustainable Development Goals. *Third World Quarterly, 38* (*1*): 16–41. Available online at: http://dx.doi.org/10.1080/01436597.2016.1166944 (accessed 23 September 2019).
Cardoso, F.H. and Faletto, E., 1979. *Dependency and Development in Latin América.* University of California Press.
Chang, H.-J., 1994. *The Political Economy of Industrial Policy.* Macmillan.
Chang, H.-J., 2003. *Globalisation, Economic Development and the Role of the State.* Zed Books.
Chimni, B., 2004. An Outline of a Marxist Course on Public International Law. *Leiden Journal of International Law, 17* (*1*): 1–30.
Chimni, B., 2008. The Sen Conception of Development and Contemporary International Law Discourse: Some Parallels. *The Law and Development Review, 1* (*1*): 3–22.
Clarkson, S., 1978. *The Soviet Theory of Development: India and the Third World in Marxist-Leninist Scholarship.* University of Toronto Press.
Collingham, L., 2017. *The Hungry Empire: How Britain's Quest for Food Shaped the Modern World.* Vintage.
Colville, R., 2016. *The Great Acceleration: How the World is Getting Faster and Faster.* Bloomsbury.
Cousins, B., Cousins, T., Hornby, D., Kingwill, R., Royston, L., and Smit, W., 2005. *Will Formalizing Property Rights Reduce Poverty in South Africa's Second Economy? Questioning the Mythologies of Hernando de Soto.* PLAAS Policy Brief No 18. The Institute for Policy, Land, and Agrarian Studies.
Craig, D. and Porter, P., 2006. *Development Beyond Neoliberalism? Governance, Poverty Reduction, and Political Economy.* Routledge.
Crane, B. and Maguire, E., 2017. First Aid: The Future of US Foreign Aid in the Trump Administration. *Conscience Magazine, 38* (*1*): 19–31.
Daly, H., 2019. Growthism: Its Ecological, Ethical and Economic Limits. *Real-World Economics Review, 2019* (*87*): 9–23.
De Soto, H., 2000. *The Mystery of Capital.* Basic Books.
Dezalay, Y. and Garth, B., 2002. *The Internationalization of Palace Wars: Lawyers, Economists and the Contest to Transform Latin American States. Chicago Studies in Law and Society.* University of Chicago Press.
Duffield, M., 2008. *Development, Security and Unending War: Governing the World of Peoples.* Polity Press.
Dussel, E., 2003. *Philosophy of Liberation.* Wipf & Stock.

Eichenauer, V.Z. and Reinsberg, B., 2017. *What Determines Earmarked Funding to International Development* Organizations? Evidence from the New Multi-Bi Aid Data. *The Review of International Organizations, 12* (*2*): 171–197.

Escobar, A., 1995/2012. *Encountering Development: The Making and Unmaking of the Third World.* Princeton University Press.

Esteva, G., 2010. Development. In Sachs, W. (ed.), *The Development Dictionary.* Zed Books, chapter. 1.

Esteva, G., Babones, S., and Babcicky, P., 2013. *Future of Development: A Radical Manifesto.* Policy Press.

Faundez, J., 2010. Rule of Law or Washington Consensus: The Evolution of the World Bank's Approach to Legal and Judicial Reform. In Perry-Kesaris, A. (ed.), *Law in the Pursuit of Development.* Routledge.

Faundez, J., 2014. *Douglass North's Theory of Institutions: Lessons for Law and Development.* Research Paper No. 2014/13. University of Warwick School of Law.

Fitzpatrick, P., 1992. *The Mythology of Modern Law.* Routledge.

Gehring, K., Kaplan, L. and Wong, M., 2018. Aid and Conflict at the Subnational Level – Evidence from World Bank and Chinese Development Projects in Africa. *Discussion Paper Series No 657. University of Heidelberg, Department of Economics.* Available online at: https://archiv.ub.uni-heidelberg.de/volltextserver/25686/3/Gehring_Wong_Kaplan_2018_dp657.pdf (accessed 23 September 2019).

Ghai, Y., Luckham, R. and Snyder, F. (eds), 1987. *The Political Economy of Law: A Third World Reader.* Oxford University Press.

Göpel, M., 2016. *The Great Mindshift: How a New Economic Paradigm and Sustainability Transformations Go Hand in Hand.* Springer.

Gudynas, E., 2013. Debates on Development and Its Alternatives in Latin America: A Brief Heterodox Guide. In Mokrani, M.D. (ed.), *Beyond Development: Alternative Visions from Latin America.* Transnational Institute/ Rosa Luxemburg Foundation.

Gupta, J. and Vegelin C., 2016. Sustainable Development Goals and Inclusive Development. *International Environmental Agreements: Politics, Law and Economics, 16* (*3*), 433–448.

Haggard, S., 2018. *Development States.* Cambridge University Press.

Haq, M., 1996. *Reflections on Human Development.* Oxford University Press.

Held, V., 2006. *The Ethics of Care: Personal, Political and Global.* Oxford University Press.

Hickel, J., 2015. *Why the New Sustainable Development Goals Won't Make the World a Fairer Place. The Conversation.* Available online at: http://theconversation.com/why-the-new-sustainable-development-goals-wont-make-the-world-a-fairer-place-46374 (accessed 23 September 2019).

Hickel, J., 2019. Degrowth: A Theory of Radical Abundance. *Real-World Economics Review, 87,* 54–68.

Hickel, J. and Kallis, G., 2019. Is Green Growth Possible? *New Political Economy, 2019,* 1–18. DOI:10.1080/13563467.2019.1598964.

Hill, W., Wald, N., and Guiney, T., 2016. Development and Neoliberalism. In Springer, S. Birch, K. and MacLeavy, J. (eds), *Handbook of Neoliberalism.* Routledge International.

Hoogvelt, A., 2001. *Globalisation and the Postcolonial World.* Macmillan.

Inglehart, R. and Oyserman, D., 2004. Individualism, autonomy and self-expression: the human development syndrome. In Vinken, H. Soeters, J. and Ester, P. (eds), *Comparing Cultures, Dimensions of Culture in a Comparative Perspective*. Brill, p. 74.

IMF, 1997. *Good Governance: The IMF's Role*. International Monetary Fund. Available online at: https://www.imf.org/external/pubs/ft/exrp/govern/govindex.htm (accessed 5 June 2019).

India-UNDAF, 2018. *UN Development Action Framework 2013–17: India*. United Nations Development Assistance Framework. Available online at: https://in.one.un.org/wp-content/uploads/2016/09/India_UNDAF202013-17_9Jul2012-1.pdf (accessed 6 June, 2019).

Jones, W., 1960. Economic Man in Africa. *Food Research Institute Studies*, *1* (*2*), 1–28.

Klein, E. and Morreo, C. (eds), 2019. *Postdevelopment in Practice: Alternatives, Economics, Ontologies*. Routledge.

Koh, H., 2017. *The Trump Administration and International Law. Faculty Scholarship Series 5213*. Available online at: http://digitalcommons.law.yale.edu/fss_papers/5213 (accessed 3 June 2019).

Kolbert, E., 2014. *The Sixth Extinction: An Unnatural History*. A&C Black.

Korten, D., 2015. *When Corporations Rule the World*. Berrett-Koehler Publishers.

Kothari, A., Demaria, F., and Acosta, A., 2014. Buen Vivir, Degrowth and Ecological Swaraj: Alternatives to Sustainable Development and the Green Economy. *Development*, *57* (*3–4*), 362–375.

Lall, S., 1995. Structural Adjustment and African Industry. *World Development*, *23* (*12*), 2019–2031.

Lee, Y.-S., 2017. General Theory of Law and Development. *Cornell International Journal of Law and Development*, *50* (*3*), 415–471.

Loomba, A., 1993. Dead Women Tell No Tales: Issues of Female Subjectivity, Subaltern Agency and Tradition in Colonial and Post-Colonial Writings on Widow Immolation in India. *History Workshop Journal*, *36* (*1*), 209–227.

Love, J., 1990. The Origins of Dependency Analysis. *Journal of Latin American Studies*, *22* (*1*), 143–168.

Lyon, D., 2001. *Surveillance Society: Monitoring Everyday Life*. Open University Press.

Mattei, U. and Nader, L., 2008. *Plunder: When the Rule of Law is Illegal*. Blackwell Publishing.

McCourt, W., 2018. Lost in Translation: The World Bank and the Paris Declaration. *Development Policy Review*, *36* (*6*), 649–668.

McNeill, J., 2014. *The Great Acceleration: An Environmental History of the Anthropocene since 1945*. Harvard University Press.

McVety, A., 2018. Wealth and Nations: The Origins of International Development Assistance. In Macekura, S. and Manela, E. (eds), *The Development Century: A Global History*. Cambridge University Press.

Mignolo, W., 2012. *Local Histories/Global Designs: Coloniality, Subaltern Knowledges, and Border Thinking*. Princeton University Press.

Mitchell, T., 2002. *Rule of Experts: Egypt, Techno-Politics, Modernity*. University of California Press.

Morosini, F. and Sanchez Badin, M. (eds), 2017. *Reconceptualizing Interntional Investment Law from the Global South*. Cambridge University Press.
Morozov, E., 2012. *The Dark Side of Internet Freedom*. Public Affairs.
Naim, M., 2007. Rogue Aid. *Foreign Policy*, *159*, 96.
North, D., 1995. The New Institutional Economics and Third World Development. In Harriss, J., Hunter, J. and Lewis, C. (eds), *The New Institutional Economics and Third World Development*.Taylor & Francis, chapter 2.
Ostrom, E., 1990. *Governing the Commons:The Evolution of Institutions for Collective Action*. Cambridge University Press.
Paliwala, A., 2007. Free Culture, Global Commons and Social Justice in Information Technology Diffusion. *Law, Social Justice & Global Development Journal (LGD)*, *2007* (*1*). Available online at: https://warwick.ac.uk/fac/soc/law/elj/lgd/2007_1/paliwala/paliwala.pdf (accessed 5 June 2019).
Paliwala, A., 2013. Netizenship, Security and Freedom. *International Review of Law, Computers and Technology*, *27* (*1–2*), 104–123.
Paliwala, A. and Kamchedzera, G., 2013. Justice Indicatorology: A New Theatre for Justice? *Law, Social Justice and Global Development Journal*, *2013* (*2*). Available online at: http://www2.warwick.ac.uk/fac/soc/law/elj/lgd/2013_2/paliwala_kamchedzera (accessed 2 May 2019).
Palma, G., 2003. Latin American Economies During the Second Half of the Twentieth Century: From the Age of Extremes to the Age of 'End of History' Uniformity. In Chang, H.-J. (ed.), *Rethinking Development Economics*. Anthem Press, chapter 6.
Pistor, K., 2019. *The Code of Capital*. Princeton University Press.
Plehwe, W., 2015. The Origins of Neoliberal Economic Discourse. In Mirowski, P. and Plehwe, D. (eds), *The Road from Mont Pèlerin: The Making of the Neoliberal Thought Collective*. Harvard University Press, chapter 7.
Pogge, T., 2002. *World Poverty and Human Rights*. Polity Press.
Quijano, A., 2007. Coloniality and Modernity/Rationality. *Cultural Studies*, *21* (*2–3*), 168–178.
Ragnedda, M., 2017. *Digital Inequalities*. Routledge.
Rajagopal, B., 2005. Limits of Law in Counter-hegemonic Globalisation: The Indian Supreme Court and the Narmada Valley Struggle. In Santos, B. and Garavito, C. (eds), *Law and Globalization from Below*. Cambridge University Press, p. 183.
Raworth, K., 2017. *Doughnut Economics: Seven Ways to Think Like a 21st Century Economist*. Random House Business Books.
Rist, G., 2008. *The History of Development: From Western Origins to Global Faith*, 3rd edition. Zed Books.
Rittich, K., 2004. The Future of Law and Development: Second Generation Reforms and the Incorporation of the Social. *Michigan Journal of International Law*, *26* (*1*), 199–243.
Robinson, F., 2011. *The Ethics of Care: A Feminist Approach to Human Security*. Temple University Press.
Roodman, D., 2011. *Due Diligence: An impertinent Inquiry into Microfinance*. Center for Global Development.

Rostow, W., 1960. *The Stages of Economic Growth: A Non-Communist Manifesto.* Cambridge University Press.
Sachs, W. (ed.), 2010. *The Development Dictionary.* Zed Books.
Said, E., 1993. *Orientalism.* Penguin.
Santos, B., 2007. Beyond Abyssal Thinking: From Global Lines to Ecologies of Knowledges. *Review, XXX (1)*, 45–89.
Sarangi, S., 2002. Crimes of Bhopal and the Global Campaign for Justice. *Social Justice, 29 (3)*, 47–52.
Sarfaty, G., 2009. Measuring Justice: Internal Conflict over the World Bank's Empirical Approach to Human Rights. In Clarke, K. and Goodale, M. (eds), *Mirrors of Justice: Law and Power in the Post-Cold War Era.* Cambridge University Press.
Sen, A., 1999. *Development as Freedom.* Oxford University Press.
Sen, A., 2009. Economics, Law and Ethics. In Gotoh, R. and Dumouchel, P. (eds), *Against Injustice: The New Economics of Amartya Sen.* Cambridge University Press, pp. 38–54.
Sen, A. 2011. *Peace and Democratic Society.* Open Book Publishers.
Schlemmer-Schulte, S., 2001. The World Bank's Role in the Promotion of the Rule of Law in Developing Countries. In Schlemmer-Shulte, S. and Tung, S.-Y., *Liber Amicorum Ibrahim F. Shihata.* Brill.
Shihata, I., 2000. *Prohibition of Political Activities in the Bank's Work, Legal Opinion of the General Counsel. Sec M95–707. Reproduced in: The World Bank Legal Papers.* World Bank.
Stiglitz, J., 2001. From Miracle to Crisis Recovery: Lessons from Four Decades of East Asian Experience. In Stiglitz, J. and Yusuf, S., *Rethinking the East Asian Miracle.* World Bank and Oxford University Press, chapter 13.
Strange, A., Dreher, A., Fuchs, A. Parks, B. and Tierney, M., 2017. Tracking Underreported Financial Flows: China's Development Finance and the Aid–Conflict Nexus Revisited. *Journal of Conflict Resolution, 61 (5)*, 935–963.
Tamanaha, B., 2011. The Primacy of Society and the Failures of Law and Development. *Cornell International Law Journal, 44 (2)*, 216–244.
Tan, C., 2011. *Governance through Development: Poverty Reduction Strategies, International Law and the Disciplining of Third World States.* Routledge.
Toye, J., 2004. Changing Perspectives in Development Economics. In Chang, H.-J. (ed.), *Rethinking Development Economics.* Anthem Press, chapter 1.
Tronto, J., 1993. *Moral Boundaries: A Political Argument for an Ethic of Care.* Routledge.
Tronto, J., 2013. *Caring Democracy: Markets, Equality and Justice.* New York University Press.
Trubek, D. and Galanter, M., 1974. Scholars in Self-Estrangement: Some Reflections on the Crisis in Law and Development Studies in the United States. *Wisconsin Law Review, 1974*: 1062 –1102.
Tully, J., 2013. Two Ways of Realizing Justice and Democracy: Linking Amartya Sen and Elinor Ostrom. *Critical Review of International Social and Political Philosophy 16 (2)*: 220–232.
UNRISD, 2016. *Policy Innovations for Transformative Change.* Flagship Report. UN Research Institute for Sustainable Development.

Wade, R., 1990/2004. *Governing the Market: Economic Theory and the Role of Government in East Asian Industrialisation*. Princeton University Press.

Wade, R., 2018. Development State: Dead or Alive? *Development and Change*, *49* (2), 518–546.

Wallerstein, I., 2004. *World-Systems Analysis: An Introduction*. Duke University Press.

WCED (World Commission on Environment and Development), 1987. *Our Common Future*. Oxford University Press.

Woods, N., 2006. *The Globalizers: The IMF, the World Bank, and Their Borrowers*. Cornell University Press.

World Bank, 1993. *The East Asian Miracle: Economic Growth and Public Policy*. World Bank.

World Bank, 1994a. *Adjustment in Africa: Reforms, Results, and the Road Ahead*. Oxford University Press.

World Bank, 1994b. *Governance: The World Bank's Experience*. World Bank.

WSIS (World Summit on Information Society), 2005. *Tunis Commitment*. WSIS05/TUNIS/DOC/7-E 18.11.2005.

Zuboff, S., 2019. *The Age of Surveillance Capitalism*. Profile Books.

Chapter 2

Ameliorating human futures through postdevelopment?

Upendra Baxi

Introduction

I place a question mark after my title because like many of us I have long been puzzled by the term 'development' in my teaching and research and have shared many a critique of the practices of development as programmes of governance that regularly appropriate (even when not outright confiscating) the spaces of social agency. I have also endorsed critiques of 'outsourcing' of the idea of 'development' by imperial hegemons and their normative cohorts, especially the international financial institutions and communities of state-like and state-transcendent multinational corporations and foreign investors. I have joined progressive voices questioning the difference between the 'old' and 'new' concepts of development and seriously queried some versions of 'alternatives to development' and 'alternate development' (Baxi, 2012). And I have dedicated most of my activist life to confronting modern day evils of state and corporate governance as practices of subjectification and economic oppression.

This rather longish preambular foray into a lifecycle becomes necessary as I confront the meanings of going 'beyond development'. What leads to this new conception — is it merely old wine in new bottles? Or does it mark a qualitative conceptual change? If the latter, what are the circumstances/conjunctures that cause or condition this change, what are itineraries of planned global social change, and what may be the first stage of the future of whatever may be said to lie 'beyond development'? Several articles (or monographs) lurk here, but it suffices to briefly address the question of 'postdevelopment'.

One understands the growing fatigue with the old and even anachronistic idea of development as comprising primarily economic change, whether centrally planned or market-driven. One also understands development as an obstacle to human freedom rather than opportunity for freedom (as Amartya Sen (1999) would have it), especially in the context of the emerging economies and the dying of a Third World that was once hoped to be a unified entity against imperialism (Galeano, 1997; Young, 2001; Prashad, 2008, 2013; Hurrell, 2013; Baxi, 2016b). But we still may ask what, if anything, may be gained by going beyond development. More importantly, we need to ask whether there is a difference of kind rather than merely one of degree between the idea of development and historical and contemporary practices of development. Put another way, does the idea of development arise from a particular set of practices or does the idea give rise to those practices? We should, in seeking answers to these questions consider the possibility that 'development has become an amoeba-like concept, shapeless but ineradicable', with 'contours so blurred it denotes nothing'.[1]

A human right to dream?

In an increasingly cruel world, at least when viewed from a worm's eye perspective, there is no room for happy surprises (Rummel, 1997; Mamdani, 2001; Mgbeoji, 2003; Santiago Nino, 1966; Osiel, 1997; Power, 2002). Nevertheless, the United Nations system seems resiliently capable of spawning new phrases and acronyms, and making these pass for deep thought. It ceaselessly creates phrase regimes that never cease to surprise or astonish. The following are some examples: sustainable development, sustainable debt, Millennium Development Goals (MDGs), Sustainable Development Goals (SDGs), common but differentiated responsibility and respective capacities, the global compact, the right to development, responsibility to protect, and latterly postdevelopment (PD). The sheer force of reiteration in a myriad United Nations General Assembly resolutions and other UN documents and fora have the cumulative effect of providing magical realities to international law, relations, and organisations.[2]

I use the term 'magic' for the creation of fictional worlds of global governance because they are fictional in the sense of the production of enchantment that overcomes the limitations of time, place, and circumstance. I also deploy the term as dream work: dreams of a human future that is truly emancipated from exploitation, drudgery and power that some people and entities exercise over most others (Mannheim, 1991; Foucault, 1997; Jacoby, 2005; Claeys, 2010). If there is one unscripted human right, it is the right of people to dream, to reimagine distant futures, and to let the dreaming wander through reality.[3]

1 In the preface to *The Development Dictionary: A Guide to Knowledge as Power*, Sachs (1992: 4) remarks that it is time to write the obituary of the very concept of 'development'.
2 Relations between law and magic call for a critical study. Axel Hagerstorm thought of law as modern magic: 'According to the Roman view', Hagerstrom maintains, 'the right of property is a mystical power over the spirit inherent in the object. This power is created, and transferred, by means of magical acts … All the ancient legal acts belonging to the original Roman law were magical acts' (Olivecrona, 1959: 133). See also Allen (2006).
3 Arturo Escobar (1995: 5) has a passing reference to this dialectic dream and nightmare in his classic work on development. 'This book', he writes, 'can be read as the history of the loss of an illusion in which many genuinely believed'; it is the story of a dream that 'progressively turned into a nightmare'.

But the question that matters is not so much about dreams but nightmares. The production of alternate futures that respect the human right to dream should also cope with a coequal human right to difference and disagreement. This raises the question whether there are moral, juristic, and legal limits to difference and disagreement? Put another way, what is at stake here is not conflict of interpretation but a threshold denial of interpretation. This hermeneutical denialism is the essence of all human rights *denialism* based upon a *grundorm* that the very idea of human rights is mortally mistaken. In this perspective, what matters is development rather than equality, freedom, dignity, or fraternal/ sororal social inclusion. What appears to matter most is social cooperation towards 'progress' and 'welfare', even when often considered indecisive or even irrelevant to governance, but these obstinate realities give rise to many a contemporary human rights and standards.

What might the positing of a human right to dream entail? At one level, it may comprise an individual and social (collective) human right to imagine different symbols, slogans, and alternative cultures and lifestyles. The difficulty with this perspective is that the dreams of some are the nightmares of others, which raises the question of the scope and content of such a right: does it extend only to dreams that are adjudged as 'reasonable'– and, if so, by whom? Or does it extend to the human right to cause nightmares? Using the trope of suffering, I wrote in *The Future of Human Rights* how the normative existence of the idea of human rights causes suffering to those who would deny them altogether for others while enjoying their bounties themselves (Baxi, 2013: 34–5).

The central question is thus the outlawing of nightmares or the authorisation of reasonable dreams. The Catch-22, as it were, is whether dream-nightmare is a binary or constitutes a continuum across which all history of human agency moves?

Constructing discursive objects of governance

Arturo Escobar (1995) developed an extension of Foucault's conceptions of an 'apparatus' and 'regimes of truth'. The discourse on development, he writes, has 'created an extremely efficient apparatus of producing knowledge about and the exercise of power over the Third World'—an apparatus that came into existence roughly in the period 1945 to 1955 and has not since ceased to produce new arrangements of knowledge and power, new practices, theories, strategies and so on' (Escobar, 1995: 9). The discourse has 'successfully deployed a regime of government over the Third World', a 'space for subject peoples that ensures certain control over it' (Baxi, 2013: 9). Development as a series of practices of governmentality, as a site of political practices of de-/re-subjectification, as a means for power to create subjects out of citizens, and generally as an arena of hegemony and dominance is the *leitmotif* of Escobar's *locus classicus* – 'development' is the elephant in the room rather than a guest artist (Escobar, 1995). This was poignantly true throughout the Cold War, as it is now in the epoch of neoliberalism.

While much can be said in criticism of the Brundtland Commission's definition of sustainable development (WCED, 1987), Escobar's sharp polemic perhaps goes too far. He argues that the Commission's report, 'inaugurated a period of unprecedented gluttony in the history of vision and knowledge', and gave rise to a new global 'ecocracy'. Escobar further criticises the assumption 'that the benevolent (white) hand of the West will save the Earth, and that it is up to the patriarchs of the World Bank, mediated by Gro Harlem Brundtland, the matriarch scientist-politician and a few cosmopolitan Third Worlders who made it onto the World Commission, to reconcile humankind with nature (Escobar, 1995: 193). One does not, however, have to rely on, or invoke, the 'benevolence' of 'ecocracy' to appreciate forms of counter-power which have furnished agendas of alternate non-dominant models of development which continue to energise the dreams of the 'commons' and 'green governance'.

In one sense neither Foucault nor Escobar specifically and directly address the issue of the necessary conditions for the emergence of discursive objects of governance (DOGs) such as sustainable development or climate change which are co-produced by expert knowledges and governmental rationalities (Allan, 2016). This is illustrated by the charmed circle of international relations theorists who have laboured to describe the ways in which DOGs are created, and influence governance functions. Their concern with DOGs is welcome but it also needs stating that legal realists (notably in Scandinavia) construed law as magic in the early 20th century and how, towards its close, the writings of Algirdas Julien Greimas (1983) crafted a new semiology of law. He pointed out that the autonomy of law lies in inventing and developing new words that did not preexist in nature or society (e.g. citizens, corporations, legal personality) and the two related but distinct realms of *production juridique* and *production verifique* (Greimas, 1983; see also Greimas, 1970/1987).

Discursive objects of governance perform the role of agenda and priority setting. The reasons why only some objects of governance become DOGs need to be explored and evaluated in each circumstance because the necessary conditions for creating them remains an open question, as recently described by Bentley B. Allan (2016). Allan broadly identifies processes of *designation, translation, and problematisation*, specifically arguing that 'knowledge and political order 'co-produce' one another in a continually changing yet self-perpetuating relationship' (Allan, 2016: 133) His analysis shows that 'scientists do not only change state interests via persuasion or institutional capture' but more crucially 'also shape state interests by wielding a productive form of power that populates the world with new entities and problems' (ibid.). Moreover, it is important to recall that 'the epistemic actors in the climate change case do not form an epistemic community because they do not necessarily share consensual causal or principled beliefs; indeed, 'heterogeneous groups of experts can participate in the constitution and governance of the same object because they deploy compatible modes of abstraction that allow transcriptions and forms of knowledge to be linked to one another' (Allan, 2016: 133, see also 139–42).

The conceptual takeaways from Allan's analysis are numerous and pertinent to discourses on the Anthropocene. The idea of the co-production of governance social realties by political and constitutional elites on the one hand and technoscience elites on the other appears as a necessary condition for the production of discursive objects of governance. Equally important is the heterogeneity of state and social actors. We also need to recognise the heterogeneity of the media and forms of 'tabloid terror' leading to the enunciation of some DOGs (Debrix, 2007; Baxi, 2009).

Postdevelopment

One of the remarkable aspects of global governance is repeated appropriation and re-appropriation, something that the practice in the UN of perambulatory recital and reiteration simultaneously signifies and mystifies. Postdevelopment is now a UN governance term, a new-fangled and contemporary discursive object of governance, just as 'development' was for four decades. It makes trite sense in terms of the prefix in that what is 'post' is what comes after 'development'. But what comes after?

It is also not immediately self-evident whether the practices of development are challenged or the very idea of development stands indicted.[4] Whereas previous development theory designated the type of development envisaged (political, economic, social) and chased their dynamic interrelationships, we do not quite know whether postdevelopment theory privileges economic development *per se*. Further, the eternal question of the relationship between theory and practice remains foregrounded; there is no threshold reason for thinking, for example, that neoliberal dogmas about development will transform theories of development from their colonial and Eurocentric moorings or that what remains of Third World approaches may help fashion altogether new approaches. Put another way, it is far from clear what postdevelopment theory emerges from all this new talk in contrast to apocalyptic narratives of anthropogenic harm which constrain us to abandon its thinking and practices.

What is abundantly clear is that new notions of postdevelopment remain deeply parasitic upon the Northern conceptions of development which generated a Eurocentric top-down idea (Esteva, 1992; Escobar, 1988; Rahnema, 1997) and divided human species into two classes: ***developers*** and ***developees***. Not merely was development conceived as an exclusionary, interventionist, and violent notion (in the sense at least of the perpetration and perpetuation of

4 See for example chapters in Klein and Morreo (2019). In the Introduction, they note that 'Postdevelopment emerged in the 1980s drawing on poststructuralist legacies in order to destabilise the discourse or apparatus of development as a hegemonic principle organising social life … Postdevelopment scholars and activists provided a cutting critique of the global development assemblage' (3–4).

developmental violence), it was also seen as a storehouse of the ways, means and constant endeavours of the former imperial powers to cancel the gains of political independence of the 'new' nations of the Third World with the advent and consolidation of the practices of the Cold War.[5] Escobar (1992: 419) approvingly cites Rahnema's (1988) description of development as 'a Frankenstein-type dream', an 'alien model of exploitation' which 'reflects urban bias'. The dream of development is over and what is now needed is not more development but 'a different regime of truth and perception' (Escobar, 1992: 412). Is the end of the long development dream a nightmare or the beginning of a new dawn? It is this concern that talk about moving 'beyond development' must address.

These polemics against development relate primarily to the practices of development. They raise the question of whether there is a distinctive theory of development that is universal. The postdevelopment response is that the idea of development is culturally conditioned and socially embedded rather than universal, and postdevelopment thinkers insist that invoking 'universal standards for classifying and evaluating societies in fact subordinates countless different perceptions and values of other people' and, moreover, that it is dangerous when global hegemons seek to transform societies according to supposedly universal standards (Ziai, 2007: 9).

The mutations of postdevelopment theory are suggested at least in the domains of enhanced autonomy and radical democratic plurality. Certainly, one of the main aims of changes to the notion of development is to put the North-centric pedagogical component of the concept to rest. As Nederveen Pieterse maintains (2000: 182), 'telling other people what to do in the name of modernisation, nation building, progress, mobilisation, sustainable development, human rights, poverty alleviation and even empowerment and participation' is no longer envisaged as development. The same applies to what has been called 'the managerialism of development' (ibid.). However, one remains anxious about what may happen to core human rights (peremptory *jus cogens* or *erga omens* obligations in customary or conventional international law). Despite this, post-development is increasingly viewed as a form of emancipation that enables Caroline Kippler to assert that it:

> implies a reclaiming of the practice and imaginary of development and firmly relocating it within a radically democratised political process which at a local level provides a means of emancipation for people by taking back a measure of control over shaping their lives.
>
> (Kippler, 2010: 3)

5 The literature on development is vast. I cull some of the best writings in Baxi (2007: 69–70, footnote 1) and the references in chapters 4 and 5. This listing is now supplanted by the literature on postdevelopment. In Baxi (2012: 79–92) I list 12 concerns about the idea of 'development' as 'planned social change'.

Kippler evokes Chantal Mouffe's (2005) central insight that the Euro-Enlightenment heritage must be moulded to 'acknowledge difference' and the thesis of Nakano about emancipation which 'in essence' is 'plural'; postdevelopment envisions the possibility of a trans-state multiplural political community (Nakano, 2007: 63–70).

From the Millennium Development Goals to the Sustainable Development Goals

The late 20th century witnessed many kinds of 'endings' — the end of the nation state, the working class, history, peasants, science, the end of books — that generated different kinds of endology, endomania, and endolatory (Baxi, 2013: 210, 279, 284, 285). We live amidst a riot of 'post-isms' in which everything is 'post' as well perhaps past. We need to distinguish at least six related but differing notions: poststructuralism, postmodernism, post-Fordism, post-neoliberalism, posthuman and postdevelopment.[6] To chase interconnections among these is a mammoth task that we do not undertake here, save to say that thinking anew about global social change in the direction of core human rights and justice in a world in the throes of transformation entails identifying fresh challenges and new approaches. Used merely as a chronological category, the prefix 'post' is not very useful and can be dangerous and even sinister when invoked as the sole basis of economic judgements about trends of future growth. With this caveat, we turn briefly to the signpost of the MDGs and their replacement by the SDGs.

The Millennium Development Goals

The eight MDGs were adopted at the Millennium Summit of the United Nations in 2000, following the adoption of the United Nations Millennium Declaration (UNGA, 2000). All 189 United Nations member states (there are currently 193) and at least 22 international organisations committed to help achieve the following MDGs by 2015. The Goals and their accompanying targets were geared specifically to eradicate extreme poverty and hunger; achieve universal primary education; promote gender equality and empower women; reduce child mortality; improve maternal health; combat HIV/AIDS, malaria, and other diseases: ensure environmental sustainability; and develop a global partnership for development. The UN's Annual Reports contain valuable accounts of international tardiness in achieving these goals and targets (UNGA, 2015a).

6 For this new-fangled conception of post-neoliberalism and postdevelopment, see Brigg (2002); Escobar (1992); Birdsall and Fukuyama (2011); Nederveen Pieterse (1996); Gibson-Graham (2005).

The MDGs were welcomed as setting an international development paradigm by privileging vulnerable humans. Expectations were high, yet the MDG timelines frequently needed extension and attainments were incommensurate with expectations.[7] The MDGs were subjected to considerable critique (Amin, 2006; Kabeer, 2005; Rosenfield et al., 2006; Attaran, 2005; Baxi, 2006: 504–8; Alston, 2005). Many found the enunciation of the goals unclear and ambivalent; others simply found them unrealistic and risked creating a 'legitimacy' trap. Some questioned the measurement and reporting methods. Still others raised the question of the efficacy of international action and collaboration (Baxi, 2006: 504–8; Kabeer, 2005; Rosenfield, Maine and Freedman, 2006; Attaran, 2005; Alston, 2005). The final UN report on the MDGs provides a typical glass-half-full, half-empty narrative of a few advances among a multitude of failures (UNGA, 2015a). As Secretary-General Ban Ki-Moon says in the short preface, although the Goals provided a new ferment which 'generated new and innovative partnerships, galvanized public opinion and showed the immense value of setting ambitious goals' and although they 'reshaped decision-making in developed and developing countries alike', the negative side is also enormous: 'inequalities persist and … progress has been slow' (UNGA, 2015a: 3). A careful study of the report shows how little was done between 2000 and 2015, and how much was undone. It shows that the MDGs constitute a pious wish list at best (Saith, 2006). Of course, the United Nations also possesses the collective right to dream on behalf of the peoples of the world but as a programme of action the MDGs should have been conceptually more coherent and clear (Saith, 2006: 1167, 1172).

The Sustainable Development Goals

The SDGs arose from the ashes of MDGs in 2015,[8] a landmark year for the United Nations as it witnessed the unanimous adoption of the 2030 Agenda for Sustainable Development (UNGA, 2015b), the Paris Agreement on climate change (UN, 2015b), the Third International Conference on Financing for Development (UN, 2015a),[9] and the Third World Conference on Disaster Risk Reduction in Sendai (UN, 2015c). Adoption of these instruments signals a new move in multilateralism despite the suspicion that all it amounts to is a shift

7 Despite a decline during the 15 years of the MDGs, approximately 700 million people remain in extreme poverty: World Food Programme, https://www.wfp.org/climate--impacts (accessed 1 November 2016). These numbers would be substantially higher but for China's growth since 1979.

8 See for an introduction to the SDGs, UNGA (2015a) (*Transforming Our World*); for critiques of the SDGs, see Jenks (2015); Loewe (2012); Osborn et al. (2015).

9 The Addis Ababa Agenda, which singularly failed to deal with concerns of developing countries such as tax avoidance and evasion by transnational corporations.

towards voluntarism. The preambulatory enunciation in the 2030 Agenda outlines a 'plan of action for people, planet and prosperity' that 'seeks to strengthen universal peace in larger freedom'. The Agenda provides a new language for multilevel governance: it integrates the three fundamental pillars of development (economic, social, and environmental), declares itself universally applicable, and includes new issues outside the old paradigms of development such as peace and climate change. Enormous work has been invested by global society actors including states and social movements as well as the United Nations in these enunciations, and the SDGs strive to be much more inclusive than the MDGs (in addition to the 193 member states, it is estimated that more than 8 million people were consulted in the preparation of the 17 goals and 169 targets) (UNDP, 2015). Whereas the UN Charter was framed in the language of 'we the peoples of the United Nations', the 2030 Agenda is declared to be a 'charter for people and planet in the twenty-first century'. The normative shift linking 'people' and 'planet' is crucial for understanding and combating anthropogenic harm and directs attention to new forms of multispecies and natural solidarity as justice to come.

A new interpretive turn and twist is provided to the three central pillars of the United Nations – peace and security, human rights, development; the preamble to the 2030 Agenda lays stress on four 'Ps': Planet, Prosperity, Peace, Partnership. The SDGs enunciate new pathways of integration among economic, social and environmental dimensions of sustainable development. The dense interrelationships between pressing concerns such as rising inequality (SDG 10), violent deaths (SDG 16), and lack of affordable housing and basic services (SDG 11) are more fully recognised than before.[10]

The innovative nature of the 2030 Agenda is not in doubt, but its likely effectiveness is. If the experience of MDGs is any guide, we would need substantial investment and greatly enhanced intergovernmental cooperation for the 17 ambitious targets to be met. The goals of PPP (public–private partnerships) are normatively welcome but financing development entails going considerably beyond self-interest and overcoming ethical Neanderthalism, especially on the part of state and corporate actors. Perhaps a detailed examination of climate finance will pave the way for a greater understanding of the types of cooperation and collaboration involved, including legal changes (Stewart et al., 2009; Johl and Lador, 2012). The aspect of financing the realisation of human rights is a question that needs to be seriously understood

10 See Independent Commission on Multilateralism (2016: 3): 'If, for example, a member state implements SDG 5 on 'gender equality and empowerment of women and girls,' it would also address targets related to poverty eradication, health, inequality, education, and peaceful and inclusive societies. Thus, the new SDG framework is a network in which all goals are interconnected'.

and urgently acted upon,[11] as does the question of financing peace (OECD, 2014; Flores and Nooruddin, 2009; Thakur et al., 2007).

Towards a theory of contradictions and evil?

It is surprising that while approaches to development and postdevelopment have addressed the underlying destruction and violence of the practices of development, these have not explored the need for a theory of contradiction and evil. The former stands relegated primarily to planning economic growth and distribution; the latter are best left to eschatology and ethics. However, any understanding of development theory, practice, and movement presupposes approaches to contradictions and evil.

By a theory of contradictions I mean something more than experiencing, living or embodying contradictions. All my life I have tried to grasp the contradictory unity of law formation: to trace its redoing emancipatory potential and to chase its Kafkaesque lies, to study the vast tragedy that is law – in both (as Robert Cover (1983) would say) its 'jurisgenerative' and 'jurispathic' (and we might add, jurispathetic) elements and dimensions.[12] To vary the phrase-regime, the law can be viewed as a force for 'creative destruction' (Schumpeter 1942; Baumol et al., 2007),[13] or the instantiation of the old and the new normal (Baumol et al., 2007), or as a means of resilience as well as destruction.[14] As we live a life of contradictions, how do we combat these? How do we understand that constitutions and laws are creative and/or destructive in the same moment?

Development, both old and new, invites a theory of contradictions that classifies at least the following seven contradictions: material, institutional, normative, cultural/civilisational, religious, or antagonistic and non-antagonistic

11 See, for an important initiative, Regulation (EU) No 235/2014 of The European Parliament and of the Council of 11 March 2014 Establishing A Financing Instrument For Democracy and Human Rights Worldwide (2014) and the contrasting views in Duke International Human Rights Clinic & Women Peacemakers Program, 2017. Available online at: https://law.duke.edu/sites/default/files/humanrights/tighteningpursestrings.pdf (accessed 25 June 2018).

12 Dr B.R. Ambebdkar, the principal architect of the Indian constitution, was most explicit in describing this contradictory unity: 'On the 26th January,1950, we are going to enter into a life of contradictions. In politics, we shall be recognizing the principle of one man one vote one value. In our social and economic life, we shall, by reason of economic structure continue to deny [this principle]. How long shall we continue to live this life of contradiction? If we continue to deny it for long, we will do so by putting our democracy in peril' (1946: Vol. XIX, 979). For a critique and reconstruction of the notion of contradiction, see Berman (2013). I add 'jurispathetic' as a third form consisting in the very denial of the idea of 'juris'— the enactment of law as an exercise of will without any reason; in essence, the denial of the very possibility of law as a restraint on power.

13 For a legisprudence example, see Stephan (1998).

14 In *Capital, Volume 1*, Marx develops this distinction well. See Baxi (1994).

contradictions as formulated by Mao Zedong (1937). David Harvey (2014) enunciates 17 contradictions in three categories: six are 'foundational', seven are 'moving' and four are 'dangerous' contradictions. Of this latter category, the portent of the 21st century is the contradiction constituted by what he calls 'universal alienation'.[15] If so, in contrast to belonging, anything that fosters alienation must be regarded as inherently evil. Adi Ophir describes evil as anything that entails 'negative consequences for one's self, one's world and one's future' and insists that 'catastrophization is a disorder, indeed, but of the world and not the mind' and is an 'avalanche of evils', which entail 'suffering and losses, humiliation and scarcity, deprivation and neglect' (Ophir, 2010: 40).

How far should we go in describing this Age of Cruelty both as an 'oppressive' and 'liberational' globalisation? On the question whether human beings have become progressively or comparatively less cruel, there is a noted difference of opinion[16]- a concern we do not examine here save to observe that what may be called developmental cruelty is peculiar to the human experience in the global South during the past 60 years (Baxi, 2013: 39, footnotes 13–23). This experience provides the historical herein of resistance, contemporary human rights standards and norms (discursivity), and even 'emancipation', while developmental cruelty doles out various forms of state authoritarianism (Baxi, 2016b). But we must also note the problem of de-westernising emancipation (Mahbubani, 2008; Ray, 2012; Barreto, 2014). If European modernity involved ecocide and epistemicide, the best way forward may be to explore the possibility of new social movements. Is it the case that such movements may, as Arturo Escobar (2004: 207) puts it, 'represent the best hope for reworking imperial globality and global coloniality in ways that make imagining after the Third World, and beyond modernity, a viable project'? What different modernities can be constructed in pursuit of emancipation? Are there alternatives to neoliberal globalisation, especially when the Second and Third Worlds are said to have suffered a historic demise, and Third Worldism – as an ideology and a state of social consciousness – is said to be in retreat (Baxi, 2016)? Ultimately, is all this talk of postdevelopment or beyond development a new discourse about the changing paradigm of law and governance?

To raise a related concern: do we also need to supplement or even develop a separate theory of evil in contrast to abundant theoretical approaches to the

15 Harvey (2014: 264–281). The Young Marx put it this way: 'Every emancipation is a restoration of the human world and of human relationships to man himself. Human emancipation will only be complete when the real individual man has absorbed into himself the abstract citizen; when as an individual man, in his everyday life, in his work, and in his relationships, he has become a species-being; and when he has recognized and organized his own powers (*forces propres*) as social powers so that he no longer separates his social power from himself as political power' (Marx, 1978: 46).

16 An evolutionary life scientist would say that humans have become less cruel: see for example Pinker (2011).

virtue of 'good'?[17] Prescinding a range of discourses, especially theological 'justifications' for evil, evil-sceptical, and evil revivalist approaches (Tooley, 2015), one may deal with moral evil — an act or omission for which the agent, whether individually, associationally or collectively may be regarded as responsible. What amounts to 'responsibility' is a vexed question and is answered in several ways that entail a judgement by the agent and others in terms of degrees of blameworthiness (Card, 2001, 2002, 2010; Garrard, 1998; 2002; Calder, 2002; Barry, 2009). Such ethical judgements are based on different grounds: evil as wrongdoing, as harm, as 'a certain sort of motivation', and as affect (Tooley, 2015). And moral evil cannot be altogether eradicated; it can only be prevented from happening or punished after it has occurred.

These are very large issues for theories, practices and movements. However, my point is simple enough: one must abandon all hopes of going 'beyond development' if approaches to understanding contradictions and evil are not well worked out.

References

Allan, B.B., 2016. Producing the Climate: States, Scientists, and the Constitution of Global Governance Objects. *International Organization*, *71*, 131–162.

Allen, J., 2006. *A Theory of Adjudication: Law as Magic.* Paper 54. New York University Public Law and Legal Theory Working Papers. Available online at: https://lsr.nellco.org/cgi/viewcontent.cgi?referer=https://www.google.com/&httpsredir=1&article=1053&context=nyu_plltwp (accessed 28 May 2019).

Alston, P., 2005. Ships Passing by the Night: The Current State of Human Rights and Development Discourse Seen through the Lens of Millennial Development Goals. *Human Rights Quarterly*, *27* (*3*), 755–829.

Amin, S., 2006. The Millennium Development Goals: A Critique from the South. *Monthly Review*, *57* (*10*), 1–15.

Attaran, A., 2005. An Immeasurable Crisis? A Criticism of the Millennium Development Goals and Why They Cannot be Measured. *PLoS Medicine*, *2* (*10*), e318.

Barreto, J.-M., 2014. Epistemologies of the South and human rights: Santos and the quest for global and cognitive justice. *Indiana Journal of Global Legal Studies*, *21* (*2*), 395–422.

Barry, P.B., 2009. Moral Saints, Moral Monsters, and the Mirror Thesis. *American Philosophical Quarterly*, *46* (*2*), 163–176.

Baumol, W.J., Litan, R.E. and Schramm. C.J., 2007. *Good Capitalism, Bad Capitalism, and the Economics of Growth and Prosperity.* Yale University Press.

Baxi, U., 1994. *Marx, Law and Justice: Indian Perspectives.* NM Tripathi/ LexisNexis.

17 An ancillary concern is how far demosprudential adjudicatory leadership can be regarded as such a social movement? See Baxi (2016a).

Baxi, U., 2006. A Report for All Seasons? Small Notes on Reading 'In Larger Freedom'. In Kumar, C. Raj and Srivastava, D.K. (eds), *Human Rights and Development: Law, Policy and Governance.* Butterworth Lexis/Nexis, p. 504.

Baxi, U., 2007. *Human Rights in a Posthuman World: Critical Essays.* Oxford University Press.

Baxi, U., 2009. Reading 'Terror': Some Reflections on Reading François Debrix, Tabloid Terror: War, Culture, and Geopolitics. *Theory & Event, 12 (3).* Available online at: https://muse.jhu.edu/ (accessed 4 April 2019).

Baxi, U., 2012. Development as a Human Right or Political Largesse. In Saleth, R.M. (ed.), *From Individual to Community: Issues in Development Studies: Essays in Memory of Malcolm Adiseshiah.* Sage.

Baxi, U., 2013. *The Future of Human Rights*, 3rd edition. Oxford University Press.

Baxi, U., 2016a. Demosprudence and Socially Responsible/Response-able Criticism: The NJAC Decision and Beyond. *National Union of Juridical Sciences Law Review, 9*, 153–172.

Baxi, U., 2016b. Some Newly Emergent Geographies of Injustice: Boundaries and Borders in International Law. *Indiana Journal of Global Legal Studies, 23 (1)*, 15–37.

Berman, P.S., 2013. Jurisgenerative Constitutionalism: Procedural Principles for Managing Global Legal Pluralism. *Indiana Journal of Global Legal Studies, 20 (2)*, 665–695.

Birdsall, N. and Fukuyama, F., 2011. The Post-Washington Consensus: Development After the Crisis. *Foreign Affairs, 90 (2)*, 45–53.

Bohoslavsky, J.P. and Cernic, J.L. (eds), 2014. *Making Sovereign Financing and Human Rights Work.* Hart Publishing.

Brigg, M., 2002. Post-Development, Foucault and the Colonisation Metaphor. *Third World Quarterly, 23 (3)*, 421–436.

Calder, T., 2002. Towards a Theory of Evil: A Critique of Laurence Thomas's Theory of Evil Acts. In Haybron, D.M. (ed.), *Earth's Abominations: Philosophical Studies of Evil.* Rodopi.

Card, C., 2001. Inequalities versus Evils. In Sterba, J.P. (ed.), *Controversies in Feminism.* Rowman & Littlefield Publishers, chapter 6.

Card, C., 2002. *The Atrocity Paradigm: A Theory of Evil.* Oxford University Press.

Card, C., 2010. *Confronting Evils: Terrorism, Torture, Genocide.* Cambridge University Press.

Claeys, G. (ed.), 2010. *The Cambridge Companion to Utopian Literature.* Cambridge University Press.

Cover, R.M., 1983. The Supreme Court, 1982 Term – Foreword: Nomos and Narrative. Paper 2705. Yale Law School Faculty Scholarship Series. Available online at: https://digitalcommons.law.yale.edu/fss_papers/2705 (accessed 19 May 2019).

Debrix, F., 2007. *Tabloid Terror: War, Culture, and Geopolitics.* Routledge.

Duke International Human Rights Clinic and Women Peacemakers Program, 2017. *Tightening The Purse Strings: What Countering Terrorism Financing Costs Gender Equality and Security.* Duke Law. Available online at: https://law.duke.edu/sites/default/files/humanrights/tighteningpursestrings.pdf (accessed 25 June 2018).

Escobar, A., 1988. Power and Visibility: Development and the Invention and Management of the Third World. *Cultural Anthropology*, *3* (*4*), 428–443.

Escobar, A., 1992. Imagining a Post-Development Era? Critical Thought, Development and Social Movements. *Social Text*, *31/32*, 20–56.

Escobar, A., 1995. *Encountering Development: The Making and the Unmaking of the Third World*. Princeton University Press.

Escobar, A., 2004. Beyond the Third World: Imperial Globality, Global Coloniality and Anti-globalisation Social Movements. *Third World Quarterly*, *25* (*1*), 207–230.

Esteva, G., 1992. Development. In Sachs, W. (ed.), *The Development Dictionary: A Guide to Knowledge as Power*. Zed Books, chapter 1.

Flores, T.E. and Nooruddin, I., 2009. Financing the Peace: Evaluating World Bank Post-Conflict Assistance Programs. *The Review of International Organizations*, *4* (*1*), 1–27.

Foucault, M., 1997. Of Other Spaces: Utopias and Heterotopias. In Leach, N. (ed.), *Rethinking Architecture: A Reader in Cultural Theory*. Routledge, p. 330.

Galeano, E., 1997. *The Open Veins of Latin America: Five Centuries of the Pillage of a Continent*. Monthly Review Press.

Garrard, E., 1998. The Nature of Evil. *Philosophical Explorations*, *1* (*1*), 43–60.

Garrard, E., 2002. Evil as an Explanatory Concept. *The Monist*, *85* (*2*), 320–336.

Gibson-Graham, J.K., 2005. Surplus Possibilities: Postdevelopment and Community Economies. *Singapore Journal of Tropical Geography*, *26* (*1*), 4–26.

Greimas, A.G., 1970/1987. *On Meaning*. University of Minnesota Press.

Greimas, A.G., 1983. *Structural Semantics: An Attempt at a Method*. University of Nebraska Press.

Harvey, D., 2014. *Seventeen Contradictions and End of Capitalism*. Profile Books.

Hurrell, A., 2013. Narratives of Emergence: Rising Powers and the End of the Third World? *Brazilian Journal of Political Economy*, *33* (*2*), 203–221.

Independent Commission on Multilateralism, 2016. Discussion Paper on the 2030 Agenda for Sustainable Development and Addressing Climate Change. Available online at: https://www.icm2016.org/the-2030-agenda-for-sustainable-development-and-addressing-climate-change (accessed 25 June 2018).

Jacoby, R., 2005. *Picture Imperfect: Utopian Thought for an Anti-Utopian Age*. Columbia University Press.

Jenks, B., 2015. *From an MDG World to an SDG/GPG World: Why the United Nations Should Embrace the Concept of Global Public Goods*. Development Dialogue Paper, No. 15. Dag Hammarskjold Foundation. Available online at: http://www.daghammarskjold.se/wp-content/uploads/2015/10/DD-Paper-no-15.pdf (accessed 28 May 2019).

Johl, A. and Lador, Y., 2012. *A Human Rights-Based Approach to Climate Finance*. Friedrich-Ebert-Stiftung Geneva. Available online at: https://ciel.org/Publications/ClimateFinance_Feb2012.pdf (accessed 28 May 2019).

Kabeer, N., 2005. Gender Equality and Women's Empowerment: A Critical Analysis of the Third Millennium Development Goal 1. *Gender & Development*, *13* (*1*), 13–24.

Kippler, C., 2010. Exploring Post-Development: Politics, The State and Emancipation. The Question of Alternatives. *Polis Journal*, *3* (*1*), 1–38.

Klein, E. and Morreo, C.E., 2019. *Postdevelopment in Practice: Alternatives, Economics, Ontologies*. Routledge.

Loewe, M., 2012. *Post 2015: How to Reconcile the Millennium Development Goals (MDGs) and the Sustainable Development Goals (SDGs)?* Briefing Paper 18/2012. The German Development Institute (DIE).

Mahbubani, K., 2008. *The New Asian Hemisphere: The Irresistible Shift of Global Power to the East*. Public Affairs.

Mamdani, M., 2001. *When Victims Become Killers: Colonialism, Nativism, and the Genocide in Rwanda*. James Currey Publishers.

Mannheim, K., 1991. *Ideology and Utopia*. Psychology Press.

Mao Zedong, 1937. *On Contradiction*. Selected Works of Mao Zedong. Marxist Internet Archive 004. Available at: https://www.marxists.org/reference/archive/mao/selected-works/volume-1/mswv1_17.htm (accessed 1 March 2019).

Marx, K., 1978. *The Marx-Engels Reader*. Norton.

Mgbeoji, I., 2003. *Collective Insecurity: The Liberian Crisis, Unilateralism & Global Order*. University of British Columbia Press.

Mouffe, C., 2005. *On the Political: Thinking in Action*. Routledge.

Nakano, Y., 2007. On the Singular Name of Post-Development: Serge Latouche's Destruktion of Development and the Possibility of Emancipation. In Ziai, A. (ed.), *Exploring Post-Development: Theory and Practice, Problems and Perspectives*. Routledge.

Nederveen Pieterse, J., 1996. The Development of Development Theory: Towards Critical Globalism. *Review of International Political Economy, 3* (*4*), 541–564.

Nederveen Pieterse, J., 2000. After Post-Development. *Third World Quarterly, 21* (*2*), 175–191.

OECD, 2014. *Development Co-operation Report 2014: Mobilising Resources for Sustainable Development*. OECD Publishing.

Olivecrona, K., 1959. The Legal Theories of Axel Hagerstown and Vilhelm Lundstedt. In Schmidt, Folke (ed.), *Scandinavian Studies in Law, vol. 3*. Almgvist & Wiksells Boktryckeri AB, chapter 3.

Ophir, A., 2010. The Politics of Catastrophization. In Fassin, D. and Pandolfi, M. (eds), *Contemporary States of Emergency: The Politics of Military and Humanitarian Interventions*. Zone Books.

Osborn, D., Cutter, A., and Ullah, F., 2015. *Universal Sustainable Development Goals: Understanding the Transformational Challenge for Developed Countries*. Stakeholder Forum. Available online at: https://sustainabledevelopment.un.org/content/documents/1684SF_-_SDG_Universality_Report_-_May_2015.pdf (accessed 28 May 2019).

Osiel, M., 1997. *Mass Atrocity, Collective Memory and the Law*. Transaction Publishers.

Pinker, S., 2011. *The Better Angles of the Nature: How Violence Has Declined*. Harper.

Power, S., 2002. *A Problem from Hell: America and the Age of Genocide*. Basic Books.

Prashad, V., 2008. *The Darker Nations: A People's History of The Third World*. The New Press.

Prashad, V., 2013. *The Poorer Nations: A Possible History of The Global South*. Verso.

Rahnema, M., 1988. On a New Variety of AIDS and Its Pathogens: Homo Economicus, Development and Aid. *Alternatives, 13* (*1*), 117–136.

Rahnema, M., 1997. Towards Post-Development: Searching for Signposts, a New Language and New Paradigms. In Rahnema, M. and Bawtree, V. (eds), *The Post Development Reader*. Afterword. Zed Books.

Ray, T., 2012. To De-Westernize, Yes, But with a Critical Edge: A Response to Gunaratne and Others. *Media, Culture & Society*, *34* (*2*), 238–249.

Rosenfield, A., Maine, D. and Freedman, L., 2006. Meeting MDG-5: an impossible dream? *The Lancet*, *368* (*9542*), 1133–1135.

Rummel, R.J., 1997. *Death by Government*. Transaction Press.

Sachs, W., 1992. *The Development Dictionary: A Guide to Knowledge as Power*. Zed Books.

Saith, A., 2006. From Universal Values to Millennium Development Goals: Lost in Translation. *Development and Change*, *37* (*6*), 1167–1199.

Santiago Nino, C., 1966. *Radical Evil on Trial*. Yale University Press.

Schumpeter, J., 1942. *Capitalism, Socialism, and Democracy*. Harper.

Sen, A. 1999. *Development as Freedom*. Oxford University Press.

Stephan, P.B., 1998. Creative Destruction – Idiosyncratic Claims of International Law and The Helms–Burton Legislation. *Stetson Law Review*, *XXVII*, 1341–1365.

Stewart, R., Kingsbury, B. and Rudyk, B. (eds), 2009. *Climate Finance: Regulatory and Funding Strategies for Climate Change and Global Development*. New York University Press.

Thakur, R.C., Aoi, C. and De Coning, C. (eds), 2007. *Unintended Consequences of Peacekeeping Operations*. United Nations University Press.

Tooley, M., 2015. The Problem of Evil. In Zalta, E.N. (ed.), *The Stanford Encyclopedia of Philosophy (Fall)*. Available online at: https://plato.stanford.edu/archives/fall2015/entries/evil/ (accessed 25 June 2018).

UN, 2015a. Outcome Document of the Third International Conference on Financing for Development: Addis Ababa Action Agenda. A/CONF.227/L.1. 13–16 July. United Nations. Available online at: http://www.un.org/ga/search/view_doc.asp?symbol=A/CONF.227/L.1 (accessed 1 March 2019).

UN, 2015b. *Paris Agreement on Climate Change*. United Nations. Available online at: https://unfccc.int/sites/default/files/english_paris_agreement.pdf (accessed 1 April 2019).

UN, 2015c. *UN World Conference on Disaster Risk Reduction*. United Nations. Available online at: https://www.wcdrr.org/ (accessed 1 March 2019).

UNDP, 2015. World Leaders Adopt Sustainable Development Goals. Available online at: http://www.undp.org/content/undp/en/home/presscenter/pressreleases/2015/09/24/undp-welcomes-adoption-of-sustainable-development-goals-by-world-leaders.html (accessed 25 June 2018).

UNGA, 2000. *United Nations Millennium Declaration*. 18 September. A/RES/55/2. United Nations General Assembly.

UNGA, 2015a. *Millennium Development Goals Report*. United Nations General Assembly.

UNGA, 2015b. *Transforming Our World: The 2030 Agenda for Sustainable Development*. 21 October. A/RES/70/1. United Nations General Assembly.

WCED (World Commission on Environment and Development), 1987. *Our Common Future*.Oxford University Press.

Young, R.J.C., 2001. *Postcolonialism: A Historical Introduction*. Blackwell.

Ziai, A., 2007. *Exploring Post-Development: Theory and Practice, Problems and Perspectives*. Routledge.

Chapter 3

Beyond development

Towards sustainability and climate justice in the Anthropocene

Sam Adelman

Introduction

In this chapter, I examine the dialectical relationship between law and development and the two components of sustainable development. One of the main aims of this volume and its companion is to interrogate the meaning of development at the moment when humanity confronts ecological collapse and the extinction of much of our planet's biodiversity (Chapter 1, this volume). Ostensibly aimed at promoting human wellbeing, development has become an end in itself (as developmentalism) and because it is intrinsically destructive of the environment, it threatens social justice in the Anthropocene.[1] Development as usual –extractive and growth-driven – threatens the material basis for all economic activity and the collapse of life-support systems on a bigger scale than war, famine or economic crisis, and is likely to cause all three.

It is now widely accepted that we live in the Anthropocene, a new climatic and geological era produced by the super-agency of a small slice of human beings, particularly since the Great Acceleration (Adelman, 2018, 2019).[2] The idea of the Anthropocene was launched in a short article in the newsletter of the International Geosphere-Biosphere Programme at the start of the millennium

1 Following Arturo Escobar (1992), I use development as an idea discovered, along with poverty and the Third World, by the West following the Second World War. Although many paths have been taken in pursuit of development, with few exceptions they have prioritised economic growth and extractive industrialisation, particularly after the end of the Cold War, the rise of neoliberalism and China's turn to state capitalism.

2 The periodisation of the Anthropocene is disputed. Some authors trace its origin to the widespread use of fossil fuels that began in the late eighteenth century. Others favour the Great Acceleration, which began in the decade after the Second World War and deposited traces in the Earth's stratigraphy of radionuclides from nuclear weapons testing and the exponential increase in the use of fossil fuels, concrete and plastic. Lewis and Maslin (2018) argue that its advent can be traced to the geological spike left in 1610 by the genocidal effects of the Columbian exchange. Geologists have not formally designated the Anthropocene as a new geological epoch, but the concept is widely accepted in Earth System Science, the natural and social sciences and public discourse.

(Crutzen and Stoermer, 2000; see also Crutzen, 2002). As the name implies, the concept is profoundly anthropocentric but it is increasingly influential at a time when bio- and ecocentric approaches are paradoxically in the best interests of human beings.[3]

Development through unequal ecological exchange

Development in the countries of the global South has been significantly undermined by unequal ecological exchange during and after colonialism as the global North expropriated their natural resources and emitted disproportionate amounts of greenhouse gases for its development (Hornborg, 2011; Bonneuil and Fressoz, 2017; Dehm, 2016). Since the Industrial Revolution the benefits of carbon-intensive development have been concentrated in the North countries most responsible for historical greenhouse gas emissions. 'Great Britain and the United States made up 60 per cent of cumulative total emissions to date in 1900, 57 per cent in 1950 and almost 50 per cent in 1980. From the standpoint of climate, the Anthropocene should rather be called the "Anglocene"' (Bonneuil and Fressoz, 2017: 82). The US accounted for 5 per cent of world energy use in 1910 but more than 60 per cent by 1970 (ibid.: 85). According to Bonneuil and Fressoz (2017: 154), 'in 1820, the poorest 20 per cent on the planet obtained 4.7 per cent of world income, falling to only 2.2 per cent in 1992'. It is difficult to disagree with their conclusion that:

> the industrial development model and its metabolism in terms of matter and energy, which altered the geopolitical trajectory of our Earth, is inseparable from the history of capitalist world-systems, of unequal ecological exchange, of colonialism and imperialism, of exploitation and underdevelopment.
>
> (Bonneuil and Fressoz (2017: 154)

The countries historically on the periphery of the core economies have provided the extraction zones from which natural resources are appropriated without full payment, disposal zones for waste and pollution, and sacrifice zones, for extractivism and environmental and climatic harms. The extraction of wealth from nature proceeded through slavery, the conquest and dispossession of indigenous peoples, colonialism and imperialism, and the 'slow violence' of carbon capitalism (Nixon 2011).

3 Capitalocene is more appropriate because it draws attention to the logic of capital and the main driver of the climate emergency and ecological collapse, but Anthropocene is more widely used in the literature and public discourse.

The picture is complicated by the rapid industrialisation of countries such as China and India since the 1980s. Half the carbon dioxide in the atmosphere has been emitted during the past three decades and more fossil fuels have been burned since the establishment of the UN Framework Convention on Climate Change in 1992 (Wallace-Wells 2019: 4). Between 1997 and 2015, China and India's emissions almost trebled.[4] On a per capita basis both might still be regarded as developing countries, but they are now among the wealthiest nations in the world. Moreover, they are significant contributors to greenhouse gas emissions, from which they derive significant benefits, including the ability to assist less developed countries. Poverty has decreased in both countries but their rapid development has been coupled with inequality and widespread ecological devastation.

Climate science dictates that developing countries must be precluded from following the paths taken by the global North to development, an injustice that can only be overcome through climate justice based upon global distributive justice and the discharging of the North's historical ecological debts, something they show little willingness to do.

Perpetual compound growth is a precondition for capitalism and leads inexorably to environmental calamity. In nature, uncontrollable growth is cancerous. Endless growth involves seizing natural wealth from both living systems and future generations. Ecological modernisers and green capitalists write optimistically about decoupling economic growth and greenhouse gases but the absolute decoupling needed to avert environmental catastrophe through a reduction in use of material resources has never been achieved and appears impossible under development that fetishises growth. As Hamilton (2003: 184) contends, 'The development mentality is the daily manifestation of growth fetishism'. As a result, green growth is as illusory as sustainable development. Sixteen years ago, Fredric Jameson (2003: 76) observed that 'it is easier to imagine the end of the world than to imagine the end of capitalism'. Today, we are confronted with a choice between capitalism and life.

4 US emissions decreased from 5705 $MtCO_2$ to 5414, China's increased from 3393 to 10357 $MtCO_2$ and India's from 917 to 2274 $MtCO_2$.: Global Carbon Atlas. CO_2 Emissions. Available online at: http://www.globalcarbonatlas.org/en/CO2-emissions (accessed 2 July 2017). Per capita emissions in 2002 were 20.0 tonnes in the US, 2.9 in China and 1.1 in India. Cumulative emissions between 1900 and 2002 were 303034, 80084 and 23083 respectively: Time for Change. CO_2 Emissions by Country. Available online at: http://timeforchange.org/CO2-emissions-by-country (accessed 2 July 2017). In 1997, cumulative emissions of CO_2 were US: 5373.11 million tonnes, China: 3472.35, India: 918.44. In 2014, the figures were 5258.58, 10300.35 and 2240.21 respectively. Ritchie and Roser, 2017. CO_2 and Greenhouse Gas Emissions. Available online at: https://ourworldindata.org/co2-and-other-greenhouse-gas-emissions/ (accessed 2 July 2017). The per capita figures for 2014 were 16.26, 7.52 and 1.72 respectively. Many OECD countries have effectively offset much of their emissions by outsourcing manufacturing to the global South.

Planetary boundaries, climate harms and injustices

Fossil-fuelled industrialisation and ecological degradation are intrinsic to all economic activity, but Western, Eurocentric models of development are conspicuously so because they are underpinned by a Baconian conception of nature as an inert set of resources (natural capital) that exists to serve the needs and interests of humankind, and the concomitant Descartian division between nature and society. These models of development have ineluctably resulted in the rupture to the Earth System that threatens all life through the breaching of planetary boundaries in the Anthropocene, particularly during the Great Acceleration following the Second World War (Rockström et al., 2009; Steffen et al., 2015).

Economic development since the Industrial Revolution has produced unimaginable wealth for a tiny slice of humanity at the expense of ecological sustainability. The models of development promoted by the international economic institutions has increased standards of living at the expense of ecological sustainability.[5] Growth-driven, extractive development pollutes the atmosphere, the land and the oceans, intensifies food, water and energy insecurity, and violates almost every human right including the right to life (Adelman, 2016), leading to increasingly vociferous demands for global human right to a clean, healthy and safe environment.[6] The planetary boundaries already breached include climate change, biodiversity loss, nitrogen and phosphorous loading, and land-use change. Two others, freshwater use and ocean acidification are dangerously threatened (Steffen et al., 2015; Hickel, 2019). Insect populations are falling precipitously, threatening agriculture and food security everywhere (Sánchez-Bayo and Wyckhuys, 2019).

Sixty per cent of biodiversity has been destroyed since 1970 in an annihilation that threatens civilisations made possible by the benign climate during the 117000 years of the Holocene (Grooten and Almond, 2018). Vast and growing consumption of food and resources by the global population is destroying the web of life upon which human society ultimately depends for food, clean air, water and everything else. The Intergovernmental Panel on Climate Change (IPCC, 2018), reflecting the 97 per cent consensus among climate scientists, warns that immediate action is required to prevent the catastrophic

5 It has lifted many out of poverty while creating new elites. Hickel (2018) challenges the numbers claimed to have been lifted out of poverty by the UN's Millennium Development Goals.

6 United Nations Human Rights Council. *Issue of Human Rights Obligations Relating to the Eenjoyment of a Safe, Clean, Healthy and Sustainable Environment.* Report of the Special Rapporteur, A/HRC/40/55, 8 January 2019. UNHRC.

consequences of global heating of more than 1.5 degrees Celsius over pre-industrial levels by 2030, superseding the 2 degrees target in Article 2 of the Paris Agreement.[7] The IPCC states that even this half a degree will significantly worsen the risks of drought, floods, extreme heat and poverty for hundreds of millions of people.[8] Unless current exploitation of resources driven by growth, fossil fuelled industrialisation and overconsumption is reversed, we would need the equivalent of 1.7 Earths. Put another way, it takes eight months to exhaust the Earth's annual budget.[9] The IPCC report calls for a 45 per cent reduction in GHG emissions by 2030 to give us any chance of meeting the 1.5 degrees target.

These warnings are reinforced in the 2019 Global Assessment by the Intergovernmental Science-Policy Platform for Biodiversity and Ecosystem Services (IPBES), which unequivocally states that 'Goals for conserving and sustainably using nature and achieving sustainability cannot be met by current trajectories, and goals for 2030 and beyond may only be achieved through transformative changes across economic, social, political and technological factors' (Diaz et al., 2019: 5). The report describes how human activity severely threatens biodiversity and ecosystems worldwide, with about a million species facing extinction within a few decades. Agriculture, forestry and urbanisation are the main causes of biodiversity loss in land-based ecosystems and rivers. Overfishing has had the greatest impact on ocean biodiversity and is exacerbated by changes in the use of the sea and coastal lands. Other negative factors include the direct use of species (through harvesting, logging, hunting and fishing), climate change, pollution, and invasive non-native species. The assessment makes clear that protecting the biosphere is impossible under current modes of production and consumption and development as usual, rendering even the weakest forms of sustainable development impossible. Simply, it is not possible to grow our way to sustainability on a finite planet. This raises the difficult question that sustainable development is designed to avoid: whether the radical transformation required to address the expanding ecological catastrophe is possible under capitalism, and if not, what ensues?

Evidence of the vicious feedback loop between underdevelopment, impoverishment and climate change is demonstrated by the devastation wrought by

7 The use of fossil fuels has constituted a dangerous experiment with our life support system just as plastic pollution has led us to treat the planet as a rubbish dump in the Garbage aka Anthropocene.

8 The article exhorts state parties to aim for 1.5 degrees.

9 Global Footprint Network. Earth Overshoot Day. Available online at: https://www.footprintnetwork.org/our-work/earth-overshoot-day (accessed 1 November 2018). Although we need more than one planet, 'we' are not equally responsible for the degradation and destruction of natural resources and greenhouse gas emissions. The tendency to ascribe responsibility to an undifferentiated humanity is a major criticism directed at the concept of the Anthropocene (Adelman, 2018).

successive cyclones in Mozambique in 2019, expanding desertification in the Sahara, and crop failure, drought and the collapse of fisheries in Guatemala, Honduras and El Salvador, which are driving people displaced by climate change towards the US and Trump's wall.[10] Since there will always be lifeboats for the rich, the central concern of climate justice must be for the most impoverished and vulnerable. Delivering climate justice requires answering the question of who owes what to whom, and why? Climate change is the quintessential collective, transboundary, super-wicked problem that cannot be resolved within the narrow, flawed logic of Westphalian sovereignty and territorialised conceptions of justice that John Rawls and others have found so difficult to reconcile. At the very least it requires distributive and global justice that delivers adequate resources from the Northern countries with the biggest ecological debts to the global South for adaptation and mitigation, capacity building and technology transfer to the global South as envisaged in the Paris Agreement. It requires reparative justice for climatic loss and damage, and procedural justice in designing and implementing adaptation policies. Every aspect of development and any attempt to deploy risky geoengineering technologies demands environmental impact assessment. (Adelman 2017). And climate justice is impossible without gender and environmental justice. This is both an immense challenge and an enormous and possibly the last opportunity to unravel the Gordian knot of ecological destruction while there is still time.

Developing countries are threatened by slow- and sudden-onset climatic harms that multiply threats that drive climate displacement and increase the likelihood of conflicts. Climate change is predicted to displace between 25 million and 1 billion people annually in the middle of the century, with 200 million the most commonly cited figure.[11] A conservative estimate is that 15 million are annually displaced by climate change (IDMC, 2018: 54). Small island developing states (SIDS) are threatened with inundation from rising sea levels. Their inhabitants have no human right to the ground beneath their feet or to relocation and resettlement under international law (Burkett, 2018). More than 65 million are threatened with displacement in SIDS alone (Bank and Frölich, 2018). Their plight is symptomatic of one of the defining conflicts

10 Markham, L., 2019. How Climate Change is Pushing Central American Migrants to the US. *The Guardian*. Available online at: https://www.theguardian.com/commentisfree/2019/apr/06/us-mexico-immigration-climate-change-migration (accessed 24 April 2019). See also Yusoff (2019: 62), who writes that 'A material and temporal solidarity exists between the inscription of race in the Anthropocene and the current descriptions of subjects that are caught between the hardening of geopolitical borders and the material de-stratification of territory'.

11 Kamal, B., 2017. Climate Migrants Might Reach One Billion by 2050. Inter Press Service New Agency. Available online at: http://www.ipsnews.net/2017/08/climate-migrants-might-reach-one-billion-by-2050/ (accessed 13 May 2019).

from now on: competition for habitable and fertile land, a core development issue intensified by climate change.

The IPCC report outlines the harms likely to result from failing to keep global temperature from exceeding 1.5°C. 'Compared to current conditions, 1.5°C of global warming would nonetheless pose heightened risks to eradicating poverty, reducing inequalities and ensuring human and ecosystem well-being' (5–4).[12] Shindell et al. (2018) calculate that approximately '150 million air quality-related premature deaths could be prevented by increasing ambition in carbon emissions reductions'. To limit the threats to all forms of economic development, greenhouse gas emissions must be reduced by 45 per cent by 2030, intensifying the difficulties of seeking growth to promote social justice in the global South. At the same time, possibly for political reasons, the report exudes faith that the 17 Sustainable Development Goals and the 169 associated targets can be achieved in an ecologically sustainable manner. Thus, 'Sustainable development broadly supports and often enables the fundamental societal and systems transformations that would be required for limiting warming to 1.5°C' (5–6). The IPCC issues the stark warning (with high confidence) that without societal transformation and rapid mitigation 'pathways to limiting warming to 1.5°C and achieving sustainable development will be exceedingly difficult, if not impossible, to achieve' (5–6). In the language of climate science, this is tantamount to admitting that contemporary neoliberal, neo-extractive development paradigms are exhausted.

A problem raised by both terms, Anthropocene and development, is the underlying assumption of the homogeneity of the human beings responsible for the former, the Anthropos, and object of the latter, those who must be rescued (from themselves). A great deal of violent injustice has been inflicted on those least responsible, the victims, through the pursuit of profit by the powerful in the name of progress through expropriation, exploitation, oppression, ecological destruction and anthropogenic global warming. A further problem with the idea of the Anthropocene is that it implies dominion over nature legitimated biblically and by Baconian manifestations of Eurocentric rationality (Adelman, 2015a, 2019).

Development

In theory, development connotes something positive, for example in relation to child development, something to which we ought to aspire. In practice, as modernisation, westernisation, endless growth and a linear, teleological conception of progress, it has led to mal- or underdevelopment, to limited reductions in poverty and inequality (Hickel, 2018), and everywhere to environmental destruction and climatic harms. The 'discovery' of development coincided with

12 References are to chapters and pages available online at: http://www.ipcc.ch/report/sr15 (accessed 1 November 2018).

the Great Acceleration, which paved the way for neoliberal globalisation. Development was 'an invention and strategy produced by the "First World" about the "underdevelopment" of the "Third World"', 'an instrument of economic control over the physical and social reality' in much of what is now referred to as the global South (Escobar, 1992: 22). Under the aegis of the international financial institutions, it has been a powerful form of governmentality and biopolitical control, a means of disciplining states and individuals (Mezzadra et al., 2013). Usually imposed rather than owned, it has been done to rather than by communities. Although the concept has metamorphosed since its 'discovery' by the West, several characteristics remain firmly entrenched: growth, progress, modernisation and industrialisation:

> Development has evaporated. The metaphor opened up a field of knowledge and for a while gave scientists something to believe in ... Neither in nature nor in society does there exist an evolution that imposes transformation towards 'ever more perfect forms' as a law ... Modern man has failed in his effort to be god.
>
> (Esteva, 2010: 20)

It was clear as early as 1972 that endless growth on a finite planet is unsustainable (Meadows et al., 1972), but growth fetishism measured by GDP remains the main aim of development, an end in itself rather than the means to other ends such as justice and wellbeing, and the primary reason why development is irredeemable. Alternative conceptions such as Amartya Sen's idea of development as freedom and his capabilities theory have influenced World Bank and IMF doxas without dislodging economic growth (Sen, 1999).[13] Countries which have sought alternative paths have been constrained by the manner of their incorporation into the global political-economy and the disciplinary power of the international financial institutions, debt and global markets.[14] Development's hold has been tenacious because it has proved capable of metamorphosing to meet the demands of the development industry, including Western donors and governments, the international economic institutions and NGOs whose interests regularly converge with those of commonly corrupt local elites. Despite sharp critiques from world system and dependency theorists in the 1960s and 1970s,

13 Despite longstanding and growing critiques of the inadequacy of gross domestic product (Fioramonti, 2013; Pilling, 2018) it remains the primary measurement of economic development. Similarly, impoverishment is measured, bizarrely and inadequately, in monetary terms, e.g. the World Bank's $1.90 per day index (for a coruscating critique, see Hickel (2018).

14 Structural adjustment programmes, poverty reduction strategies, debt and a range of other conditionalities have been imposed by the IMF, the World Bank, the WTO, state and private lenders and vulture capitalists to entrench what Baxi (2006) calls trade-related, market-friendly human rights.

the rise of neoliberalism in the early 1980s symbolised by the Washington Consensus suffocated alternatives in the rush for growth and profits. In 2010, Wolfgang Sachs (2010: xv) wrote 'The last forty years can be called the age of development. This epoch is coming to an end. The time is ripe to write its obituary.' Development's obituary has been written many times but, zombie-like, it stalks the planet like the undead. As Ashis Nandy puts it:

> The problem with the idea of development is not its failure. The idea has succeeded beyond the dreams of its early partisans who never imagined that they had hit upon something whose day had come. Developmentalism has succeeded where western colonialism and evangelical Christianity failed. It has established itself as one of the few genuine universals of our time.
>
> (Nandy, 2003: 171)

The illusory freedom from nature's determinism promised by modernity is exposed in the Anthropocene, making it all the more imperative to finally break free from the tentacles of developmentalism. The ecological emergency is not an unintended by-product of development and neoliberal globalisation but the inevitable consequence of economic models that are literally unsustainable, so that it follows that the answer lies in alternatives *to* development as Escobar (1992), Esteva (2010) and others have long argued.

Sustainable development

Food, water and energy security, reducing impoverishment, social justice, livelihoods and wellbeing are contingent upon a safe and healthy environment. If the aim of development is human wellbeing, it is failing on any criterion beyond the crude and limited measurement of per capita GDP. The dead end to which development has delivered us is reflected in the current dominant framing of sustainable development, the putative solution to development, social justice and ecological collapse (Adelman 2018, 2019). Old wine in a new bottle, sustainable development has become the hegemonic form of development that promises to overcome the deficiencies of previous incarnations by combining economic growth, social justice (primarily through poverty reduction) and environmental protection. Since endless growth is impossible without breaching planetary boundaries, sustainable development has justifiably been condemned as a dangerously delusional oxymoron (Daly, 1990: 1; Sachs, 2010; Redclift, 2005; Adelman, 2018). Sustainable development's advocates along with evangelisers of ecological modernisation, assure us that the solution to the depredations of neoliberalism and neo-extractivism is more of the same (Curran, 2018). The problem, it seems, is not capitalism but not enough of it, to which green capitalism is the ostensible solution.

The concept came to prominence in 1987 with the report of the Brundtland Commission to the World Conference on Environment and Development, which famously defined sustainable development as 'development that meets the needs of present generations without compromising the ability of future generations to meet their own needs' (WCED, 1987: 43). The Commission prescribed sustainable development as the solution for 'an environmental crisis, a development crisis, an energy crisis. They are all one' (ibid.: 4). Its inherently contradictory nature was revealed in its call for 'a new era of economic growth –growth that is forceful and at the same time socially and environmentally sustainable' (ibid.: xii). The Commission based its analysis upon needs, but mistakenly identified impoverishment as a cause rather than a symptom of unsustainability, and the limitations 'imposed by the state of technology and social organization on the environment's ability to meet present and future needs' (ibid.: 43) rather than biophysical limits and planetary boundaries. As Escobar (1996: 54) argues, the concept 'focuses not so much on the negative consequences of economic growth on the environment, as on the effects of environmental degradation on growth and the potential for growth'. Within five years, more than 70 definitions of sustainable development had been proposed, demonstrating the vague capaciousness of the concept that enables states and transnational corporations to greenwash unsustainable activities.

Following the 1992 Earth Summit and the establishment of the United Nations Framework Convention on Climate Change (UNFCCC), sustainable development was entrenched in international environmental law and the climate regime (Adelman, 2013).[15] Principle 12 in the Rio Declaration declares that 'States should cooperate to promote a supportive and open international economic system that would lead to *economic growth and sustainable development* in all countries' (my emphasis).[16] It is a leitmotif in the Paris Agreement, which 'aims to strengthen the global response to the threat of climate change, in the context of sustainable development and efforts to eradicate poverty (art 2).[17]

In September 2015, the UN General Assembly adopted the Sustainable Development Goals (SDGs), which are intended to be achieved by 2030. I have critiqued the SDGs at length elsewhere (Adelman, 2018) and confine my discussion here to one of their major contradictions. Goal 8 calls for increased annual GDP growth in least developed countries and higher levels of economic productivity everywhere. Remarkably, sustained unsustainability is combined in the oxymoronic call for '*sustained*, inclusive and *sustainable* economic growth, full and productive employment and decent work for all' (my emphasis). Goal 8.1 aims to 'Sustain per capita economic growth in accordance with national circumstances and, in particular, at least 7 per cent gross domestic product

15 United Nations Framework Convention on Climate Change, UNGA A/RES/48/189, 20 January 1994,

16 Rio Declaration on Environment and Development, UN Doc. A/CONF.151/26 (vol. I); 31 ILM 874, 13 June 1992.

17 United Nations Framework Convention on Climate Change Conference of Parties, Twenty-First Session, Adoption of the Paris Agreement, UN Doc. FCCC/CP/2015/L.9/Rev.1, 12 December 2015.

growth per annum in the least developed countries'. This will be catastrophic unless they are provided with resources to achieve this using renewable energy and environmentally devastating in any event. Goal 8.4 envisages decoupling economic growth from environmental degradation through improvements in 'global resource efficiency in consumption and production'. This is essential if the SDGS are to be achievable – but extremely unlikely (Hickel and Kallis, 2019).

The universal application of the SDGs implies that all countries are developing. Just as the Anthropocene destabilises conventional conceptions of time and history, it also highlights spatial and geographical disjunctions that will become more acute as transboundary environmental problems subvert the territorial and conceptual boundaries of Westphalian sovereignty. Today most countries are characterised by pockets of wealth in gated communities surrounded by swathes of exclusion, inequality and poverty – global North and South cheek by jowl. Climate change will blur distinctions between developed and developing countries, although the former have far greater resources and adaptive capacity and there will be lifeboats for the rich. This is why climate justice must be primarily concerned with the poor and vulnerable.

Towards social and climate justice

The central injustice of climate change is that less developed countries with the least historical responsibility for creating the problem are most vulnerable to its harms due to a combination of underdevelopment, the legacies of colonialism, accidents of geographical location, poor infrastructure, low adaptive capacity, weak governance, and the structural inequalities baked into the global economy under neoliberal globalisation.

Awareness of the super-agency of human beings highlighted by the idea of the Anthropocene destabilises most of the conventional ontological, epistemological and ethical thinking of modernity. The ecological cataclysm is the result of intertwined failures. The failure of business as usual in the combination of growth-driven, extractive development and neoliberal globalisation and, at root, of a mode of production intrinsically antithetical to the environment. And the failure of law as usual, as a system of rules and regulations that naturalises and facilitates environmental degradation. The fiduciary duty to prioritise the interests of shareholders drives growth in pursuit of profit and facilitates environmental destruction. The failure of epistemologies of dominance and mastery manifested in mainstream models of development are rooted in the Cartesian dualisms and deep anthropocentrism of Eurocentric rationality (Adelman, 2015a). Ultimately, however, the cataclysm is the result of politics as usual, of the failure of politicians to tell the truth about climate change and what that inexorably implies; the failure to acknowledge that how we produce, what we consume, and the fate of the future generations and the planet are not inevitabilities but choices.

Alternatives to development

The scale and urgency of the crisis dictate the need for the fundamental restructuring of law, politics and economics in what Bruno Latour (2018) calls the New Climatic Regime. There are no easy answers to the hard questions posed by climate change and ecological devastation. Almost thirty years ago, Arturo Escobar argued that the 'present crisis does not call for a "better" way of doing development, not even for "another development"' (Escobar, 1992: 22); instead, we need another way, for which possibilities exist. For a start, the West's hubristic rejection of alternatives *to* development must be overcome. In Latin America, Andean cosmovisions such as *buen vivir* (roughly translated as living well) offer alternatives *to* development. Many indigenous knowledges that have no concept similar to the Western idea of development seek to dissolve the society-nature dualism, anthropocentrism and legal hierarchies, and move beyond growth fetishism, and misplaced conceptions of progress (Adelman, 2019; Walsh, 2010). *Buen vivir* is a decolonial, a-growth concept that includes material and spiritual commitments on quality of life, and 'Communities are defined in an expanded sense, which includes some non-human elements or even the whole environment. In some cases this ends in the concept of *Pachamama* (Mother Earth), as an all-encompassing social-ecological set' (Gudynas, 2016: 727).

> *Buen Vivir* is a non-essentialist position, which not only rejects growth as an end in itself, but also disregards the idea of development in any of its expressions. It does not seek to join the linearity of a Western history. It accepts the plurality of valuations and recognizes the values intrinsic in Nature. Therefore, its perspectives on values are very different from those of modernity.
>
> (Gudynas, 2017: 5)

It promotes sustainability on the basis that wellbeing is only possible in harmony with nature and a biocentric understanding of life that accords rights to nature and to Mother Earth. *Buen vivir* has been incorporated into the constitutions of Ecuador in 2008 and Bolivia in 2009, albeit in contradictory ways that demonstrate the difficulties of breaking free from neo-developmentalism (Gudynas, 2016). Above all, it offers a path to sustainable development that is ecologically sustainable rather than a means of sustaining growth and profits.

Ramírez-Cendrero distinguishes between 'pure' post-developmental conceptions such as *buen vivir* or those based on the rights of nature and others based on alternatives to capitalism. Alternative development envisages development in a different form that *might* transcend capitalism whereas alternatives to development reject the idea of development as irredeemable. He acknowledges that 'post-developmentalist criticism has contributed decisively to the awareness of the physical and environmental limits of capitalism's production and consumption patterns' but argues that 'the risks of neo-extractivism associated with new development strategies in some Latin American countries are merely new forms of capitalist modernization' (Ramírez-Cendrero, 2017: 15).

IPBES's 2019 global assessment confirms that biodiversity loss and ecosystem functioning is much less pronounced on lands managed by indigenous peoples and local communities, and recognises the significant role of indigenous knowledge, governance systems and culturally-specific worldviews which adopt a stewardship approach to managing natural systems (Adelman, 2015a, 2019).

We need to consider ideas such as steady state economics, degrowth and approaches such as Kate Raworth's that seek to construct models of development that respect planetary boundaries and move beyond GDP as the primary measure of economic success (Kallis et al., 2012; Raworth, 2017).

A paradigm shift in law and legal theory

With few exceptions, successive discourses on law and development have been overly concerned with law and economic growth but far less troubled by unsustainability. These discourses have willingly embraced formal, hierarchical, positivist and mechanistic jurisprudence trapped in sovereign rationality, private property and contract (Capra and Mattei, 2015) and 'good' governance that have served the needs of local elites and global capital more than the poor and environmental commons (Meyer, 2018). The idea of the Anthropocene points to the need to treat law as embedded, plural and contingent in ways that decentre appropriation and exclusion and, indeed, human beings. Sustainable development can only pay lip service to ecological sustainability and climate justice if its primary agent is *Homo economicus* – law's abstract, acquisitive, anthropocentric, competitive and predatory Anthropos (Grear, 2015) – is law's Anthropos. His untrammelled pursuit of profit, rather than that of an undifferentiated humanity, regardless of the planet, through development as never-ending growth is now an existential threat to all of us. Constructed to facilitate this heedless pursuit, international law today operates to impede attempts to change course (Anghie, 2007). The construction of European identity through colonialism and exclusion (Fitzpatrick, 1992) led to the othering of humans and nature on the pretext that both lacked reason. Universalising their particular interests during the putative Age of Reason, colonising powers ironically claimed the appellation *Homo sapiens* while demonstrating how unwise human beings can be and celebrating their civilisations in acts of barbarism. As Walter Benjamin argued, 'There is no document of civilization which is not at the same time a document of barbarism' (Benjamin, 1968: 7th Thesis, 258).

Law as usual isn't working, but paradoxically remains indispensable because effective regulation and governance are preconditions for ecological sustainability and climate justice. Environmental law, both domestic and international, has had limited effects in preventing and punishing ecological degradation because it seldom forces polluters to fully internalise negative externalities or prevent future harms (De Lucia, 2019). It is particularly ineffective in relation to climate change. Law as usual will not stave off ecological collapse, but it is still worthwhile taking international environmental law seriously despite its many inadequacies. Enforcing the polluter pays principle and the precautionary approach (which is now virtually redundant) and striving to make the Paris Agreement effective (it is binding but unenforceable) are worthwhile goals, but these are essentially reformist measures when a paradigm shift leading to radical transformation is required.

Arguments for climate justice have commonly been based upon the interconnected criteria of historical responsibility, the benefits derived from fossil-fuelled industrialisation, and the concomitant ability to provide resources for adaptation, mitigation and, latterly, loss and damage (Adelman, 2016). Requiring the countries of the global North to discharge their ecological debts according these criteria is a precondition for global distributive justice that meets the needs of the South. This feeds into the principle of common but differentiated responsibilities and respective capabilities (CBDR-RC) in light of national circumstances. This is both the core equity issue and the most controversial aspect of the climate regime, and giving it teeth is a central concern of developing countries in relation to climate justice. The Paris Agreement requires developed countries to take the lead in meeting the common obligation to reduce greenhouse gas emissions and to provide financial and other resources for adaption, capacity building and technology. Developed countries have committed to contribute $100 billion annually to the Green Climate Fund, far less than they gave to the banks that exploded the global economy in 2008 and nowhere near what is required for climate justice and ecologically sustainable development.[18] The evolution of the principle during the history of the UNFCCC also opens up possibilities of South–South cooperation and solidarity through which rapidly industrialising countries such as China and India can advance climate justice in less developed countries consistent with the obligations that flow from their rising emissions and increasing wealth.

But the failure of law goes much deeper because law naturalises and facilitates environmentally destructive behaviour. Scratching the surface of state-centric, formal, positivist legal systems reveals the extent to which law negates environmental sustainability by privileging private property and credit, debt, interest and rent–which all require endless compound growth. Unsustainability is baked into the law through devices such as limited liability, the prioritisation of the rights of shareholders over communities and ecosystems, and human rights over those of nature.

A paradigm shift that overturns the anthropocentric, dualistic and hierarchical character of most contemporary legal systems is required to enable the progressive use of law in pursuit of justice and sustainability. This must include

18 And further undermined by Trump's intention to withdraw from the Paris Agreement, reinforcing the conclusion that the US is a rogue state on climate change and much else.

expanded conceptions of property, for example through commons governance, and rights, for example by granting rights to nature (Grear, 2012; Adelman, 2015b). It might involve New Materialist approaches that acknowledge the agency of nature, other species and even inert things that influence and shape both natural and built environments through concepts such as natureculture (versus nature-culture) (Davies, 2017). Andreas Philippopoulos-Mihalopoulos (2015: 57) calls for a critical environmental law that 'exerts a radical critique of traditional legal and ecological foundations, while proposing in their stead a new, mobile, material and acentric environmental legal approach'. Dialectically linked to each other, we need equally radical transformation in law beyond development before time runs out.

Conclusion

Ecologically unsustainable development is ethically wrong, and economically illiterate and counterproductive because it undermines the material conditions for life. It is unachievable on a planet disfigured by historical structural inequalities and injustices which are multiplied by climate change, biodiversity loss and the destruction of ecosystems. The scale of the ecological crisis is both daunting and an unprecedented opportunity because dealing with it is impossible in isolation. This must include removing subsidies for fossil fuels, stopping tax avoidance and evasion, abolishing unsustainable debt, building capacity and transferring renewable technologies to the global South, and sanctioning environmentally destructive rogue states and companies. It involves taking international environmental law seriously rather than allowing polluters to evade soft law rules and principles, and taking human rights seriously – not least a right to relocation and resettlement for those displaced by climate change. It requires humility and openness to alternative, sustainable ways of being, living and seeing such *buen vivir*. It requires developed countries with most responsibility for historical emissions to discharge their ecological and colonial debts by paying compensation and making reparations for climatic harms. These are necessary but insufficient because neither reformed capitalism nor technological miracles make it possible to avoid the stark choice between fundamental transformation and ecological collapse. We need a paradigm shift in law and drastic rethinking that goes beyond development to prevent growing global injustices as planetary boundaries are breached.

The charlatans, liars, climate deniers and libertarians may be entitled to their opinions in a post-truth world, but they cannot deny the indisputable facts in the IPCC and IPBES reports that warn that we are on the precipice of ecological collapse. Ecological modernisers and neoliberal green capitalists regard the climate crisis as an opportunity for a good Anthropocene (Hamilton, 2016), which can only come at the expense of the poor and vulnerable. First, a fundamental transformation in how we produce, what we consume, how we understand development and how we use law is needed if the Brundtland Commission's hope that sustainable development would deliver justice for current and future generations has any meaning. A habitable planet is incompatible with current growth-driven, extractive, carbon-based modes of development and production. Second, achieving social justice is impossible under business, law and politics as usual. Climate justice is conceptually different but inextricably linked to environmental justice, and both are contingent upon global distributive justice, gender justice and procedural justice, not least in relation to the growing cacophony of voices calling for climate engineering as a technical fix for the failed experiment of using the planet as a rubbish heap. In addition, corrective and reparative justice, fiercely resisted by those most responsible for climate change, must be reformulated for climate justice to be meaningful. Above all, we have to move beyond growth-driven, extractive development.

References

Adelman, S., 2013. Rio+20: Sustainable Injustice in a Time of Crises. *Journal of Human Rights and the Environment*, *4* (*1*), 6–31.

Adelman, S., 2015a. Epistemologies of Mastery. In Grear, A. and Kotzé, L. (eds), *Research Handbook on Human Rights and the Environment*. Edward Elgar, chapter 2.

Adelman, S., 2015b. Tropical Forests and Climate Change: A Critique of Green Governmentality. *International Journal of Law in Context*, *11* (*2*), 195–212.

Adelman, S., 2016. Climate Justice, Loss and Damage and Compensation for Small Island Developing States. *Journal of Human Rights and the Environment*, *7* (*1*), 32–53.

Adelman, S., 2017. Geoengineering: Rights, Risks and Ethics. *Journal of Human Rights and the Environment*, *8* (*1*), 119–138.

Adelman, S., 2018. The Sustainable Development Goals, Anthropocentrism and Neoliberalism. In French, D. and Kotzé, L. (eds), *Global Goals: Law, Theory and Implementation*. Edward Elgar, chapter 2.

Adelman, S., 2019. Modernity, Anthropocene, Capitalocene and the Climate Crisis. In Bollier, D. and Grear, A. (eds), *The Great Awakening: New Modes of Life Amidst Capitalist Ruins*. Punctum Press.

Anghie, A., 2007. *Colonialism, Sovereignty and the Making of International Law*. Cambridge University Press.

Bank, A. and Fröhlich, C., 2018. Forced Migration in the Global South: Reorienting the Debate. GIGA Focus Global, 3 (Special Issue). Available online at: https://www.giga-hamburg.de/en/publication/forced-migration-in-the-global-south-reorienting-the-debate (accessed 3 October 2019).

Baxi, U., 2006. *The Future of Human Rights*. Oxford University Press.

Benjamin, W., 1968. On the Concept of History. In Arendt. H. (ed.), *Illuminations*. Schocken Books.

Bonneuil, C. and Fressoz, J.-B., 2017. *The Shock of the Anthropocene: The Earth, History and Us*. Verso.

Burkett, M.C., 2018. Justice and Climate Migration. *Climate Refugees, 73* (*88*), 73–88.

Capra, F. and Mattei, U., 2015. *The Ecology of Law: Toward a Legal System in Tune with Nature and Community*. Berrett-Koehler Publishers.

Crutzen, P.J., 2002. Geology of Mankind. *Nature*, *415*, 23.

Crutzen, P.J. and Stoermer, E.F., 2000. The Anthropocene. *IGBP Newsletter*, *41*, 17.

Cullinan, C., 2011. A History of Wild Law. In Burdon, P.D. (ed.), *Exploring Wild Law: The Philosophy of Earth Jurisprudence*. Wakefield Press, p. 12.

Curran, G.A., 2018. Ecological Modernisation. In Castree, N., Hulme, M. and Proctor, J.D. (eds), *Companion to Environmental Studies*. Routledge, chapter 6.2.

Daly, H., 1990. Toward Some Operational Principles of Sustainable Development. *Ecological Economics*, *2* (*1*), 1–6.

Davies, M., 2017. *Law Unlimited: Materialism, Pluralism and Legal Theory*. Routledge.

Dehm, J., 2016. Carbon Colonialism or Climate Justice: Interrogating the International Climate Regime from a TWAIL Perspective. *Windsor Yearbook of Access to Justice*, *33*, 129–161.

De Lucia, V., 2019. *International Environmental Law: Genealogy and Biopolitics*. Routledge.

Diaz, S., Settele, J. and Brondízio, E., 2019. *Summary for Policymakers of the Global Assessment Report on Biodiversity and Ecosystem Services of the Intergovernmental Science-Policy Platform on Biodiversity and Ecosystem Services*. IPBES.

Escobar, A., 1992. *Encountering Development: The Making and Unmaking of the Third World*. Princeton University Press.

Escobar, A., 1996. Constructing Nature: Elements for a poststructural political ecology. In Peet, R. and Watts, M. (eds), *Liberation Ecologies: Environment, Development, Social Movements*. Routledge.

Esteva, G., 2010. Development. In Sachs, W. (ed.), *The Development Dictionary: A Guide to Knowledge as Power*. Zed Books, chapter 1.

Fioramonti, L., 2013. *Gross Domestic Problem: The Politics Behind the World's Most Powerful Number*. Zed Books.

Fitzpatrick, P., 1992. *The Mythology of Modern Law*. Routledge.

Grear A., 2012. Human Rights, Property and the Search for Worlds Other. *Journal of Human Rights and the Environment*, *3* (*2*), 173–195.

Grear, A., 2015. Deconstructing Anthropos: A Critical Legal Reflection on 'Anthropocentric' Law and Anthropocene 'Humanity'. *Law and Critique*, *26* (*3*), 225–249.

Grooten, M. and Almond, R.E.A. (eds), 2018. *Living Planet Report 2018: Aiming Higher*. World Wildlife Fund.

Gudynas, E., 2016. Beyond Varieties of Development: Disputes and Alternatives. *Third World Quarterly*, *37* (*4*), 721–732.

Gudynas, E., 2017. Value, Growth, Development: South American Lessons for a New Ecopolitics. *Capitalism Nature Socialism*, *30* (*2*), 234–243.

Hamilton, C., 2003. *Growth Fetish*. Pluto Press.

Hamilton, C., 2016. The Theodicy of the 'Good Anthropocene'. *Environmental Humanities*, *7* (*1*), 233–238.

Haraway, D.J., 2016. *Staying with the Trouble: Making Kin in the Chthulucene*. Duke University Press.

Hickel, J., 2018. *The Divide: Global Inequality from Conquest to Free Markets.* W.W. Norton.
Hickel, J., 2019. Is it Possible to Achieve a Good Life for All within Planetary Boundaries? *Third World Quarterly, 40* (*1*), 18–35.
Hickel, J. and Kallis, G., 2019. Is Green Growth Possible? *New Political Economy, 2019,* 1–18.
Hornborg A., 2011. *Global Ecology and Unequal Exchange: Fetishism in a Zero-Sum World.* Routledge.
Howe, H., 2017. Making Wild Law Work – The Role of 'Connection with Nature' and Education in Developing an Ecocentric Property Law. *Journal of Environmental Law 29* (*1*), 19–45.
IDMC (Internal Displacement Monitoring Center), 2018. *Global Report on Internal Displacement.* IDMC. Available online at: www.internal-displacement.org/global-report/grid2018/down-loads/2018-GRID.pdf (accessed 31 May 2018).
Jameson, F., 2003. Future City. *New Left Review, 21,* 65–79.
Kallis, G., Kerschner, C. and Martinez-Alier, J., 2012. The Economics of Degrowth. *Ecological Economics, 84,* 172–180.
Latour, B., 2018. *Down to Earth: Politics in the New Climatic Regime.* Polity Press.
Lewis, S. L. and Maslin, M., 2018. *Human Planet: How We Created the Anthropocene.* Yale University Press.
Meadows, D.H., Meadows, D.L., Randers, J. and Behrens III, , W.W., 1972. *The Limits to Growth: A Report for the Club of Rome's Project on the Predicament of Mankind.* Universe Books.
Meyer, T., 2018. Multiple modernities and good governance. In Meyer, T. and de Sales Marques, J.L. (eds), *Multiple Modernities and Good Governance.* Routledge, chapter 1.
Mezzadra, S., Reid, J. and Samaddar, R. (eds), 2013. *The Biopolitics of Development: Reading Michel Foucault in the Postcolonial Present.* Springer.
Nandy, A., 2003. *The Romance of the State: And the Fate of Dissent in the Tropics.* Oxford University Press.
Nixon, R., 2011. *Slow Violence and the Environmentalism of the Poor.* Harvard University Press.
Philippopoulos-Mihalopoulos, A., 2015. Actors or Spectators? Vulnerability and Critical Environmental Law. In Grear, A. and Grant, E. (eds), *Thought, Law, Rights and Action in the Age of Environmental Crisis.* Edward Elgar, chapter 2.
Pilling, D., 2018. *The Growth Delusion: The Wealth and Well-being of Nations.* Tim Duggan Books.
Ramírez-Cendrero, J.M., 2017. Limits and Contradictions of Post-Developmentalism as a Heterodox Approach to Capitalist Development. *Capitalism Nature Socialism, 29* (*4*), 68–87.
Raworth, K., 2017. *Doughnut Economics: Seven Ways to Think Like a 21st-Century Economist.* Random House.
Redclift, M., 2005. Sustainable Development (1987–2005): An Oxymoron Comes of Age. *Sustainable Development, 13* (*4*), 212–227.
Rockström, J. Steffen, W., Noone, K., Persson, Å., Chapin III, , F.S. et al., 2009. Planetary Boundaries: Exploring the Safe Operating Space for Humanity. *Ecology and Society, 14* (*2*), 32–55.

Sachs, W. (ed.), 2010. *The Development Dictionary: A Guide to Knowledge as Power.* Zed Books.
Sánchez-Bayo, F. and Wyckhuys, K.A.G., 2019. Worldwide Decline of the Entomofauna: A Review of Its Drivers. *Biological Conservation, 232*, 8–27.
Sen, A., 1999. *Development as Freedom.* Oxford University Press.
Shindell, D., Faluvegi, G., Seltzer, K. and Shindell, C., 2018. Quantified, Localized Health Benefits of Accelerated Carbon Dioxide Emissions Reductions. *Nature Climate Change, 8* (*4*), 291–295.
Steffen, W., Richardson, K., Rockström, J., Cornell, S.E., Fetzer, I. et al., 2015. Planetary Boundaries: Guiding Human Development on a Changing Planet. *Science, 347* (*6223*), 1259855–1259851, 1259855–1259810.
Wallace-Wells, D., 2019. *The Uninhabitable Earth: A Story of the Future.* Allen Lane.
Walsh, C., 2010. Development as Buen Vivir: Institutional Arrangements and (De) colonial Entanglements. *Development, 53* (*1*), 15–21.
WCED (World Commission on Environment and Development), 1987. *Our Common Future.* Oxford University Press.
Yusoff, K., 2019. *A Billion Black Anthropocenes.* University of Minnesota Press.

Chapter 4

In search of nothing

'Unseen empires' and the law beyond development

Peter Fitzpatrick

'Unseen empires'

Two interlinked perspectives underscore the argument of this chapter. As Quijano (2007: 177) suggests:

> First of all, epistemological decolonization, as decoloniality, is needed to clear the way for new intercultural communication, for an interchange of experiences and meanings, as the basis of another rationality which may legitimately pretend to some universality. Nothing is less rational … than the pretension that the specific cosmic vision of a particular ethnie should be taken as universal rationality, even if such an ethnie is called Western Europe because this is actually [to] pretend to impose a provincialism as universalism.
>
> (Quijano, 2007: 177)

This is reinforced by Blanchot (1988: 29) 'the world which is ours for being nobody's'.

But first some refinement of the target which, given the title of this collection, has to be development. The initial and admittedly loaded setting chosen for this phenomenon comes from the 'unseen empires' which Pope Francis identified in his address to the European Parliament on 25 November 2014:

> Keeping democracies alive is a challenge in the present historic moment. The true strength of our democracies – understood as expressions of the political will of the people – must not be allowed to collapse under the pressures of multinational interests which are not universal, which weaken them and turn them into uniform systems of economic power at the service of unseen empires.
>
> (Francis, 2014)

He preceded this by saying that '[i]t is no secret that a conception of unity seen as uniformity strikes at the vitality of the democratic system' (2014).

Pope Francis then, and for present purposes, offers several 'challenges'. How may we identify and know empires that are 'unseen'? How is democracy, how is 'the political will of the people', subsumed in 'the service' of these empires? What is it that has to be sustained, 'kept alive' to counter that? And to add a further challenge, at least in a preliminary way: what is the part of law in all this?

While modern occidental empires often lacked coherence, and while these empires did at times incline towards the 'unseen', as with so-called empires of trade and so-called indirect rule for example, they were still in an ultimate way emanations of an explicit imperium. In contrast, their 'unseen' successors would advance 'uniformity' through commonalities of requisite instrumentality and effect thus generating an 'imperialism of the same', as Levinas may render it (1969: 87), while still sustaining an insistent differentiation. With this more 'informal imperialism', borrowing Tully's depiction (2008: ch. 5), those not presently or entirely of the elect are to undergo a process of development oriented towards overcoming that existential deficiency, and to do so by way of a plethora of organisations and, writes Escobar, by way of 'an endless number of practices' (1984: 387).[1] These seek to orient developing nations consensually yet they do so more intrusively, more intimately, than the modes typical of the prior and more 'formal' imperialisms. While this overall process can assume a large symbolic, aspirational and programmatic range and secure a wide measure of acceptance, and while it adopts systematic and scientistic modes of operation, nonetheless it remains organisationally diffuse.

Development, with its innumerable 'practices', has come to merge with an encompassing domain of 'governance', a governance that has been 'often defined as government without readily identifiable governors' (Klabbers and Piiparinen, 2013: 38). Or, somewhat similarly, it is accommodated within a 'globalization' the combining of an indefinite pervasion with a distinctness of its 'local' components (e.g. Fitzpatrick, 2001: 197–8). This could be aligned with the much observed decline of the nation state as a cohering and supposed totality, with the generative connections between 'global cities', and with the burgeoning of international institutions. Or it could be refined in terms of Brown's depiction of a global neoliberalism as 'ubiquitous and omnipresent, yet disunified and nonidentical with itself' (2015: 48). All of which mysteries can be found typifying Foucault's governmentality (his invented and self-confessed 'ugly word') (2007: 161).[2]

1 More particularly, see the indispensable critical engagement provided by Celine Tan (2011).

2 'Governmentality' would be 'a more exact title', said Foucault, for his series of lectures *Security, Territory, Population* (2007: 108). The most concentrated account of governmentality comes with lectures three and four (2007: 57–114, 108). In this chapter Foucault's work on 'biopower' is also drawn on as integral to governmentality (e.g. 2008: 21–2).

For Foucault governmentality has 'in the West' come to take on a 'pre-eminence over all other types of power – sovereignty, discipline, and so on' (2007: 108). It is an elusive pre-eminence, however. Governmentality is integral to the diversity it governs and does not assume a positioned power or a singular cohesive force set apart from that diversity. And while governmentality is identified in its 'pre-eminence over all other types of power' (2007: 108),

> we should not see things as a replacement of a society of sovereignty by a society of discipline, and then a society of discipline by a society, say, of government. In fact we have a triangle: sovereignty, discipline, and governmental management.
>
> (2007: 107)

Indeed, for Foucault, '[s]overeignty and discipline, legislation, the right of sovereignty and disciplinary mechanics are in fact two things that constitute – in an absolute sense – the general mechanisms of power in our society' (2003a: 39).

A seeming paradox enters the scene. Governmentality is pre-eminent over all other types of power yet, so it seems, it is also intrinsically tied to, even dependent on them. In somewhat the same vein, governmentality is an encompassing unity, yet that unity assumes no distinct form. Rather, governmentality is infused with the diversity of powers and sites through and in which it takes effect. Bluntly, governmentality has constituently to surpass that on which it constituently depends. This inviting paradox now inhabits the rest of the present chapter.

Dimensions

First, the dependence. The diversity and range of this dependence could evoke that depiction of development offered earlier by Escobar – development as involving 'an endless number of practices' (1984: 387). Taking, however, the two emphasised by Foucault, sovereignty and discipline, and starting with sovereignty, for Foucault sovereignty is 'absolutely not eliminated' by the transition to governmentality but is, rather, 'made more acute than ever' (2007: 107). Or, in terms of his more frequently quoted declaration, 'we still have not cut off the head of the king' (1981: 88–9). Yet the sovereign state is likewise constrained, occupying within governmentality a position more pointedly delimited than its own sovereign pretension would allow.

One has to be more prolix when dealing with discipline with its own 'innumerable practices', but a way of concentrating these would be to focus on a key naturalised 'object ... specific to government', the individual (Foucault, 2008: 22). While, as befits a participant in the liberal economy, the individual for Foucault was free and possessed of individual rights, an 'entrepreneur of himself', that same 'sovereign' individual was also an 'enslaved sovereign', someone normalised and the subject of what is frequently called 'responsibilization'

(Foucault, 2008: 226; 1970: 312).[3] Even as individuals are 'normalized' through tentacular disciplinary powers, these powers are diffuse, 'exercised rather than possessed' (Foucault, 1979: 26). Disciplinary power is exercised through individuals, 'it invests them, is transmitted by them and through them; it exerts pressure upon them, just as they themselves, in their struggle against it, resist the grip it has on them' (Foucault, 1979: 27). Governmentality would seem to subsist, then, in compounded profusion – not only the profusion of disciplinary powers but also the profusion of individuals bringing them to bear. To which could be added the profusion of emplaced sovereignties, those of the nation states with their national populations.

There are however, and as Foucault finds, a host of forces, historical and existent, endowing governmentality with an operative coherence, even if an elusive coherence. Most comprehensively, governmentality is a 'science of government' (2007: 104). It is brought to bear on specific entities such as populations, through specific endowing functions such as effecting security, and within specific shaping sites such as economy (2007: 103–5). All of which will typically involve the regularizing of what otherwise may seem distinct and diverse phenomena. A telling comparison is offered in Foucault's finding a match for the disciplined individuals of governmentality by way of Christian 'pastoral power' in its embedding a 'government of souls and conduct', a power infusing individuals who yet remain ultimately responsible for their own salvation (2007: 88, chs 5–9).

This match poses a constituent challenge for governmentality. A pastoral primer sourced in a boundless transcendence is not an available reference in modernity – at least in a modernity of the occidental variety. Yet with governmentality we have still and somehow to render modes of power that are 'indefinite', 'without limit', 'never closed', or 'naturally opaque and naturally non-totalizable' (Foucault, 1979: 227; 2008: 282). Not only unseen but unseeable. Nevertheless, governmentality is a determinable 'matter of taking control of life', of achieving 'overall states of equilibrium or regularity', and all through 'this very specific albeit very complex power' (Foucault, 2003a: 246; 2007: 108). So, progress in resolving the paradox posed at the end of the previous section is hardly evident.

It may not immediately help matters to suggest that the paradox is self-solving. Governmentality is admittedly reliant for its content on state sovereignty, on innumerable sites of discipline, on individuals, on population 'with its own regularities', and much more (Foucault 2007: 104).[4] It could heighten such reliance to add, with Foucault, that 'the end of government is internal to the

3 An instance plucked from the innumerable: the cult of 'metrics' as it operates in many European universities increasingly secures the 'responsibilization' of the individual academic (Berg et al., 2016). I am grateful to Abdul Paliwala for this reference and for much else.

4 For a compressed indication of this manifold and multitudinous 'more' see Rose (1996: 43).

things it directs', and '"[g]overnment" designated the way in which the conduct of individuals or of groups might be directed' (2007: 99; 2001b: 341). It directs that on which it depends. And, in a contrast with sovereignty frequently drawn by Foucault, governmentality does not seek to incorporate its contents within itself (e.g. 2007: 99). Rather, '[t]here is a sort of polymorphism at work here … a syncretism of that function of control of existence' (1983a: 82). Such 'control' would seem, then, to inhere in or as the very plurality of entities on which it relies.

There are several ways in which this inviting, if still paradoxical, resolution could be pursued in Foucault's work, but, hopefully, doing so through the idea of plurality will prove reflectively apt and adequate. By way of a connection, there is Foucault's equating 'government' with his comprehensive concept of power – power as a 'plurality', as coming 'from below', 'a multiplicity of force relations emanent in the sphere in which they operate and which constitute their own organisation' (2001b: 341; 1981: 92, 94, 96). Yet Foucault also describes power in its general extent in such situated terms as structure, strategy, convergence and hegemonic effects (1981: 94, 99). Which may be beginning to look like repetition but, in search of a 'solution', our guiding paradox could be mapped onto plurality. A plurality can be a simple plurality – a term denoting more than one, many – but the prime meaning given to 'plurality' in the *Oxford English Dictionary* is '[t]he state of being plural; the fact or condition of denoting, comprising, or consisting of more than one.'[5] This condition, this consisting and relating in and as a plurality, would for Donald Davidson 'make sense … only if there is a common coordinate system on which to plot' the different entities relating plurally, 'yet the existence of a common system belies the claim to dramatic incomparability' (1985: 130). This, however, is a compliant commonality which accommodates a seeming aporia within plurality. If, say, entities are to relate in and as a plurality then the element in commonality cannot be only within each of them because this would leave them as a simple plurality, leave them in dissipation. So the commonality has to be, and be set, in some way determinately apart from them. Yet the determinate commonality cannot be so much apart from them in their singularity that it ceases to relate responsively to them – ceases constituently to absorb the changeful commonality generated by their relation to the commonality and to each other.

This commonality, then, is generated in an apparent aporia. It has to be capable of vacating itself and changing in this responsiveness while enabling some determinate manifestation in and as itself. Even as that manifestation is enabled, it does not and cannot assume an invariant, much less comprehensive, hold on the commonality. And what is manifest will always be partial and contingent on the ultimate plurality with-in the commonality.

5 *Oxford English Dictionary*, CD ROM Version 4.0, 2nd edition, 'plural'.

To endow this abstract scenario with more substance, it may be as well to look at a recognisable, an operative, instance of this plurality. That instance is community. It could, then, seem perverse to begin with Nancy and his description of community as 'inoperative' (1991a). The inoperative in and as community is, for Nancy, set starkly against standard conceptions of community as manifest, determinate, even contained. For Nancy, community 'necessarily takes place' in an 'unworking'– an unworking of any ostensibly realised 'work' of community, an unworking that is 'before or beyond the work' (1991a: 31). And this working is not only before or beyond the work but 'begins and ends infinitely within and beyond the work' (Nancy, 1991b: 73). Yet this infinity, Blanchot would add, has to be rendered finitely if it is to operate within and as a community of finite beings (1988: 6).[6] Nancy would agree but also stress that the 'limit' marking a community 'is not a place … there is no common place' (1991b: 73). The concentrated relation, the sharing, between finite beings 'making up' community cannot be 'placed', cannot be positively contained. So, Blanchot could add, the claim to sovereignty is a negation of community (1988: 20). Any totalised comprehension projected onto community would be a denial of it.

Perhaps, then, this depiction of plurality and community can evoke possible paths around the aporetic together with the prospect of some such paths inhabiting governmentality. The range and connectivity of the 'plurality of specific ends' (2007: 99) of governmentality would intimate that there was some commonality between them. A trail of connection could begin with what for Foucault is a leading player, the economic and especially economies of the liberal, neoliberal and ordoliberal kinds. Liberalism, in turn, assumes an illimitable effectiveness, yet 'the form of governmental technology we call liberalism … [has] its own self-limitation' as its objective (Foucault, 2008: 297). Liberal governmentality, then, assumes an illimitable capacity of self-limitation. The same could be said of that figure of the individual we have already met early in this section. This same individual could be seen as a product of neoliberalism, of a 'neoliberal rationality' that 'configures human beings exhaustively as market actors, always, only, and everywhere as *homo economicus*' (Brown, 2015: 32). Such individuals were also formed by powers of disciplinary normalisation, powers that in turn were exercised through them – powers to which they are never entirely or ultimately subordinate (Foucault, 1979: 27). The individual is, to repeat somewhat, a surpassing 'sovereign' even if also 'enslaved' (Foucault, 1970: 312). What could be called the genealogy of this individual is traced by Foucault from 'the developing concern in early modern Europe for coordinating the government of individuals with the government of a human collectivity understood as population' (Gordon, 2001: xxv, emphasis in original). There is a combined 'individualization and totalization' (Foucault, 2001c: 325). Another

6 This simply, doubtless too simply, will be a constructed conversation derived from the empathic debate between Nancy and Blanchot in these works. See also Nancy (2016).

possible connection to the commonality, 'science:' it was through the development of the science of government that the economy could be re-focussed on a level of reality that we now describe as the economic; and it is again through the science of government that the specific problem of population could be identified and, it could be added, disciplinary power brought to bear (Foucault, 2007: 104).

Economy, in turn, obliged by making it 'possible to think, reflect, and calculate the problem of government outside the juridical framework of sovereignty' (Foucault, 2007: 104).

Development

Something of an intruder into governmentality and its commonality would be a mantric 'development'. While Foucault's 'power' would accommodate 'apparatuses and institutions', or 'the various power apparatuses that operate at various levels of society' (1981: 96; 2003a: 13), Foucault tends to confine the governmentality within which they operate to a configuration of the nation state and the individual: the 'fundamental phenomenon in the history of the West' is 'the governmentalization of the state' (2007: 110). It is the state to which 'all other forms of power relation must refer ... because power relations have come more and more under state control' (2001b: 345). Yet development encapsulates a commonality of the 'endless number of practices' signalled earlier (Escobar, 1984: 387), a commonality of the numerous 'apparatuses and institutions' the existence and efficacy of which have always exceeded the reach of the state. Conspicuously, the components of governmentality extend beyond the situated state – extended by way of such as the economy, neo-liberalism, science and disciplinary power. Its modes of power, as we saw, are 'indefinite', 'without limit', 'never closed' (Foucault, 1979: 227). Along with its imperial antecedents, and beyond the state, development would be more aptly related to a 'biopolitics' with-in governmentality where 'power is situated and exercised at the level of life, the species, the race and the large-scale phenomena of population' (1981: 137).

More expansively, for Foucault governmentality extends beyond any combinatory coherence. While governmentality assumed determinate existence in the multiple of distinct entities through which it operated, it was also a governmentality which subsisted beyond them. It governed 'at a distance' (Rose, 1996: 43, 57). In so doing, governmentality assumed a surpassing power over these entities and was unified in so doing, yet it was illimitable and without determinate positioning. Even as 'life and its mechanisms' are brought 'into the realm of explicit calculations', still '[i]t is not that life has been totally integrated into the techniques that govern and administer it; it constantly escapes them' (1981: 143). It cannot be a matter 'of immobilizing life' (Foucault, 1980: 60). Yet the emphasis can shift. Governmentality can be a determinate 'matter of taking control of life', of achieving 'overall states of equilibrium or regularity', 'a sort of homeostasis' (Foucault, 2003a: 246, 249). So, in a more 'applied' vein there is 'the essential function of security' brought to bear by governmentality – protecting 'the security of the whole:' 'the essential function of security ... is to respond to a reality in such a way that this response cancels out the reality to which it responds – nullifies it, or limits, checks or regulates it' (Foucault, 2007: 47; 2003a: 249).

Governmentality then is identified in terms that would control and stabilise life – life that still cannot in any way be subsumed. Yet to do so, even if confined to an operative aspiration, governmentality has to portend an incipient comprehension of life, one that can match, or purport to match, the 'plenitude of the possible' as and when there is specific provocation (Foucault, 1981: 145). To do this, governmentality has to be held entirely responsive and expectant, and as such it does not assume a forceful and explicate determinacy. Even as its 'political rationality' impels it towards 'totalization', there is still no site of surpassing control, no 'primary existence of a central point ... from which secondary and descendent forms could emanate' (Foucault, 2001c: 325; 1981: 93). Such governmentality could be categorised as 'a new totalitarianism', incorporating the idea from Lacoue-Labarthe and Nancy (1997: 129).[7] This is a totalitarianism that does not issue forth from some pertinent power above. Rather, it 'would itself proceed from the dissolution of transcendence, and henceforth come to penetrate all spheres of life now devoid of any alterity' (Lacoue-Labarthe and Nancy, 1997: 129). And alterity could disappear with governmentality, disappear in the incorporated potential of its control of life, its shaping of existence. All of which would leave no room, as it were, for the alterity intrinsic to community, even as there is a commonality sufficiently evoked within the plurality that is governmentality.

In sum, governmentality provides a referential commonality that is not only receptive but could also project a potential completeness of control, but it has no positively explicate existence or force. It is, nonetheless, 'very specific albeit very complex' (Foucault, 2007: 108). Yet this specificity has to exert a constantly potential totality of control over life. In the cause of 'security', as we have just seen, it has to encompass, negate and shape 'reality'. Its comprehension of the economic, to take another cognate content, has to cover an 'economic world [that] is naturally opaque and naturally non-totalizable' (2008: 282). The same could be said of other cognate contents such as disciplinary power and sovereignty. Understandably then, no cohesive content is given to its specificity. For governmentality to encompass and effect a governing of the illimitable, it cannot itself be restrained by any delimited positivity. It has to remain an insistent nothing.

A seeming resolution comes with Foucault's emplacing all this, at least in relation to its origin and perhaps its continuing impetus, within 'the West'. For

7 Foucault may disapprove of the use of 'totalitarianism' within this context (see 2007: 373; 2008: 87; 91; cf. 2001c: 325).

example: 'by "governmentality" I understand the tendency, the line of force, that for a long time, and throughout the West, has constantly led towards the pre-eminence over all other types of power' (Foucault, 2007: 108) and governmentality is a 'fundamental phenomenon in the history of the West' (Foucault, 2007: 110). Derrida would render the imperious affirmation of 'the West' as a 'globalatinization' that 'is at the same time hegemonic and finite'–an irreducible 'extensiveness' (2002a: 51–2, 67). Such a 'globalatinizing tradition', Derrida would add

> appears inseparable in the modernity following the Enlightenment from an ambiguous secularization (and secularization is always ambiguous in that it frees itself from the religious, all the while remaining marked in its very concept by it, by the theological, indeed, the ontotheological.
>
> (2005: 28)

A compounded compatibility between governmentality and the West ensues. As 'hegemonic and finite', as a situated illimitability, the 'modern' West has to be a 'hidden' imperium. It assumes the operative dimensions of a monotheistic substitute yet cannot be explicate in this given its supposed secularity. This seeming impasse follows the aporetic paths of governmentality. Governmentality assumes an affirmative, determinable efficacy. It can be pointedly 'specific' in this (Foucault, 2007: 108). Yet it is also illimitable and irreducible to any delimited positivity.

Since governmentality is a 'fundamental phenomenon in the history of the West' (Foucault, 2007: 110), the redemptive claim could be that it is immanent to the West and, as Nancy has suggested, the 'totalitarianism' recently touched on could be rendered as 'immanentism' (1991: 3). But immanence – the immanence evoked here as well as immanence generally – is illimitable and, as Deleuze and Guattari would caution, 'whenever immanence is interpreted as immanent *to* Something, we can be sure that this Something reintroduces the transcendent' (1994: 45, emphasis in original). An occidental 'Something' would share with governmentality and its informing powers the presumption of operatively containing the illimitable with-in a limited, a specific domain – yet, and again, this domain is intrinsically incapable of being positively, coherently existent. Borrowing from Lacoue-Labarthe and Nancy, its 'unappearance is proportionate to its all-powerfulness' (1997: 126).

Negation

We could begin with Franz Fanon's perceptive statement 'When I search for Man in the technique and the style of Europe, I see only a succession of negations of man' (1967: 25).

Despite or because of its imperious reach, governmentality cannot be rendered ultimately in terms of any positive presence. What is resorted to instead is a negative universal reference. This reference can initially be located within the racism that Foucault would find within a 'biopower' inhabiting governmentality, a power in which 'starting from the eighteenth century, modern Western societies took on board the fundamental fact that human beings are a species' (Foucault, 2007: 1). While this biological fact imported 'the integrity, superiority, and the purity of the race', it also imported a basic division within the unity: '[t]hat is the first function of racism: to fragment, to create caesuras within the biological continuum addressed by biopower' (Foucault, 2003a: 81, 255). Such caesuras are inexorably sharp. The 'enlightened' and exclusive claim to the universal has to exclude utterly. As such it constituently excludes that much of the preceding West (such as the religious) found to be incompatible with the occidental modern.

For Foucault racial division was 'the first historico-political discourse on society', being 'ultimately … a way of normalizing society' – a 'universally disciplinary and regulatory society' (2003a: 49, 61, 259). The initial and initiating exclusion in terms of race persists of course along with its updating in terms of religion, culture and terrorism. Yet in the service of a 'normalizing society' the particular appropriation of the universal has not only to exclude completely but also to include completely. So the erstwhile excluded are bidden also, following the Enlightenment's injunction, to 'improve' or, later, to 'progress' or reform, or in some other way achieve inclusion. Further, with the espousal of the universal, the antithesis resides potentially within the bearers of the universal along with their potentially failing the requirements of that 'universally disciplinary and regulatory society'.

It is at this ultimate point of inclusion that Foucault's expansive idea of racism becomes crucial. The 'universally disciplinary and regulatory society' of governmentality, with its all-encompassing modes and ends, is oriented towards nothing less than the control of life. Those excluded from the multiple range of the norm become both 'interior and foreign', the carriers of 'an inclusion through exclusion', the source of 'a natural order of disorder' (Foucault, 1970: xxiv; 2001a: 78; 1981: 44). With a 'normalizing society' the excluded comprise the 'abnormal', 'the evil,… the non-normal' (Foucault, 2003a: 316–17). The normal, then, absorb or sustain their positive content in negation of the abnormal who become 'another people within the same people' (Foucault, 1979: 253). A 'case' in point would be a 'development' impelled by the dictate of 'progress' and, eventually, a layered shift from progress to an imperative of becoming 'disciplinary', a 'controlling' discourse (e.g. Skouteris, 2009: 163, 222–6). Progress, then merges into a 'development' characterised by tentacular regulation (Buchanan and Pahuja, 2004: 73). In this, development exemplifies the current phase of the negative universal reference by elevating a universal norm through 'the creation of "abnormalities" such as the "underdeveloped," … which it would, later treat and reform' (Escobar, 1984: 387).

In all, the formative force of negation can be drawn into the diffusion of governmentality, endowing it and its universalised cohorts with a negatively impelled identity. The inescapable issue then becomes one of how these entities, including governmentality, could be rendered as operatively positive when they are operatively constituted in negation. The answer involves a culminating regard for law.

Law

Resorting to law may not be immediately promising. Its 'modern' manifestation would seem to be thoroughly implicated with, even subsumed within, governmentality, and this to such an extent as to leave no scope for it to act upon and supplement governmentality itself. Governmentality and law emerged conterminously. The law of a modern occident took identity in compound negations – the negation of the 'savages', the negation of prior European modes of sociability fictively attributed, and the negation of significant prior modes of law such as custom and natural law. These negations were not chasmic. Law retained an actual or incipient connection to the negated. What was crucially different was the ability of law now to re-shape these, 'to release norm-contents from the dogmatism of mere tradition and to determine them intentionally' (Habermas, 1976: 86). This positioning in negation extends to the freeing of law from any ultimately determinate ties except the tie to the sovereign nation-state. As the expression of the 'will' of this remodelled sovereign, law becomes an objective embodiment of the Enlightenment domestication of the deity. Law's range of determination in this cause becomes infinite and as such cannot ultimately be contained in it.[8] It assumes a universalised, encompassing dimension and the ability, potentially, to self-situate determinately by negating or incorporating anything.

While for Foucault, as we saw when considering development, the 'fundamental phenomenon in the history of the West' is 'the governmentalization of the state', when it comes to the ruling 'triangle' of 'sovereignty, discipline and governmental management' there is a marked diminishing of the pivotal significance of sovereignty, something that Foucault frequently emphasised in relation to law –'law' conceived within 'the juridical framework of sovereignty' (2007: 104, 107). And especially as far as such law is concerned, diminishing correlated with the advance of disciplinary power. As Foucault has it, '[t]he discourse of discipline is alien to that of law'– to that of law as 'juridical' (2003a: 38). Yet something of a redemptive ambivalence is lurking here. So, while the

8 A conventional jurisprudence could envisage law liberated from this servitude by a work professing to do so, a work that is, in Brian Simpson's apt assessment, 'the most successful work of analytical jurisprudence ever to appear in the common law world'– Hart's *The Concept of Law* (1961: 1st edition; Simpson, 2011: 1). But this law itself is soon enslaved. The meaning of any of its rules is set by an enduring 'core of certainty'; and after taking identity in opposition to the 'primitive', it becomes amenable to the dictates of an omnipotent officialdom (Hart, 1961: 89–91, 112–14, 119).

disciplinary 'action of the norm' advances 'at the expense of the juridical system of law', this would seem to be 'norm' as depicting what is normally so in a 'disciplinary society' something that takes on a 'positive' and 'technical', 'natural', 'clinical', even factual quality (1979: 223; 1981: 144; 2003a: 38; 2003b: 50). Yet what would seem to be the opposite is also confidently claimed. The determination of the norm is not only a matter of observation since 'there is an originally prescriptive character of the norm' (2007: 57). That much is imported by law's operating 'more and more as a norm' in its relation to disciplinary power (1981: 144). A fusion results – a 'scientifico-legal complex' for example, or an 'epistemologico-juridical' formation' (1979: 23). And there are numerous instances where a distinct legal presence is marked such as the noting of 'a judicial power' within the discipline, 'a microcourt' inseparable from a disciplinary 'micropower', a noting of 'the emergence of a new form of "law": a mixture of legality and nature', a noting of our being 'in the society of the teacher-judge, the doctor-judge, the educator-judge, the "social worker"-judge', a noting of the asylum doctor being 'Father and Judge, Family and Law', and the observation that '[t]he psychiatrist really becomes a judge', all within the context of disciplinary powers (1979: 304; 2001a: 86; 2009: 37). And, returning to the formative force of negation, what for Foucault is 'final' in the constitution of the norm is the 'division between the normal and the abnormal'– the constitution of the normal in its opposition to the abnormal (2007: 57). That outcome is not simply something observed. It requires, rather, creation, interpretation, and decisive judgment. It requires, in a 'final' applied way, law.

The engagement with development also emphasised an insistent theme of this chapter: that is, an illimitable governmentality distinctly surpasses the diversity of powers and sites through which it assured operative existence. Despite its own claim to the illimitable, the nation-state was seen to be surpassed in the range of a 'development' impelled by a governmentality that is a product of 'the West'– one that asserts 'a pre-eminence over all other types of power – sovereignty, discipline, and so on' (2007: 108). Of course, the sovereign state and disciplinary power will play a constituent and operative part in and as development, as will other powers drawn on by 'governmental management' such as those embedded in the economic. Yet the dependence of governmentality on law for ultimate and positive affirmation would persist.

There is of course an abundance of laws involving development in the sphere of what could loosely be called the international. Taking the instance of international law proper, its enabling of a determinate governmentality extends beyond its emanent connection to the nation-state. Selecting from numerous 'applied' instances, there is the domain of *jus cogens*, that domain of peremptory norms of international law binding on every state whether or not it has agreed to them. Then there are obligations *erga omnes*, obligations deemed to be 'towards all' in that the obligation is one 'to the whole of the international community' in requiring, for example, the 'enforcing and protecting [of] fundamental human rights' (Bantekas, 2010: 13). Perhaps most telling is the 'recognition' by other nation-states which goes to create a nation-state in accord with criteria laid down in international law – criteria such as those contained in Article 1 of the Montevideo Convention on the Rights and Duties of States of 1933. Furthermore, no matter what the difficulty in theorizing its 'recognition', a 'state may exhibit all the hallmarks of statehood yet be denied recognition by other states by reason of the circumstances of its creation offending fundamental norms of the international legal order' (Shearer, 1994: 87).

What underlines all these types of law – juridical, disciplinary, international – is the affinity between law and governmentality. Since governmentality is illimitable and without its own discrete content it has to engage in a 'self-limitation' of its insipient range so as to enable and situate specific modes through which it has effect.[9] Somewhat similarly, the universalised range of law post-Enlightenment frees it from any constraining connection, except to the sovereign state, even as it remains able to situate itself determinately. There are, however, two differences to be observed. One is that in giving effect to an illimitable governmentality, an illimitable law is not tied to some sovereign 'will'. The second deserves a new paragraph.

While both are illimitable as well as situated, governmentality and law are also radically different. Governmentality is ever surpassing and apart in its directed comprehension of life, its shaping of reality. It can be seen, returning to Lacoue-Labarthe and Nancy, as a 'new totalitarianism' with its 'unappearance' being 'proportionate to it all-powerfulness' (1997: 126, 129). Given that range of appropriation, and as we saw, governmentality would absorb alterity and in so doing would deny it any ultimacy. For law, in contrast, alterity is ultimate. Returning to Foucault, we find law extending a 'silent and infinitely accommodating welcome' in which it becomes of 'the outside that envelops conduct, thereby removing it from all interiority' (1987: 34, 38). Yet even as law assumes its 'impalpable substance' as exteriority, it is put 'beside itself' as it separates itself (turning to Blanchot now) 'via the very separation that institutes it as form, in the very movement by which it formulates ... exteriority as law' (1987: 35; 1993: 434). To effect this creative combination, as Derrida sees it, one '*must* ... [*il faut*] calculate, negotiate the relation between the calculable and the incalculable' (2002b: 257, emphasis in original). Derrida proceeds to concentrate '[t]he order of this *il faut*' by finding that 'it does not *properly* belong either to justice or to law' – 'justice' here being the infinitely accommodating law and 'law' being the law determinate: rather, that order 'only belongs to either realm by exceeding each one in the direction of the other – which means that, in their very heterogeneity, these two orders are undissociable *de facto* and *de jure*' (2002a: 257, emphasis in original).

9 For a summary of Foucault's 'self-limitation' of governmentality, see Raffnsøe et al. (2016: 283–4). The 'self limitation' in the text above extends that notion somewhat.

A question remains, one that has haunted much of this chapter. The incompatibility of transcendence and a secular modernity was noted serval times. Yet the law just described in its exteriority, its infinite accommodation, its utter responsiveness, evokes, or is even identifiable with, transcendence. It could be that in practice law avoids this attribution since its exteriority, its impalpability, frees it from any enduring content. Law, Blanchot finds, 'affirms itself as law and without reference to anything higher: to it alone, pure transcendence' (1992: 25). It may be doubted, however, whether that aspect of law would be demotically definitive. A more acceptable accounting for such a practical transcendence could be the correspondence between the heterogeneity that goes to create law and the generative components of community described earlier. There is a much-noted inseparability, or even identity, of law and community or sociality. Proponents of such a coupling would include Rousseau (1968: Bk II, ch. 7, 87), Nancy (1991a: 28), and Derrida (1997: 231). Would that something of a palindromic pursuit were possible: then this chapter could be recast as an engagement with the relation between law and community.

References

Bantekas, I., 2010. *International Criminal Law*, 4th edition. Hart Publishing.

Berg, L., Huijbens, E. and Larsen, H., 2016. Producing Anxiety in the Neoliberal University. *The Canadian Geographer*, *60* (*2*), 168–180.

Blanchot, M., 1988. *The Unavowable Community*. Translated by Joris, Pierre. Station Hill Press.

Blanchot, M., 1992. *The Step Not Beyond*. Translated from French by Nelson, L. State University of New York Press.

Blanchot, M., 1993. *The Infinite Conversation*. Translated from French by Hanson, S. University of Minnesota Press.

Brown, W., 2015. *Undoing the Demos: Neoliberalism's Stealth Revolution*. MIT Press.

Buchanan, R. and Pahuja, S., 2004. Legal Imperialism: Empire's Invisible Hand? In P.A. Passavant and J. Dean (eds), *Empire's New Clothes: Reading Hardt and Negri*. Routledge.

Davidson, D., 1985. On the Very Idea of a Conceptual Scheme. In J. Rajchman and C. West (eds), *Post-Analytic Philosophy*. Columbia University Press, p. 129.

Deleuze, G. and Guatarri, F., 1983. *Anti-Oedipus: Capitalism and Schizophrenia*. Translated from French by Hurley, R., Seem, M. and Lane, H.R. University of Minnesota Press.

Deleuze, G. and Guattari, F., 1994. *What is Philosopy?* Translated from French by Burchell, G. and Tomlinson, H. Verso.

Derrida, J., 1997/2005b. *Politics of Friendship*. Translated from French by Collins, G. Verso.

Derrida, J., 2002a. Faith and Knowledge: The Two Sources of 'Religion' at the Limits of Reason Alone. Translated from French by Weber, S. In G. Anidjar (ed.), *Acts of Religion*. Routledge, p. 42.

Derrida, J., 2002b. Force of Law: The 'Mystical Foundation of Authority'. Translated by Quaintance, M. In G. Anidjar (ed.), *Acts of Religion*. Routledge, p. 228.

Derrida, J., 2005. *Rogues: Two Essays on Reason*. Translated from French by Brault, P.-A. and Naas, M. Stanford University Press.

Escobar, A., 1984. Discourse and Power in Development: Michel Foucault and the Relevance of his Work to the Third World. *Alternatives, 10* (Winter), 377–400.

Fanon, F., 1967. *The Wretched of the Earth*. Penguin.

Fitzpatrick, P., 2001. *Modernism and the Grounds of Law*. Cambridge University Press.

Foucault, M., 1970. *The Order of Things: An Archaeology of the Human Sciences*. Tavistock.

Foucault, M., 1979. *Discipline and Punish: The Birth of the Prison*. Translated from French by Sheridan, A. Penguin.

Foucault, M., 1980. Georges Canguilhem: Philosopher of Error. *Ideology & Consciousness, 7* (Autumn), 51–62.

Foucault, M., 1981. *The History of Sexuality Volume One: An Introduction*. Translated from French by Hurley, R. Penguin.

Foucault, M., 1987. Maurice Blanchot: The Thought from Outside. Translated from French by Massumi, B. and Mehlman, J. In M. Foucault and M. Blanchot, *Foucault/Blanchot*. Zone Books.

Foucault, M., 2001a. Truth and Juridical Forms. Translated from French by Hurley, R. *et al.* In M. Foucault, *Power: Essential Works of Foucault 1954–1984 (Volume 3)*. Penguin, pp. 1–89.

Foucault, M., 2001b. The Subject and Power. Translated from French by Hurley, R. *et al.* In M. Foucault, *Power: Essential Works of Foucault 1954–1984 (Volume 3)*. Penguin.

Foucault, M., 2001c. 'Omnes et Singulatim': Toward a Critique of Political Reason. Translated from French by Hurley, R. *et al.* In M. Foucault, *Power: Essential Works of Foucault 1954–1984 (Volume 3)*. Penguin, pp. 298–325.

Foucault, M., 2003a. *'Society Must Be Defended': Lectures at the Collège de France 1975–1976*. Allen Lane.

Foucault, M., 2003b. *Abnormal: Lectures at the Collège de France 1974–1975*. Picador.

Foucault, M., 2007. *Security, Territory, Population: Lectures at the Collège de France 1977–1978*. Palgrave Macmillan.

Foucault, M., 2008. *The Birth of Biopolitics: Lectures at the Collège de France 1978–1979*. Palgrave Macmillan.

Foucault, M., 2009. *History of Madness*. Routledge.

Francis, Pope, 2014. *Address to the European Parliament in Full*. Catholic Herald. Available online at: http://www.catholicherald.co.uk/news/2014/11/25/pope-franciss-address-to-the-european-parliament-in-full (accessed 18 June 2017).

Gordon, C., 2001. Introduction. In M. Foucault, *Power: Essential Works of Foucault 1954–1984 (Volume 3)*. Penguin.

Habermas, J., 1976. *Legitimation Crisis*. Translated from German by McCarthy, T. Heinemann.

Hart, H.L.A., 1961. *The Concept of Law*. Oxford University Press.

Klabbers, J. and Piiparinen, T., 2013. Normative Pluralism: An Exploration. In J. Klabbers and T. Piiparinen (eds), *Normative Pluralism and International Law. Exploring Global Governance*. Cambridge University Press, p. 141.

Lacoue-Labarthe, P. and Nancy, J.-L., 1997. The 'Retreat' of the Political. In S. Sparks (ed.), *Retreating the Political*. Routledge, ch. 7.

Levinas, I., 1969. *Totality and Infinity: An Essay on Exteriority*. Translated by Lingis, A. Duquesne University Press.

Nancy, J.-L., 1991a. The Inoperative Community. Translated from French by Connor, P. et al In J.-L. Nancy (ed.), *The Inoperative Community*. University of Minnesota Press, p. 1.

Nancy, J.-L., 1991b. Literary Communism. Translated from French by Connor, P. et al In J.-L. Nancy (ed.), *The Inoperative Community*. University of Minnesota Press, pp. 1–42.

Nancy, J.-L., 2016. *The Disavowed Community*. Translated by Armstrong, P. Fordham University Press.

Quijano, A., 2007. Coloniality and Modernity/Rationality. *Cultural Studies*, *21* (*2*), 168–178.

Raffnsøe, S., Gudmand-Høyer, M. and Thaning, M.S., 2016. *Michel Foucault: A Research Companion*. Palgrave Macmillan.

Rose, N., 1996. Governing 'Advanced' Liberal Democracies. In A. Barry, T. Osbourne and N. Rose (eds), *Foucault and Political Reason: Liberalism, Neo-liberalism and Rationalities of Government*. University of Chicago Press, ch. 2.

Rousseau, J.-J., 1968. *The Social Contract*. Translated by Cranston, M. Penguin Classics.

Shearer, I.A. (ed.), 1994. *Starke's International Law*, 11th edition. Butterworths.

Simpson, A.W.B., 2011. *Reflections on The Concept of Law*. Oxford University Press.

Skouteris, T., 2009. *The Notion of Progress in International Law Discourse*. T.N.C. Asser Press.

Tan, C., 2011. *Governance Through Development: Poverty Reduction Strategies, International Law and The Disciplining of Third World States*. Routledge-Cavendish.

Tully, J., 2008. *Public Philosophy in a New Key: Volume 2, Imperialism and Civic Freedom*. Cambridge University Press.

Part II

The academy and social activism

Chapter 5

Southern voices

Extending a project

William Twining and Abdul Paliwala

Introduction

We, William Twining and Abdul Paliwala, had conversations about how to extend William's original project on Southern Voices, whose central question was what was needed to deparochialise Northern academic practices concerning theoretical approaches to law in an era of globalisation (Twining, 2009b). A key initiative has been the production by William of the book *Human Rights: Southern Voices: Francis Deng, Abdullahi An-Na'im, Yash Ghai, Upendra Baxi* based on detailed study of four important Southern human rights scholars (Twining, 2009b). Abdul feels the same about infusing Northern scholarship with Southern voices, but suggests an additional agenda of promoting South–South communication of Southern perspectives in ways that promote global justice. This results in some differences between us. For William, the intention is pluralist – to open up infinite possibilities for Southern voices. For Abdul, while pluralism is important, there is an underlying need to de/anti-colonialise discourses globally in order to promote global justice, and to differentiate between Southern discourses which have a unique Southern perspective and others that are derivations of Northern perspectives. While this is not intended to disqualify dependent Southern discourses from consideration, Abdul believes that the main value of Southern discourses lies in their de/anti-colonial nature.

We have not looked for an anodyne compromise between two salient perspectives. William's Northern perspective is significant in its attempt to deparochialise the North; Abdul's Southern perspective is equally concerned with how Southern perspectives challenge the impact of the parochial North but also how this can promote Southern conversations. In the next two sections we have therefore provided space for each perspective to be stated separately. This is followed by a concluding section on how to further develop the original Southern Voices project.

Deparochialising Northern[1] legal scholarship: William's perspective

A person encountering the vast heritage of Northern legal scholarship and theorising is likely to feel daunted. So many authors, so many topics, so many schools and -isms, so many contested questions. To take but one example: one English jurist, Jeremy Bentham, wrote well over a million words; the few students who study his writings in the original usually focus on a few chapters of one early work, *An Introduction to the Principles of Morals and Legislation* (1781). This represents less than 1 per cent of his *Collected Works*, which will in time extend up to 68–70 substantial volumes.[2] The index of names in the fifth edition of Lloyd's *Introduction to Jurisprudence* (Freeman, 2014) lists over a thousand authors. And that is just jurisprudence, the more abstract part of the academic literature on law. If one extends the panorama to include writings within the Romanist and Scandinavian traditions those available in English are only the tip of an immense iceberg.

From this perspective it may seem bold even rash for someone to criticise this vast, rich heritage of texts and ideas for being narrowly focused and parochial. Yet the project under discussion started from the suggestion that 'during the twentieth century and before, Northern academic legal culture has tended to be state-oriented, secular, positivist, Northo-centric, unempirical, and universalist in respect of morals' (Twining, 2009a: 6).[3] If one adopts a global perspective, these generalisations, subject to a few caveats, are quite easily defended. Suffice to say here that most of our inherited theories of law exclude most kinds of religious and customary law except insofar as they are recognised as part of a state legal system. In the predominant view, teachers of Islamic law, Hindu law, Jewish law, the Confucian tradition, or 'African law' are not teaching law properly so-called; even those who try to accommodate some version of 'non-state law' in their theories barely cite any non-Northern authors or texts. Look at the indexes of names of

1 We have used the term Northern rather than Western as it forms a better contrast with Southern in the context of this book.

2 Recent student readers on Jurisprudence, such as the eighth edition of Lloyd and Freeman's *Introduction to Jurisprudence* (Freeman, 2014) and Penner, Schiff and Nobles' *Jurisprudence and Legal Theory* (Barron et al., 2005) heroically try to give a broad conspectus by giving a historical perspective, by regularly crossing disciplinary boundaries, by moving beyond Anglo-American authors and transnational classics such as Aquinas, Kant, Kelsen and Weber, to include modern Continental Europeans, such as Derrida, Foucault, Lacan, Bourdieu, Habermas, and Luhmann. Although both extend over 1,000 pages, their authors lament that they have been forced to make significant omissions for reasons of space.

3 The quoted statement from Twining's *General Jurisprudence* (2009a) is hedged around by a few caveats: 'Of course, all of these generalisations are crude and subject to exception – indeed none has gone unchallenged within the Western legal tradition – and issues surrounding nearly all of them constitute a high proportion of the contested agenda of modern Western jurisprudence' (ibid.).

Lloyd's Jurisprudence (Freeman, 2014) or *Introduction to Jurisprudence and Legal Theory* (Barron et al., 2005) or any other standard work within the common law and civil law traditions and count the number of persons cited who might be categorised as 'Southern' or 'non-Northern' writing about law in countries in the global South or however one wishes to characterise outside the West. Furthermore, much Northern-based scholarship on law in those parts of the world has been criticised for being 'orientalist' along the lines of the well-known critique by Edward Said and others: rightly or wrongly much of such scholarship is dismissed as patronising, colonialist and Eurocentric (Said, 2003).There is, perhaps, one major exception to these generalisations. This relates to the intellectual tradition of macro-comparative law, exemplified by David and Brierley (1978) or Zweigert and Kötz's account of 'legal families' (1998). These panoramic overviews at least tried to encompass the whole world. Unfortunately, they were widely recognised to be theoretically problematic and vulnerable to criticisms of being too simplistic, too abstract or over-generalised. Many comparative lawyers were embarrassed by these weaknesses and opted to practice more respectable micro-comparison, mainly between the common law and civil law of particular Northern countries. The late Patrick Glenn's brave *Legal Traditions of the World* (2014), backed by a sophisticated, if controversial, concept of tradition has revived interest in this important area. But our Northern traditions have not equipped us with adequate concepts, data or methods to make reliable generalisations about most aspects of law in the world as a whole. The main reason for this is that, with the major exception of Roman Law, nearly all Northern legal scholarship and education has focused on the state legal system of a single country or jurisdiction.

It is an undeniable fact that 'Southern voices' have been largely unheard in the heritage of Northern jurisprudence and legal scholarship. One can quibble about details and categories, but this was the starting-point of the current project. As a legal theorist adopting a global perspective – i.e. viewing law in the world as a whole – I was concerned about the narrowness or parochialism or insularity of the mainstream heritage of nearly all Northern Jurisprudence and the accompanying dangers of ethnocentrism and Eurocentric universalism in its practices. My central question was: what steps might be taken towards trying to deparochialise our practices in thinking, talking, debating, and teaching about theoretical questions concerning law in an era of globalisation?

I canvassed options about where to start. These included stimulating a series of book-length studies of non-Northern jurists;[4] a project to facilitate translations of texts inaccessible to linguistically deprived Anglophones; and encouraging the establishment of a greater number of academic posts devoted to the analysis of relevant issues. I decided on a modest plan to try to make a few specific jurists

4 As Editor of the *Jurists* series I invited proposals for books on non-Western jurists; I received several proposals and even more promises, but so far only one book has been published: Colin Imber's, *Ebu's-Suud: The Islamic Legal Tradition* (1997).

and texts better known in the Anglophone West. Limitations of my expertise and linguistic competence narrowed the options. Possibly within my competence, however, was an edited collection of important texts by African nationalist leaders, such as Kwame Nkrumah, Julius Nyerere, Kenneth Kaunda, Nelson Mandela, and founders of the *négritude* movement, including Léopold Senghor and Aimé Césaire. After considering a range of candidates I cut my list to four individuals whom I respected, whose background was already familiar and whom I knew personally as colleagues and friends. Although I am not a specialist in human rights, the four I chose from a shortlist of seven or eight had the great advantage that all were both activists and writers about human rights and each of them, despite some striking similarities, had a distinctive approach to the subject. After some preliminary research, I started with the MacDonald public lecture in Alberta in 2005. The following is the abstract for that occasion.

> In the context of 'globalization,' Western jurisprudence has largely ignored non-Northern viewpoints, interests, and traditions. This article takes a modest step towards de-parochializing our juristic canon by introducing writings about human rights of four 'Southern' jurists: Francis Deng (Southern Sudan), Abdullahi An-Na'im (Sudan), Yash Ghai (Kenya), and Upendra Baxi (India). All were trained in the common law and have published extensively in English, so their work is readily accessible, but their perspectives show some striking differences. Deng argues that traditional values of the Dinka of the Southern Sudan are basically compatible with the values underlying the international human rights regime. For An-Na'im, a 'modernist' interpretation of Islam is mostly reconcilable with international human rights, but acceptance of such ideas depends far more on conversations within Islam than on cross-cultural dialogue or external efforts. Ghai questions claims to universal human rights; however, from his materialist stance and his experience of postcolonial constitution-making, human rights discourse can provide a framework for negotiating settlements in multi-ethnic societies. Baxi argues that as human rights discourse is professionalized or hijacked by powerful groups, it risks losing touch with the suffering and needs of the poor and the oppressed, who are the main authors of human rights.
>
> (Original lecture published in Twining, 2009a: ch. 13).

The distinctiveness of their contributions can be summarised as follows.

- For a case study of the relationship between an exotic traditional nomadic culture and the international human rights regime, read Francis Deng.
- If you wish to learn how a devout Muslim scholar has developed a strategy for reconciling Islamic beliefs with Western liberal democratic ideals, read Abdullahi An-Na'im.
- If you are interested in a pragmatic, materialist argument about the practical value of using human rights discourse to reach political settlements and

compromises in multi-ethnic or other conflicted societies and its role in constitution-making more generally, read Yash Ghai.

- And, if you are interested in an impassioned plea that human rights discourse should first and foremost be interpreted and used to further the interests of the worst-off, read Upendra Baxi (Twining, 2009b: 220).

These four thinkers are both significantly similar and strikingly different and are therefore suitable objects for comparison.[5] They belong to a single postcolonial generation (three were born, coincidentally, in 1938; An-Na'im is a decade younger, but started early).[6] All four have been concerned with the problems of racism, colonialism, post-independence politics, weak and corrupt regimes, poverty, and injustice in the global South. They have given expression to ideas that are rooted in these concerns without claiming to represent any particular constituency. All four were trained in the common law, have spent substantial periods in the United States and the United Kingdom, and write in English. They have all been activists as well as scholars, but in quite varied ways. Each has a distinctive voice and says different things. They make a fascinating study in contrasts. But although they differ, they do not disagree on most fundamentals; rather they complement each other.

In recent years their ideas seem to have converged in some significant ways. First, all four are acutely aware that we live in a world characterised by a diversity of beliefs and culture. So far as I can tell, each of them would opt for what Patrick Glenn calls 'sustainable diversity' rather than some bland homogenisation in which one size is made to fit all (Glenn, 2014: ch. 10). Second, the fact that they accept pluralism (of beliefs, cultures, traditions) as an intractable social fact raises issues that are fashionably discussed in terms of universalism versus cultural relativism, especially in relation to human rights (Twining, 2009a: 129–32). My sense is that all four are impatient about such debates. Each steers a path between strong versions of universalism and particularism. All four reject strong cultural relativism.[7] None of them treats the

5 For extracts from each author's work see Twining (2009: chs 2–5).

6 All four belong to the post-Independence generation of public intellectuals in their own country or region. India became independent in 1947, in Baxi's eighth year; the Sudan in 1956, when Deng and An-Na'im were still at school; Kenya became independent in 1963, the year that Ghai took up his first teaching post at Dar-es-Salaam, where Tanzania had attained Independence two years earlier. For each of them, local, regional, and international post-Independence politics formed a crucial part of the context of their intellectual development.

7 'They respect cultural diversity and value tolerance, but this involves no commitment to "tolerating the intolerable". Each believes in the value of dialogue, but with different emphases: Deng, the diplomat, has always relied on persuasion and mediation; An-Na'im stresses the importance of internal dialogue; Ghai points to the value of human rights discourse as a framework for political negotiation and compromise between people with different interests, concerns, and ethnicities; Baxi, more pugnacious, sees dialogic human rights as the gentler part of struggle.' (Twining, 2009b: 218)

existence of a pluralism of beliefs as a ground for abdicating moral commitments or refusing to criticise particular cultural practices. On ethical universalism, their positions are somewhat different: all four are politically committed to fighting for the basic values embodied in the Universal Declaration of Human Rights. An-Na'im comes close to espousing a religion-based form of ethical universalism; Deng emphasises human dignity as a basic value, but seems to use international human rights documents as consensual working premises rather than embodiments of a single set of universal moral precepts; Ghai and Baxi pragmatically plugged into human rights discourse quite late in their careers because it was so dominant in the spheres in which they operated. Ghai sees the UDHR as a historically contingent workable framework for negotiating constitutional and political settlements and developing constitutions through genuinely democratic constitutive processes, but he emphasises material interests rather than cultural differences as the main recurrent basis of conflict. Baxi also treats human rights as a form of discourse and emphasises their potential for abuse and obfuscation, passionately arguing for them to be allowed to be the medium for expressing 'voices of suffering', especially of the half of the world that is deprived of food, water, health, education, and other necessities for a life worth living.

The lecture in Alberta was productive. I learned that the topic could be made interesting and intelligible to people who were both geographically and intellectually remote from it, and that my chosen subjects were sufficiently similar and sufficiently different to provide the basis for some illuminating comparisons. However, a single lecture, published in an excellent but obscure Canadian journal, would not do much to further the cause of making these authors and texts better known. Although I had provided a few quotations in a handout, I had summarised their ideas. If their voices were to be heard more widely, it was important that they would be communicated in their own words, rather than through secondhand summaries. I therefore designed a book intended to be a model for similar projects in a form that would make it usable in teaching as a resource or as a text. The ingredients were a substantial selection of original key texts; an introduction to the project as a whole; a short biographical and contextual introduction to each text; and a concluding chapter which, rather than criticising or analysing each text in detail, suggested how they related to each other and to the broader context of mainstream Northern human rights literature. It also outlined some preliminary thoughts as to how the project might be extended.

As editor I had several advantages. I knew each of the four thinkers personally and where they were coming from. I interviewed three of them and sent written questions to the fourth. A research grant enabled me to bring them together at a symposium in Belfast in June 2008 when they exchanged views and discussed issues such as the meaning of 'Southern' and 'voice'. They agreed that they were not *representing* anybody, that they were cultural hybrids, and that they were all concerned with 'Southern' interests and points of view and had extensive experience of dealing with actual problems on the ground. Some of these advantages will not be easily repeated and so this model cannot be followed exactly. However, I am convinced that the contextual material and the grouping of several individuals together added to the value of the book.

What might be the next step in the project? I was well aware of the strict limitations of this first effort. First, the primary audience was Northern. Second, they were all male, common law trained jurists of the immediate post-independence generation (born between 1938 and 1946) in former British dependencies, writing in English about human rights for Anglophone audiences. I thought of including the acceptance speeches of two Nobel peace prize winners, Shireen Ebadi and Aung Sang Suu Kyi, but decided that this would be mere tokenism. Instead I tried to stimulate at least one sister volume and still hope that this will emerge in due course – there could easily be several. I encouraged friends to take up the challenge. Oscar Guardiola-Rivera has responded with a fascinating piece on applying the approach to Latin America.[8] Abdul Paliwala has plans for a project based at Warwick, including a website and a small library and archive. In the next section he outlines possible next steps from his perspective. We both realise the possibilities are endless, for apart from replicating my model, one could proceed along different paths by changing single aspects that confined/limited the initial project: Why confine the audience to Anglophone jurists and human rights lawyers? Why only texts written in English? And so on.

In Italo Calvino's *Invisible Cities*, The Emperor Kublai Khan and his guest, Marco Polo, contemplate a wooden chess board. The Great Khan is concerned to reduce his Empire to order by confining it to 64 geometrical squares, or preferably a single piece of wood. Marco Polo is of a different temperament: he wants to open up infinite possibilities:

> Then Marco Polo spoke: 'Your chessboard, sire, is inlaid with two woods: ebony and maple. The square on which your enlightened gaze is fixed was cut from the ring of a trunk that grew in a year of drought: you see how its fibres are arranged? Here a barely hinted knot can be made out: a bud tried to burgeon on a premature spring day, but the night's frost forced it to desist ...' And Polo goes on to talk about ebony forests, rafts laden with logs that come down the rivers, of dock, of women at the windows.
>
> (Calvino, 1974: 131–2)

I side with Marco Polo.

8 Guardiola-Rivera (2015: ch. 5). He cites many other works by himself and others but greatly exaggerates my influence on them.

Southern Voices for the South: Abdul's perspective

William Twining and I agree that applying Marco Polo's broad pluralistic scenario to our Southern Voices project leaves us with enticingly inclusive prospects. From William's perspective, the need is for the North to be deparochialised. For me, there is an equal need for Southern scholars to deparochialise *themselves* – and develop a critical understanding of the ways in which Southern voices can make a distinctive contribution to the global South's own understanding of human rights and social justice.

The four voices of Deng, An 'Naim, Ghai and Baxi, whose intellectual locations straddle the North and the South, fulfil our pluralist approach in their ability to speak to both Southern and Northern audiences (Twining, 2009b). However, should everyone writing about the South be included? Does the writing need to have distinctly Southern perspectives, and if so, which best represent Southern voice(s)? Should they be restricted to the voices of intellectuals and professionals or those of the people? If the latter, how can people's voices be communicated?

An underlying issue is the dominant North's orientalisation and othering of the South and Southern perspectives. For Edward Said (2003), much Northern work on Islamic and other 'oriental' civilisations is an attempt to sustain Northern intellectual domination. The Northern 'orientalist' claims to understand the Orient in a superior manner to that of the Southern 'orientals'. In this way, Southern voices have been discriminated against, undermined, marginalised and silenced or ignored in patronising and pejorative misrepresentations. Santos characterises this as epistemicide or abyssal thinking (2014). Walter Mignolo suggests:

> My discomfort with modernity and Western civilization (two faces of the same phenomenon) is not with Western modernity's contribution to global history, but rather with the imperial belief that the rest of the world shall submit to its cosmology, and the naïve or perverse belief that the unfolding of world history has been of one temporality and would of necessity lead to a present that corresponds to the Western civilization that Hegel summarized in his celebrated lessons in the philosophy of history. Both the political and economic expansion of Western civilization have gone hand in hand with the management of all spheres of knowledge. Or, worded differently, Western civilization's ability to manage knowledge explains its success in expanding itself politically and economically.
>
> (2012: ix)

For Mignolo, it is necessary to decolonise the North's 'monoculture of the mind' through the device of border thinking. The epistemic border is the intersection between colonial/modern/global perspectives and local histories of the colonised, located on the other side of the border. Border-thinking thus requires thinking from within the border from the perspective of the colonised other as opposed to thinking about the border (Mignolo, 2012: xvi). In this respect thinking within the border enables the building of decolonial local histories in ways which delink and decolonise Northern epistemological knowledge, undermine its hegemony and enable Southern epistemological approaches. Acceptance of a 'border' imposed by the North can result in the ghettoising rather than the transcendence of the Southern voice. For Alexander Weheliye, it is the relational ethic of the historically oppressed Southern voice, which provides the scope of a cultural transcendence of both South and North from an individualist 'man' to a relational 'human': 'My principal question, phrased plainly, is: what different modalities of the human come to light if we do not take the liberal humanist figure of Man as the master- subject but focus on how humanity has been imagined and lived by those subjects excluded from this domain?' (Weheliye, 2014: 8).

Enrique Dussel (2013) sees the potential for liberation in philosophies othered by the North. For him the classification of Greek texts as philosophy but the orientalisation of other texts such as the Egyptian Book of the Dead, semitic and Hebrew texts, the Upanishads or Lao Tzu as mythological is perverse. He creates a temporal and territorial cartography of the parallel development of two broad systems of ethics, each located within global cultures, but one being a more formal 'helleno-centric' system and the other based on radical critique culminating in anti-colonial ethics of liberation, an ethic located in the perspective of the other. For example, Dussel's rejection of 'helleno-centrism' enables the location of the origins of Egyptian ethical systems in African Bantu culture. He locates similar autonomous developments in Meso-America, China and South Asia (Dussel, 2013: 29–31). Formal ethical systems in all cultures tended to emphasise the status quo resulting in justification of domination and oppression of the poor and the marginalised. Consequently they rebelled 'against the condition of their slavery and humiliation, brandishing a critical ethics' of justice as proposed by Buddhism, Christianity and Islam (Dussel, 2013: 17–19). He cites the example of the Qur'an:

> Did He not find you an orphan and give you shelter? And find you lost and guide you? And find you in want and make you to be free from want? Therefore, as for the orphan, do not oppress him. And as for him who asks, do not chide him.
>
> (Dussel, 2013: 19)

For Dussel, European domination of modernity from the reinvention of the Greeks to Descartes, Kant and Weber and its critique by Marx, Nietzsche, Foucault, Levinas and the ethics of liberation are a Northern discourse with the South as an external observer (Dussel, 2013: 37). The North classifies the South and its discourses as barbarian, pre-modern or in the process of being modernised. Yet, while the North also lays claim to the counter-discourse of liberation, the origins of the discourse are often located in the South. Thus, the Spaniard Bartolome de Las Casas's critique of the oppression of indigenous native Americans was developed through his experiences in the Americas and the Southern voices he heard. But whereas Northern *translators* such as Las Casas were published and accepted as legitimate, Southern voices such as that of the Mexican Francisco Xavier Clavijero, a contemporary of Kant, with a rich 'anti-hegemonic global vision' were unable to publish their work (Dussel, 2013: 45). The discovery of Southern Voices is thus located in a 'philosophy of liberation' as a counter-discourse – 'a critical philosophy born in the periphery (from the perspective of victims, the excluded), which has the intention of being relevant on a global scale' (Dussel, 2003: 47).

The submergence of Southern voices by the colonial/imperial North is particularly evident in most Southern approaches to law. In the section above, William notes the absence of a general appreciation of Southern perspectives with some honourable exceptions. Patrick Glenn's stimulating *Legal Traditions of the World* tries to integrate Northern and Southern works as different but continuously developing traditions through porous interaction (2014). While there are similarities with Dussel's broader socio-ethical perspective, Glenn's political neutrality is significantly different to Dussel's anti-orientalist, anti-colonial vision (2013). On the other hand, Peter Fitzpatrick (1992) spectacularly described the denigration and othering of non-European laws through forms of denial, denigration and marginalisation. The denial of the law of the supposed savage, particularly property law, enabled Europeans to view their lands as *terrae nullius*, expropriate these lands and establish their own right to property as the essence of modern law. Instead of giving due weight to cultures and civilisations in the colonies:

> The European created the native and the native law and custom against which its own identity and law continued to be created. The small, static, kin-group, bound by a barely explicit, almost instinctual and indolent custom, was created both in a fantastic inversion of European identity and by colonial regulation.
>
> (Fitzpatrick, 1992: 110)

Fitzpatrick's main aim was not so much to speak to the South, but to the North by illustrating how the othering mythology of the uncivilised enabled its inverse, the creation of the myth of the superior civilised modern law.

William indicates his preference for a specific future Southern gender voices project, rather than engaging in tokenism in the original Southern Voices project. Southern women have made profound epistemological contributions to feminist and subaltern struggles. A significant North-centric literature developed on Women and Development and subsequently on Women in Development and their implications for law. Even though this included Southern women writers, the role of women was assumed to be that of recipients of Northern emancipation from native patriarchy involving a modernisation perspective which linked well with neo-liberal globalisation (see critique by Stewart, 2011: 40–3; Orford, 2002; Nnaemeka, 2003). An alternative approach led by Chandra Mohanty (2003) and Gayatri Spivak (1998) viewed Southern subaltern women's subjectivity or voice as a crucial component of feminism. Spivak's germinal chapter 'Can the Subaltern Speak?' challenged the perspective of Northern feminists that viewed white men and women as the rescuers of brown women from brown men's oppression (1998). It also challenged the othering of Southern women into a homogenous entity as part of the West's civilising mission (Abdalkafor, 2015). Southern women were 'quarantined' in a specific country or issue by a commodity chain of researchers feeding their Northern sisters (Stewart, 2011: 40). For Nnaemeka:

> African women (as researchers/scholars and as the researched) are instrumentalized: as researchers/scholars they are the instruments for collecting the raw data with which foreign scholars manufacture knowledge; as the researched they are the instruments through which scholarship is produced and careers built.
>
> (2003: 367)

Oloka-Onyango and Tamale (1995: 698; cf Orford, 2002) challenge the worth of a romanticised notion of a homogenous sisterhood in building a global international feminist coalition. They describe how Southern feminists perceive themselves as being at the vantage point of the 'other', both in relation to the law and to a homogenising feminism. They therefore have the potential to 'defamiliarize feminist theory as we know it and assist it not only in interrogating, understanding, and explaining the unfamiliar but also in defamiliarizing and refamiliarizing the familiar in more productive and enriching ways' (Nnaemeka, 2003: 381; Stewart, 2011: 40). Thus, Southern feminist voices do not necessarily represent different epistemologies, but rather different standpoints from which to interrogate, understand, defamiliarise and then refamiliarise international feminist voices.

There is another respect in which Southern feminism presents an epistemic challenge to the North. Spivak's challenge was how to *let the subaltern speak!*: not the voice of the Southern intellectual, but rather that of the Southern subaltern woman (1998; Abdalkafor, 2015). This awareness of the subaltern voice reflects both the position of Southern feminists such as Spivak and distinct approaches in the subaltern studies movement whose objective was to give voice to all subalterns in the South (Guha and Spivak, 1988).[9] The Subaltern Studies group in India located the subaltern in colonised groups oppressed by class, caste, gender or office requiring detailed historical and legal analyses from a

9 The term 'subaltern' was itself given a political connotation by Gramsci (1996: N3, §48) as referring to groups in society who were under the hegemony of the ruling classes.

postcolonial perspective. In 'Chandra's Death' by Ranajit Guha (1987), villagers were involved in an abortion which led to the death of the pregnant mother, Chandra. Guha carefully deconstructs colonial records to give voice to the villagers involved in the tragic events, including the village's dispute settlement system, the Panchayat, and the colonial system. The excavated voice and perspective that emerges is not of the authorities, but that of the villagers themselves in their claim for social justice.

In postcolonial times, the representation of peoples' voices can conflict with the voices of new elites as Shahid Amin (1995) demonstrates in his analysis of Chauri Chaura events when villagers killed colonial police in India. While orthodox interpretations have regarded the killings as a stain on the anti-colonial Satyagraha, Amin's historical research represents a much more complex perspective thus giving voice to subaltern resistance in oppressive circumstances.

The subaltern voices of indigenous peoples have become significant in recent years in their mobilisation against colonial and postcolonial injustices. Law has been one avenue for the revelation of these voices, for example in the celebrated *Mabo* cases in Australia and the *Delgamuukw* case in Canada.[10] In Latin America, previously oppressed indigenous minorities are not only speaking, but also celebrating the profoundly significant incorporation of their voices in national constitutions in Ecuador and Bolivia. Thus the Ecuador Constitution has adopted the three concepts of *Pachamama* (ch. 7, derechos de la naturaleza or rights of nature), Sumak Kawsay (*buen vivir* or good living) and plurinationality.[11] The process of incorporation has been influenced by a variety of factors, including indigenous, national Ecuadorian and global activism. As an activist environmental lawyer in the movement demanding recognition of these rights argues:

> the difficult part was pointing out to [indigenous groups] that this was not already recognized in the juridical system. That didn't make sense to them…'but of course, nature is our mother, she has rights'. Similarly they considered that the economy 'ought to be based on ancestral principles like "Sumak Kawsay"', which values reciprocity and is set in contrast to accumulation as the ultimate end of economic activity. The economic development model, rather than exploiting nature and viewing it purely as a source of commodities, should thus recognize that 'nature is the Pachamama, that we are part of it, and therefore relationships with the natural environment need be respectful'.
>
> (Gudynas, 2013: 21)

10 *Mabo v Queensland* 1988; *Mabo v Queensland* (NO 2) 1989 in Australia and *Delgamukuw v British Columbia* [1997] 3 SCR 1010. The story continues in recent cases: see e.g. *Northern Territory v Mr A. Griffiths (deceased) and Lorraine Jones on behalf of the Ngaliwurru and Nungali Peoples* [2019] HCA 7 (13 March 2019).

11 Bolivian Constitution 2009, Art 1.

In Africa, the concept of Ubuntu is seen not as a subaltern idea but as a national ethic or ideology for African countries, especially in Southern Africa. Its roots lie in the principle of relationality between individuals and groups and among groups found in African societies that found ideological expression in the 1970s (Eze, 2010). Eze expresses the principle as 'humanity is not embedded in my person solely as an individual; my humanity is co-substantively bestowed upon the other and me. Humanity is a quality we owe to each other. We create each other and need to sustain this otherness creation' (2010: 190–1). In 1993 the Interim Constitution of South Africa recognised the concept in its *post-amble* which called for transcendence over divisions and strife, gross violations of human rights and humanitarian principles and declared: 'These can now be addressed on the basis that there is a need for understanding but not for vengeance, a need for reparation but not for retaliation, a need for ubuntu but not for victimisation' (Act No. 200 of 1993).

The Constitutional Court relied on the conception in the 1995 landmark case of *S v Makwanyane*[12] in unanimously deciding that the death penalty was unconstitutional. The judges viewed Ubuntu as a 'golden thread across cultural lines' that emphasised human rights and human values. Although the final Constitution of 1996 does not mention Ubuntu specifically, courts have continued to use the principle as enshrining African customary values embedded through the Constitutional recognition of customary law. What distinguishes Ubuntu from Northern notions of human rights and values is its emphasis on relationality. Thus, in *MEC for Education: KwaZulu-Natal v Pillay*,[13] Langa CJ emphasised the person in community aspect of Ubuntu in the Zulu phrase *umuntu ngumuntu ngabantu*, or 'a person is a person through other people' (Himonga et al., 2017: 382).

There are obvious links between principles such as Ubuntu, Andean cosmovisions and other indigenous espistemologies such as those of Maori communities in Aotearoa/New Zealand (Huambachano, 2015; Spiller et al., 2011). The underlying principle resides in relational ontologies which challenge the duality of individualistic modernism and emphasise the integral relationality between and among people and things, especially nature. This contrasts with the anomic and Cartesian separation of personal relations and relations of environment through forms of contractualism and commodification most evidenced by free market neoliberalism (Gudynas, 2013; Santos, 2014). For Santos (2014: 23), the underlying problem is the fundamental contradiction between an integral environmental perspective and modernism's idea of 'infinite growth and the unstoppable development of productive forces'.

My consideration of the varieties of Southern voices has revealed a number of tendencies. Firstly, the focus has been on voices which give primacy to Southern

12 1995 3 SA 391 (CC).
13 2008 CC, para. 53.

perspectives without necessarily ignoring Northern scholarship. This is different from the mainstream Southern scholarship which umbilically links itself to existing Northern discourses on human rights and development. While this scholarship should not be ignored, my intention is to indicate the relevance of otherwise othered scholarship for an understanding of Southern perspectives in distinction from North-based approaches. There are divergences, but the main unifying trend is a critique of colonial/imperial/postcolonial hegemony. As Santos (2014: 237) suggests, 'cognitive justice' or, in our terms, the assertion and just balancing of Southern voices, is crucial to the struggle for global social justice.

There are of course differences within these Southern perspectives, a key one being perspectives which emphasise cultural anti-imperialism such as Ubuntu and Buen Vivir and those which emphasise critical Southern political economic perspectives. Thus, the Third World Approaches to International Law (TWAIL) group's main concern is with the imperialist domination of international law discourses (Chimni, 2011). In *The Concept of Human Rights in Africa* (1989), Issa Shivji does not locate himself in African culture but in African political economic history in relation to Northern imperialism. The four *Southern Voices* discussed by Twining (above and 2009b) integrate Northern epistemologies into Southern social justice perspectives.

The second distinction is between those who start with a general theoretical or epistemological framework based in political economy, ethics or culture, and those whose main concern is with ensuring that the voices of the subaltern are heard (Spivak, 1998; Guha and Spivak, 1988).

These distinctions are significant, but not always divisive. For example, *Sumak Kawsay* and *Pachamama* may be considered part of a cultural assertion movement, but involve an ontology of deep critique of the imperial/colonial discourses which are dependent on Cartesian notions of separation of things, people and the environment. They are also rooted in indigenous struggles. Similarly, those promoting subaltern voices and struggles are engaged in struggles for social justice as are those such as the TWAIL group. Yet, their gaze is different. Nevertheless, the point of this chapter is not to construct a false and unachievable unifying epistemology of the global South, but to consider the range of voices which challenge a Northern epistemological hegemony which privileges the individualist neoliberal 'man' as opposed to the relational 'human' (Weheliye, 2014). While the relational ethic can also be found in Northern dissident voices, South–South dialogue of mutual engagement between these different Southern perspectives is essential to advance the struggles against global social injustices.

Extending the Southern Voices project

The conversation between William and Abdul in this chapter is about how to extend the original Southern Voices project. From different perspectives, we agree on the need to inform both the North and the South about Southern perspectives. However, we have emphasised different priorities. For William, the priority is to inform the North of the infinite range of possibilities offered by Southern discourses. For Abdul, the priority is for Southerners to inform each other in order to advance social justice.

Language is a key issue ameliorated by the increasing global dominance of English, which is used by a growing number of sophisticated Southern scholars. But this dominance of English raises questions about linguistic injustice (Alcalde, 2015; Piller, 2016; de Schutter and Robichaud, 2015). The main medium of intellectual expression is not English in much of the world. Even when authors from regions such as East Asia, the Francophone countries, Latin America and the Middle East write in English, authors are acting as mediators and what they write may not represent the full range of perspectives available. There is therefore a need for translation to represent those who do not write in English. Yet, for citizens of the global South who wish to understand other Southern perspectives, translation into the globally dominant language(s) needs to be accompanied by translation into national languages. Thus, the political, economic and intellectual rise of China has been facilitated by translation of myriad, mainly Northern, texts into Chinese. Nevertheless, this sinification of Northern discourses raises questions of power in the practice of translations (Qi, 2012; Liu, 1994). A different problem relates to historical documentation. Much of the submergence of Southern voices is a consequence of the absence of availability of significant texts in acceptable translations. For example, it was only when original research was done in Arabic texts by Lebanese scholars, such as the Makdisis, that it was possible to communicate to the Northern and Southern audiences the influence of Islamic Law in the origins of the English Common Law and the Inns of Court (Makdisi, 1991; Makdisi, 1999). So how can we make available subaltern or peoples' voices which are seldom rendered in global languages? Power determines whose voices are mediated and how this is done (Spivak, 1998).

A second issue concerns the mode of communication. The original Southern Voices project resulted in a book (Twining, 2009b). It is of course possible to extend the project in the form of further books as the feminist project imagined by William above. However, while there are advantages of the book form in South–North communication, South–South communication is only accessible to elite legal education institutions. Books published in the South only exceptionally transcend national or regional borders and do not reach other Southern jurisdictions. Today, and more significantly, communication of a vast global literature requires electronic media. The advantage of a Southern Voices website is that it can accommodate a variety of forms of communication and languages, thereby facilitating the diversity we advocate. Much will depend on planning for effective South–South as well as South–North communication.

There is need to develop priorities and identify relevant texts, modes of access and communication, including translation as appropriate. For the widest North and South appeal, the network has to be a conduit for the collection and communication of information. Extending the original Southern Voices project therefore requires difficult pragmatic decisions.

First, what should be prioritised? We suggest that the project should inform both Southern and Northern scholars about Southern scholarship. Restricting it to manageable levels may require a focus on social (in)justices directly related to human rights and gender justice. A key issue is the role of the scholar as translator learning from subaltern de/anti-colonial voices from below.

Who would be responsible for organisation? The idea of an extended project developed from the Twining paper at the *Warwick International Symposium on Beyond Development: New Imaginaries of Social Justice* in 2016.[14] It is therefore appropriate that it should be taken forward by Warwick while involving scholars from the North as well as the South. We suggest an initial small group including experts in key global South regions which would organise the project and define its parameters.

The variety of tasks for the project include identification of globally significant sources of Southern scholarship; development of a network of scholars; development of a website and an archive; the organisation of conferences and seminars, and the production of support publications. In the context of this book, the role of this chapter has been to argue the need for a project to advance knowledge of Southern voices. We believe that if we are to take discussion of the law in relation to the global South beyond Law and Development and into wider concerns with global social justice, it is essential for Southern voices to provide a transformative impetus to Northern orientalism. If their voices are to be heard more widely, it is important that they would be communicated in their own words, rather than through secondhand summaries. Of equal if not greater significance is the need for the global South to inform itself of its own voices, especially its subaltern voices.

References

Abdalkafor, O., 2015. *Gayatri Spivak: Deconstruction and the Ethics of Postcolonial Literary Interpretation*. Cambridge Scholars Publishing.

Alcalde, J., 2015. Linguistic Justice: An Interdisciplinary Overview of the Literature. Amsterdam Working Papers in Multilingualism No. 3. pp. 27–96. Available online at: http://ssrn.com/abstract=2630104 (accessed 24 August 2017).

Amin, S., 1995. *Event, Metaphor, Memory: Chauri Chaura, 1922–1992*. University of California Press.

Barron, A., Collins, H., Jackson, E., Lacey, N., Reiner, R., Ross, H., Teubner, G., Penner J., Schiff, D. and Nobles, R., 2005. *Jurisprudence and Legal Theory*. Oxford University Press.

14 See: http://www2.warwick.ac.uk/fac/soc/law/research/events/conferences/beyond_development (accessed 24 August 2017).

Bentham, J., 1781. *An Introduction to the Principles of Morals and Legislation.* Francis & Law.

Blommaert, J., 2001. Review: Linguistic Genocide in Eduction – or Worldwide Diversity and Human Rights? *Applied Linguistics, 22* (*4*), 539–542.

Calvino, I., 1974. *Invisible Cities.* Harcourt Brace.

Chimni, B. (ed.), 2011. Third World Approaches to International Law. *Trade, Law and Development, 3* (*1*) Special Issue.

David, R. and Brierley, J.E., 1978. *Major Legal Systems in the World Today: An Introduction to the Comparative Study of Law.* The Free Press.

de Schutter, H. and Robichaud, R. (eds), 2015. *Linguistic Justice: Van Parijs and His Critics.* Routledge.

Dussel, E., 2003. *Philosophy of Liberation.* Wipf & Stock.

Dussel, E., 2013. *Ethics of Liberation: In the Age of Globalization and Exclusion.* Duke University Press.

Eze, M., 2010. *Intellectual History in Contemporary South Africa.* Palgrave Macmillan.

Fitzpatrick, P., 1992. *The Mythology of Modern Law.* Taylor & Francis.

Freeman, M., 2014. *Lloyd's Introduction to Jurisprudence.* Sweet and Maxwell.

Glenn, P., 2014. *Legal Traditions of the World: Sustainable Diversity in Law.* Oxford University Press.

Gramsci, A. (ed.), 1996. *Prison Notebooks, vol. 3.* Columbia University Press.

Guardiola-Rivera, O., 2015. Human Rights and Latin American Voices. In U. Baxi, C. McCrudden and A. Paliwala (eds), *Law's Ethical, Global and Theoretical Contexts.* Cambridge University Press, p. 90.

Gudynas, E., 2013. Debates on Development and Its Alternatives in Latin America: A Brief Heterodox Guide. In M.D. Mokrani (ed.), *Beyond Development: Alternative Visions from Latin America.* Transnational Institute/Rosa Luxemburg Foundation, p. 15.

Guha, R., 1987. Chandra's death. In R. Guha (ed.), *Subaltern Studies* (*No. 5*). Oxford University Press, p. 135.

Guha, R., and Spivak, G., 1988. *Selected Subaltern Studies.* Oxford UniversityPress.

Himonga, C., Taylor, M. and Pope, A., 2017. Reflections on Judicial Views of uBuntu. *Potchefstroom Electronic Law Journal/Potchefstroomse Elektroniese Regsblad, 16* (*5*), 370–427. Available online at: https://www.ajol.info/index.php/pelj/article/view/101890 [Accessed 23 September 2019].

Huambachano, M., 2015. *Food Security and Indigenous Peoples Knowledge: El Buen Vivir-Sumaq Kawsay in Peru and Tē Atānoho, New Zealand, Māori-New Zealand.* Common Ground Publishing. See also: https://researchspace.auckland.ac.nz/handle/2292/2879/discover (accessed 1 October 2018).

Imber, C., 1997. *Ebu's-Suud: The Islamic Legal Tradition.* Edinburgh University Press.

Lang, M., and Mokrani, D. (eds), 2013. *Beyond Development: Alternative Visions from Latin America.* Transnational Institute/ Rosa Luxemburg Foundation.

Liu, L., 1994. *Translingual Practice: Literature, National Culture, and Translated Modernity – China, 1900–1937.* Stanford University Press.

Makdisi, G., 1991. *Religion Law and Learning in Classical Islam.* Routledge.

Makdisi, J., 1999. The Islamic Origins of the Common Law. *North Carolina Law Review, 77* (*5*), 1635–1739.

Mignolo, W., 2012. *Local Histories/Global Designs: Coloniality, Subaltern Knowledges, and Border Thinking*. Princeton University Press.

Mohanty, C., 2003. *Feminism without Borders: Decolonizing Theory, Practicing Solidarity*. Duke University Press.

Morris, R., 2010. *Can the Subaltern Speak?: Reflections on the History of an Idea*. Columbia University Press.

Nnaemeka, O., 2003. Nego-Feminism: Theorizing, Practicing, and Pruning Africa's Way. *Signs: Journal of Women in Culture and Society, 29* (*2*), 357–385.

Oloka-Onyango, J. and Tamale, S., 1995. 'The Personal is Political', or Why Women's Rights are Indeed Human Rights: An African Perspective on International Feminism. *Human Rights Quarterly, 17* (*4*), 691–731.

Orford, A., 2002. Feminism, Imperialism and the Mission of International Law. *Nordic Journal of International Law, 71* (*2*), 275–296.

Piller, I., 2016. *Linguistic Diversity and Social Justice. An Introduction to Applied Sociolinguistics*. Oxford University Press.

Prada, R., 2013. Buen Vivir as a Model for State and Economy. In M. Lang and D. Mokrani (eds), *Beyond Development: Alternative Visions from Latin America*. Transnational Institute/Rosa Luxemburg Foundation.

Qi, S., 2012. *Western Literature in China and the Translation of a Nation*. Springer.

Rathgeber, E., 1990. WID, WAD, GAD: Trends in Research and Practice. *The Journal of Developing Areas, 24* (*4*), 489–502.

Said, E., 2003. *Orientalism*. Penguin.

Santos, B., 2014. *Epistemologies of the South: Justice Against Epistemicide*. Routledge.

Schuler, M. (ed.), 1995. From Basic Needs to Basic Rights: Women's Claim to Human Rights. *Women, Law and Development International, 3* (*2*), 609–620.

Spiller, C., Erakovic, L., Henare, M., and Pio, E., 2011. Relational Well-Being and Wealth: Māori Businesses and an Ethic of Care. *Journal of Business Ethics, 98* (*1*), 153–169.

Spivak, G., 1998. Can the Subaltern Speak?. In C. Nelson and L. Grossman (eds), *Marxism and the Interpretation of Culture*. Macmillan, p. 271.

Stewart, A., 2011. *Gender, Law and Justice in a Global Market*. Cambridge University Press.

Twining, W., 2009a. *General Jurisprudence: Understanding Law from a Global Perspective*. Cambridge University Press.

Twining, W., 2009b. *Human Rights: Southern Voices: Francis Deng, Abdullahi An-Na'im, Yash Ghai, Upendra Baxi*. Cambridge University Press.

Weheliye, A., 2014. *Habeas Viscus: Racializing Assemblages, Biopolitics, and Black Feminist Theories of the Human*. Duke University Press.

Zweigert, K. and Kotz, H., 1998. *Introduction to Comparative Law*, 3rd edition. Clarendon Press.

Chapter 6

Practice teaches paradigm

Reflections on radical and liberal law perspectives

*Issa G. Shivji**

Grounding with the people

This essay is a short tale of radical scholarship and its relation to practice. I draw upon my experiences in legal aid practice and as the chairman of the Tanzanian Presidential Commission of Inquiry into Land Matters (The Commission) (Tanzania, 1994) to reflect critically upon what we thought were radical legal paradigms. A significant number of colleagues at Warwick Law School and the Dar es Salaam Faculty of Law have come from the radical tradition of law. The tradition variously took the form of law in context, law in development, critical human rights and different versions, both vulgar and subtle, of Marxist approaches to state and law.

Law in Context had a dual genesis. The disaffection of British and US scholars against black letter traditions

> led to the linking of law to the social sciences; a dialectical approach to every issue; a highly intellectualized but nevertheless realistic approach to legal practice and the law in action; a demonstration of the interdependence of theory and practice; and a concern for justice.
>
> (Twining, 1997: 7)

In Dar es Salaam, this was given a specific impetus by Julius Nyerere's urging that 'we should teach East African Law in context – and context here meant the historic break with colonialism, local circumstances and problems, and the ideology of the first Independence Government' (Twining, 2017: 38). Under the broad Law in Context umbrella could be observed several specific trends. The first, represented by Twining and McAuslan, was a liberal adaptation of British law to East African conditions. Scholars from the United States such as Robert Seidman promoted versions of Law and Development which involved

* My sincere thanks to Natasha Shivji for her meticulous reading of the draft and incisive comments.

instrumental transfer of Western values to East Africa as the basis for development (Seidman and Seidman, 1978). On the other hand, critical scholars such as Sol Picciotto, Yash Ghai and Akilagpa Sawyerr developed critiques based partly in Marxist inspired political economy. This was especially so in the case of Picciotto (1986), less so in the case of Ghai (1986) and Sawyerr (1988). For young Tanzanian scholars who became the dominant influence at the Dar Faculty of Law from the late 1960s to the late 1980s, it was the Marxist inspiration which became significant. In the left tradition, law was seen as a terrain of struggle and analysed in socio-economic and historical contexts. In Dar es Salaam, many of us viewed law as ultimately serving vested interests in the service of the status quo (Shivji, 1986). As we declared in the editorial of the Eastern Africa Law Review:

> A lawyer intellectual has to analyse the legal forms to reveal the real substance – the exploitative economic and political dominant/dominated relationships that underlie much of law. Failing this critical role, the lawyer is likely to become an 'intellect worker'; a technocrat in the service of the ruling class.
>
> (Shivji, 1972: 1)

Yet, this Marxism was far from monolithic and fissures developed between an approach which saw analysis purely in terms of national struggle against finance capital-based imperialism and a more nuanced analysis which considered the complex class inter-relationships between local bourgeoisies and imperialist classes. The left tradition had significant presence in both law schools. However, from the 1980s neoliberalism began to influence legal scholarship and in Dar es Salaam the left tradition was unceremoniously routed reflecting a similar shift in politics in Tanzania (Shivji, 1986; Paliwala, 2017).

Several academics from the Dar Faculty had joined Warwick law school and were involved in the development of Law in Context approach in Britain (Twining, 1997). This was a largely pluralist tradition which included both the liberal law in context dimension established by Twining and McAuslan and the more radical Marxist inspired political economy perspective signified by Picciotto and Ghai. Neoliberal approaches began to affect academic discourse, but the left tradition retained its influence especially in the Law in Development programme of the Law School.[1]

Neoliberal approaches were pragmatic and instrumental. Law was seen as a toolkit from which the lawyer was expected to select appropriate tools to give effect to policy changes required for neoliberal transformation through what from the 1980s onwards were euphemistically called Structural Adjustment Programmes (SAPs) (Shivji, 2006). In Dar es Salaam, neoliberalism took the defining sting out of the radical tradition, especially its Marxist strain, by

1 Currently International Human Rights Law and Development.

delinking law from analyses of state and class. (Shivji, 1986; Adelman and Paliwala, 1993).

Admittedly, our radicalism belonged to the classroom and generally had little connection with real life situations. This realisation led some of us in the Dar law school to undertake serious legal aid work that brought us face to face with working people. Planning legal strategies with our clients and fighting legal battles under procedures adverse to them provided lessons a thousand times more instructive and humbling than grand classroom lectures and faculty seminars. We gradually learned the art of engaging in working class struggles. 'Give the masses systematically what you get from them confusedly', Mao Zedong had said many decades ago (Mao Zedong, 1967 cited in Shivji, 2009: 186). Little anecdotes from the courtroom taught a lot but more importantly they brought home the reality of our elitist legal education. Legal aid showed how alienating conventional legal practice can be. Militant workers were treated as supplicant ignoramuses in the dock when they faced a barrage of inane but stinging questions in cross-examination. Radical sensitivities were hurt, but rage against the bourgeois legal system was aroused and reinforced the will to change. There were also happier moments in which the age-old 'simple' wisdom of the people poked fun at years of school education. On one occasion, when counsel arrogantly asked an elderly semi-literate witness why he had volunteered to give evidence, obviously implying an ulterior motive, the old man broke into a limerick:

> macho yangu yameona,
> masikio yangu yamesikia,
> yale niliyaona,
> yale niliyosikia,
> kichwa changu kimeweka na
> leo mzigo huu ni nakuleteeni hapa.
> my eyes saw,
> my ears heard
> what I saw
> what I heard
> my head recorded
> that record I'm playing before you.

This is a near-perfect poetic rendering of the meaning of evidence under the Evidence Act, 1967 (No. 6 of 1967). Needless to say, it passed over the heads of the learned gentlemen. Had it been said by one of them, it would have become a quotable quote.

On another occasion, a well-known defence counsel was haranguing a legal-aided working woman with a volley of questions in an election petition filed by her against a big shot who had won the election. In what he thought was a triumphant final barb, he declaimed: 'You have dared to bring a frivolous matter to this honourable court because you have been given a *free lawyer*!' With lightning speed, the witness retorted, 'You have dared to tell *that* lie to this honourable court because you have been *paid* to do so!' Legal aid practice opened my eyes to the reality of social problems faced by the downtrodden.

The Land Commission

In 1991 I was appointed chair of the Presidential Commission of Enquiry into Land Matters. This exposed me to the reality of the lives of small producers – peasant and pastoral communities – who constitute the majority of the Tanzanian population and the most exploited segment of our society. I share the personal experiences of the Commission which made me critically interrogate many dearly held radical legal paradigms and perspectives. The Commission had a wide-ranging mandate (Tanzania, 1994). This first land commission following independence in 1961[2] was appointed in the period of transition from nationalism to neoliberalism. The expectations of various players, including the government and the World Bank, were that the Commission would come up with recommendations that would facilitate the privatisation and commodification of land.

Tanganyika was a trust territory under a League of Nations mandate with a stipulation that the trustee would administer land in the interest of 'natives'.[3] Immediately after the British took over the territory, the colonial power passed the Land Ordinance 1923 and the Master and Native Servants Ordinance 1924. The latter was intended to facilitate a supply of labour and the former to regulate land, placing land and labour at the disposal of the state in the interest of the colonial state and British capital. The British are masters at legal craftsmanship. In 17 brief sections, the ordinance laid the foundations of the land tenure system that survived for three-quarters of a century. All lands were declared 'public lands' to be disposed of at the colonial governor's discretion. Because Tanganyika was not a colony, land could not be vested in the Crown as was the case in neighbouring Kenya. Instead, radical title was vested in the colonial state. Contrary to popular and scholarly myth, socialist Julius Nyerere, the first president of independent Tanzania, never nationalised the land. This was done in 1923 by the colonial state. The law gave powers to the governor to allocate land by what was known as right of occupancy, defined as the right to occupy and use land for a

2 The previous commission had been appointed by the colonial government in 1953–5 (East African Royal Commission, 1955).

3 Britain initially administered the territory as an occupying power after seizing it from Germany in 1916. On 20 July 1922 British administration was formalised under the League of Nations mandate. From 1946, it was administered as a United Nations trust territory.

term of years not exceeding 99 years. In substance, the right was like a lease but with greater government control than in a typical lease.

The law declaring all lands public lands was silent on the rights of indigenous occupiers and owners of land, but what it left out the courts dutifully filled in. Native occupiers were considered to occupy and use land under deemed rights of occupancy with the implied consent of the governor. Two categories of rights of occupancy thus emerged, statutory or granted rights and deemed rights. Immigrant communities, foreign companies and other non-natives occupied land under granted rights of occupancy. Their right was contractual and statutory law regulated their use of the land. Natives occupied and used land under their customary laws and had no rights. Their occupation was considered permissive (in the sense that they occupied land by an implied permission of the governor) and governed administratively. The basic contours of the land tenure system were simple and neat. They rested on a triangular relationship. The relation between the statutory landholder and the state was civil and contractual, and set out the rights and obligations of the contracting parties. Breach of contract on either side led to damages, a civil remedy. The relation of the customary holder to the state was administrative, with obligations but no rights. In contrast, use of land by customary owners was regulated by criminal law with breach resulting in penal sanctions. The relation between customary and statutory users was hierarchical. A statutory owner's title was superior and prevailed over customary title in cases of conflict. Customary law that defined rights and obligations under customary remedies regulated the relation between customary owners *inter se*. Native courts administered customary law and civil courts administered statutory law. Natives were subjects and European settlers were citizens; Asian immigrants were in-between.

When land from statutory holders was to be acquired, the state had to follow due process as stipulated in the Land Acquisition Ordinance. When land from customary owners was required by the state for any purpose, whether public or private, due process did not apply (Seidman, 1969). Natives occupied public land by *deemed* consent of the governor. When land was alienated from them, under whatever circumstances, the governor's consent was *deemed* to have been withdrawn. Legal craftsmanship and judicial craftiness lent a veneer of legality, if not political legitimacy, to British colonial rule.

On independence, the President replaced the governor but in other respects the land tenure system remained intact. When the state carried out massive resettlements of rural populations between 1971 and 1973 through forced villagisation, no legislative process was involved. It was assumed that the President had effectively withdrawn consent for the villagers to occupy their original lands. In any event, Nyerere's state did not derive its legitimacy from law but instead from its nationalist genesis and socialist ideology crowned by the President's personal integrity and political popularity (Shivji and

Majamba, 2005). In outline, this is the land tenure system that the Land Commission, appointed by Nyerere's successor Ali Hassan Mwinyi was mandated to examine.[4]

The Commission travelled throughout the country, mostly to the rural districts in which 80 per cent of the population derived their livelihoods from the land. The commissioners held public hearings in mass meetings, received private petitions, letters and memoranda, interviewed land officers and patiently listened to grievances and complaints. Back in Dar es Salaam, reports on the hearings were meticulously documented, discussed and analysed. At the end of the process, a two-volume report was published and 20 volumes of evidence deposited in the library of the University of Dar es Salaam (Tanzania, 1994).

Everywhere we heard the same grievance articulated – insecurity of land. Everywhere the same demand was heard – democratic decision-making over access to and tenure on land. As towns, national parks and reserved lands expanded, they swallowed up peasant and pastoral lands. Prisons and parastatals, the military and government ministries, bureaucrats and businessmen all appropriated peasants' land with or without consent and usually without their participation. Land acquired in the name of public interest was converted to private use. Nepotism was pervasive, corruption in land deals was rampant, courts took years, if not decades to resolve disputes, and administrators sat on land files until they fell apart or disappeared. The Commission's task was to make sense of this massive amount of evidence and deliver a coherent set of recommendations. In Mao's phraseology, the commissioners had to give back to the people systematically what it had received from them confusedly (Mao Zedong, 1967, cited in Shivji, 2009: 186).

Subtle if not overt pressure was placed on the Commission. Neoliberalism was knocking on Tanzania's door in the form of LIMP – liberalisation, marketisation and privatisation. Peasants wanted security of tenure and democratic decision-making about land distribution while politicians and government functionaries, prodded by donors and financial institutions, wanted land to be put on the market. How should the Commission resolve these contradictory demands? What criteria should guide it? Existing legal paradigms, radical or otherwise, proved to be inadequate. What was called for was not only radical law but radical politics grounded in equally radical political-economy analysis. Lenin's dictum that politics is the concentrated expression of economics was extended by us to law being the concentrated form of politics (Lenin, 1965, XXXII: 32). A national-popular people oriented perspective rather than a neoliberal profit oriented prescription had to take command. In the concrete case of Tanzania

4 The Commission consisted of nine persons, all of whom were either former ministers or principal secretaries or members of parliament. There was one female and one academic (myself).

people meant peasants. We had to chart a peasant path of development which meant a process of accumulation from below (Neocosmas, 1993).

Section C in chapter 14 of the Commission's report entitled 'Paths of Development' succinctly lays down the three major premises that informed our detailed recommendations (Tanzania, 1994: 137–9):

> Premise 1: Tanzania is a country of smallholders (peasant and herdsmen) and is likely to remain so for the foreseeable future.
>
> (Tanzania, 1994: 137)

In the 1960s and 1970s the disappearance of the peasantry and pastoralists in sub-Saharan Africa was envisaged through large-scale industrial and agrarian development. Peasant production was considered inefficient and marred by low productivity. Contrary to the accepted wisdom, the high productivity of large-scale farmers and plantations, for example in Zimbabwe and Kenya, was based directly upon state subsidies and indirect 'subsidies' from the peasant sector. The peasant sector acted as a reservoir of cheap labour, an important source of food and social security for plantation labour (Lofchie, 1975; Worsley, 1976). The peasant sector was the sponge that absorbed and made possible the super-exploitation of plantation labour. Nevertheless, at the behest of the World Bank, the post-independence government in Tanzania experimented with village settlement programmes and rangelands development which proved to be unmitigated disasters. In passing, the law and development guru then teaching at the Dar es Salaam Faculty of Law, Professor Robert Seidman, considered the USAID-funded Range Development Act as a positive piece of social engineering (cf. Seidman and Seidman, 1978). So much for the law and development school of jurisprudence, which was then touted as progressive and radical.

> Premise 2: If we begin from the premise that Tanzania is a country of smallholders, our second premise follows inexorably. Tanzania must feed itself, which means first and foremost, the peasantry must feed itself and secondly, feed the country.
>
> (Tanzania, 1994: 137)

The Commission's position was that an investor from outside a village is unlikely to invest in food production and even if they did, it would be in pursuit of profits from the temperate or Gulf markets rather than the domestic market. On the other hand, the Commission argued that within the peasant and pastoral communities there were social forces such as rich peasants 'capable of generating, accumulating and reinvesting in the rural sector' (138). Rich peasants could be possible agents of accumulation from below in a national strategy of agrarian and pastoral development, albeit under capitalism rather than socialism.

> Premise 3: The Commission's third premise was that since the rural community in mainland Tanzania is organised in villages, this should be the point of departure in designing a new land tenure structure. Ownership and governance of land should be located at the village level. The village, in other words, should be the site of production as well as the domain of democracy.
>
> (Tanzania, 1994: 198)

After the forced villagisation between 1971 and 1973, when more than 5 million rural people were moved into villages, the government passed legislation providing for village governance. Two organs were created: village assemblies consisting of all adult residents and a village council of 25 people elected by the village assembly. In effect, the village became the lowest rung of governance exhibiting features of both direct and representative democracy. The Commission recommended and proposed legislation to the effect that the village assembly would be given corporate status and the usual attributes of legal personality. It further recommended that the assembly be included in the Constitution as part of Tanzania's governance structure. With the aim of combining resource and representative democracy as villagers had demanded, the Commission argued that village lands should be vested in the village assemblies while national lands – all lands which are not designated village lands – should be vested in a Board of Land Commissioners accountable to Parliament. The monopoly of radical title vested in the President, as an inheritance from colonialism, would be diversified thereby democratising the land tenure system and simultaneously giving the village assembly elevated constitutional status as a main organ of direct grassroots democracy with a key role in the land tenure system.

Not unexpectedly, the government firmly rejected the recommendation divesting the Executive of radical title on the specious ground that the system of vesting radical title in the President bequeathed by the former colonial power was 'fundamentally sound' and that the government should not be 'turned into a beggar for land' needed for development purposes:

> The President as Head of State is responsible for the development of the country and the well-being of the people, and land being an important element for development has to be controlled by the President. If land is vested in [the] Board of Land Commissioners and the Village Assemblies then the Government will be turned into a beggar for land when required for development. Instead of simply acquiring land for public purpose under the Land Acquisition Act the Government will now be required to apply to the Board of Land Commissioners. In the villages the Government is an outsider and can only be given land of not more than three acres at a time for less than ten years. The Government will not implement its policies in that way. The Investment Promotion Policy will be impossible when the Government does not have a say in land matters. Land has to remain in

> the hands of the Government... the Commission has not given enough reasons for the departure.
>
> (Quoted in Sundet, 1997: 109)

This is a quintessential statement rationalising 'development from above'. But more important, it reflects the interests of the post-colonial classes for whom the state becomes the site of accumulation in conjunction with global neo-liberal land grabs. The bureaucratic class did not want to surrender control over the main resource of the country from which it reaped rents. For different reasons, what was 'fundamentally sound' for the colonial metropolitan bourgeoisie was also 'fundamentally sound' for the post-colonial comprador bourgeoisie. Eventually, the government's position was cast in legal stone in the elaborate land laws drafted by the late Professor Patrick McAuslan, whose consultancy contract was financed by a grant from the British government. The Village Land Act (Act No. 5 of 1999) and the Land Act (Act No. 4 of 1999) stipulated that all lands are vested in the President to be held in trust for the people of Tanzania. This could only be a political trust not a legal one.[5] No one could possibly take the President to court for breach of trust and succeed. In effect, therefore, the position remained as it was in the colonial and pre-1999 land legislation.

Coincidentally McAuslan also taught at both Dar and Warwick. He was well known as a land and planning expert (for a sympathetic view of McAuslan's work in Africa see Adams, 2017) He subscribed to the 'law in context' and 'law and/in development' schools that were considered radical. In a major feat of social engineering, he drafted very elaborate principal legislation and even a more extensive subsidiary legislation of regulations, rules and forms. The draft ran into some 300 pages necessitating its division into two Acts. A coalition of civil society organisations called National Land Forum (NALAF) responded to McAulsan by issuing a declaration condemning the undemocratic process involved in drafting the bill and its undemocratic content (reprinted in Shivji, 1998: 111–18). Invited consultants, academics, bureaucrats and NGOs discussed drafts of the bill. The Declaration claimed, 'The Bill does not take into account the interests of the large majority of land users. The Bill takes away the basic right of the citizens to be consulted and to participate effectively in decision-making processes' (112). McAuslan was understandably not amused. In a subsequent academic lecture he tried to justify his work as not opposed to the Commission's recommendations (McAuslan, 1996). Unintentionally the debate on land law became a contest of perspectives and schools of law between two academics – one in his capacity as the chairman of the Commission and the other in his capacity as a consultant - with similar backgrounds but diametrically opposite perspectives (Manji, 2006).

5 For the difference, see *Tito v Waddell (No 2)* [1977] ch. 106.

Among other things, McAuslan criticised the Commission for not providing a detailed draft law to implement its recommendations. He extolled his draft thus:

> The real revolutionaries therefore might turn out to be not those who propose radical policies but those who, through the NLP[6], propose a radical legal methodology for implementing policies; namely a detailed and inevitably lengthy new land code in which legal rules and checks and balances replace reliance on administrative and political action based on good will and common-sense.
>
> (1996: 39)

McAuslan summed up his lecture with how he saw the role of lawyers in land reform in sub-Saharan Africa where he provided consultancy services on land matters:

> In sum, while land law reform might, just, still be the preserve of the lawyer, the products of that reform – the new laws – are the property of the nation and the nation must be stimulated whole-heartedly to embrace those laws. Only in this way can law be made to work to restructure land relations in Africa.
>
> (1996: 39)

Two years after McAuslan's lecture, while his draft was still a bill, from the perspective of the former chairman of the Commission, I suggested:

> The perspectives of justice, rights and equity embedded in the law reform recommended in the Commission's Report are contradictory to those underlying the draft Land Bill. They are not only contradictory, but locked in struggle with them. In this contest one of the perspectives is undoubtedly becoming dominant by the logic of force (the state).
>
> (Shivji, 1998: 108–9)

McAuslan's draft eventually became law in 1999 while the Commission's report gathered dust. The 1999 land laws laid the legal framework for neoliberal reforms that ensued and were amended a couple of times to facilitate the commodification and alienation of land to so-called investors (Mwami and Kamata, 2011; German et al., 2013). After almost two decades, Tanzania's land problems have multiplied; small producers' insecurity has become worse; land disputes are rampant while bureaucrats continue to abuse power and reap rents. As neoliberal

6 NLP (National Land Policy) (Tanzania, 1995) was drafted by the Ministry of Lands including two professors-turned-bureaucrats. The Commission had recommended that the ministry be abolished and substituted by a Board of Land Commissioners.

triumphalism is wearing down, there are signs that the land question is being revisited (Massay, 2016; Kusiluka et al., 2011; German et al., 2013). A younger generation of lawyers, hopefully, may dust off the Commission's report to assess it and draw lessons to restart the grand debates of the 1960s and 1980s when lawyers thought big, beyond 'law in context' and 'law and development' perspectives.[7]

Learning from practice

When we were first-year students, we read Glanville Williams, *Learning the Law* (now Smith 16th edition, 2016), as a compulsory text. The radical orientation of the Dar es Salaam campus then taught us, or rather, we taught ourselves, how to dissect and demystify law. We learnt a great deal more in radical political economy and history of class struggles outside the classroom in ideological classes organised by the University Students' African Revolutionary Front (see generally Hirji, 2010). We also learnt and paid homage to learning from practice, but in the abstract. We talked of and in the name of workers and peasants but had little contact with them. And when we did come into contact with them we were anxious to teach rather than learn. Our reading of Mao's *Where Do Correct Ideas Come From?* was textual not temporal (Mao Zedong, 1967). We were enamoured by its spirit but failed to grasp its materiality. The legal aid work woke us up. It brought us face to face with the role of law in mystifying power and the role of its procedures in legitimising it.

Procedures are presented as fair, just and equitable disguising the substance whose very bedrock is unequal, inequitable and unjust. Procedures deliver legal justice with one hand and take away social injustice with the other. Many a time, we won on procedure and lost on substance, but rarely lost on procedure and won on substance. Loss on procedure means you have lost your day in court. Our erstwhile 'law-in-context' and 'law-in/and-development' gurus, sought to wreak a revolution through procedures, no doubt, with the best intentions in the world but then, the road to hell is paved with good intentions.

Second, legal aid practice shook our paradigms but did not challenge them. It made us believe in the reform of law. It made us uncritical adherents of rights-ideology. It was only the practice of interacting with the working people and listening to them patiently – peasants, pastoralists, small producers etc. – through the Commission's work that drove home the point that law is the most sophisticated of bourgeois inventions that combines in it the blind faith of religion, the popular legitimacy of mythology and the rhetorical power of Socratic persuasion to disguise the rapaciously unequal and unjust capitalist system. We came face to face with systemic forces that appear to work behind the

7 For consideration of this history, see the chapters by key scholars in Shivji (1986) and Paliwala (2017).

backs of actors, both the exploited and the exploiters. We truly learnt from the people. What we got from them confusedly we gave them back systematically. Our radical recommendations did not seek to wreak a revolution (unlike McAuslan's claim for his draft bill). We were under no such illusion. Our recommendations had a limited aim: to bring the terrain of social struggles closer home to the working people in their villages and neighbourhoods in the hope that they would become the 'schools of conscientization' as Paulo Freire (1970/2018) would have it. Just as for Marx trade unions were the schools of developing socialist consciousness, not an instrument of socialist revolution, for us, village assemblies would be schools of raising democratic consciousness, not an apparatus for building socialism.

But now we must descend to a lower level of abstraction to sum up how the Commission's work and recommendations made us shift from our pre-conceived paradigms, however, radical.

Paradigmatic shifts

First, we moved away from the rights-based paradigm because this paradigm works within the bourgeois system of commodity exchange. Its legal expression is the contract, with two parties holding a bundle of rights and exchanging them in an apparently free transaction. So, if we had applied the rights-based paradigm – right to sell or let land etc. – we would first have had to accept the rules of commodity exchange, including the fiction that parties to a contract are equal, and second, that land is either already a commodity, or if it is not, it must be commodified. And, as Karl Polanyi told us long ago, land is not an actual commodity (1944). It is not a product of labour. It has to be made a commodity through law and state action. It is an artificial, or fictitious, commodity. To this day, land in much of Africa is still not a commodity. A central premise of neoliberalism is that the state should play a central role in making natural endowments such as land, resources, water, forests, air, environment and bio-resources into commodities (Polanyi, 1944; on land, see Akram-Lodhi, 2007).

Second, by making village assemblies the foundation of democracy and integrating political governance with resource governance, we questioned one of the fundamental premises of bourgeois constitutional ideology or theory: separation between politics and economics. We were extending Lenin's dictum, which says politics is a concentrated expression of economics (Lenin, 1965, XXXII: 32) by suggesting that law is a concentrated form of politics and thus economics.

Third, by making the village assembly, an organ of direct democracy, part of the governance structure, we were exposing the limits of representative democracy and the whole structure of multi-party system of liberal democracy built on it.

Fourth, of course none of this assumed a different system than the existing capitalist one. Even if our recommendations were accepted, it would not mean an end of class struggle, nor of the capitalist system of production. However, by demystifying issues around neutrality, impartiality and equality before the law they would locate law and democracy as part of the central terrain of struggle.

Fifth, it provided new weapons in the struggle to create anti-hegemony. Not yet counter-hegemony; anti-hegemony constitutes a form of resistance and struggle towards building counter-hegemonic struggles.

Finally, let me say a word on the emerging identity discourse whose origin lies in the West but is being picked up in Latin America with respect to land. This 'shift-of-paradigm' is more recent than the work of the Commission and was interestingly articulated at the Warwick International Symposium on Beyond Development in 2016 (Duer, 2016). In a paper on the resistance of the Menoko people of Chile against the forestry industry, land as property was juxtaposed to land as identity and this was presented as a radical shift of discourse on land. I would argue that in land-as-property, land is objectified. It becomes an object to possess, to own, to sell, buy or hoard. In the so-called shift of paradigm to land-as-identity, which is a cultural construct, land is subjectivised. To the extent that it helps to mobilise traditional resources of belief and mythology around land (sanctity of land as mother *Pachamama*, or where ancestors are buried etc.) for resistance, for struggle, it has its role. But such struggles remain local. Worse, they fragment communities and forces of resistance along *ethnic* lines. Therefore, they fail to transit to the national level as well as to solidarise as class struggles of the peasants and other working people. Invariably, they are defeated. The question I ask myself is: how do we look at these local struggles? I would like to suggest that unless a universalist counter-hegemonic project leads local struggles, they cannot really transform the system as we would like it to. What is more, unless led by such a project, they also harbour within them the seeds of fragmentation. The least that can be said is that radicals and progressives should be wary of applying identity politics to land and land struggles.

Practice matters. For a society-conscious lawyer, legal practice enrages as social practice enlightens. When combined, they assail the scholar's venerable paradigms. What was once considered radical scholarship turns out to be left liberal in the good old tradition of bourgeois enlightenment. Theory too matters. '[E]very practice produces a theory', Amilcar Cabral said, 'and … if it is true that a revolution can fail even though it be based on perfectly conceived theories, nobody has yet made a successful revolution without a revolutionary theory' (1969: 75). The location – both social and geographical – of the scholar also matters. In the erstwhile division of the world between imperialist centres and dominated peripheries, production of knowledge is as divided as the production of goods and services. Scholars of the periphery produce data; scholars of the centre process the data and produce theory. Radical scholars are not immune. Some of the arrogance of theory of mainstream scholars of the centre brushes on radicals too. And in the context of erstwhile class divided societies, we must perhaps also interrogate what it means to learn from practice. Our elite, petit-bourgeois background makes us believe in our own wisdom; that we have a lot to teach the ignorant masses while little to learn from them. Our theories and paradigms inevitably share our class outlooks. The least we can do is to be conscious of it and choose our sides accordingly.

These are then a few lessons I draw from this short narrative which should humble us all – radical scholars of both the centre and the periphery.

References

Adams, M., 2017. The Vagaries of Consulting on Land Policy and Land Law Reform in Africa, 1994–2006. In T. Zartaloudis (ed.), *Land Law and Urban Policy in Context: Essays in Honour of Patrick McAuslan*. Routledge, p. 79.

Adelman, S., and Paliwala, A. (eds), 1993. *Law and Crisis in the Third World*. Hans Zell Publishers.

Akram-Lodhi, A. Haroon, 2007. Land, Markets and Neoliberal Enclosure: An Agrarian Political Economy Perspective. *Third World Quarterly*, *28* (*8*), 1437–1456.

Cabral, A., 1969. The Weapon of Theory. In A. Cabral (ed.), *Revolution in Guinea: An African People's Struggle*. Stage 1, p. 73.

Duer, M., 2016. *The Protection of the Menoko against the Advancement of the Forest Industry: The Case of Machi Francisca*. International Symposium on Beyond Development: New Imaginaries of Law and Social Justice. University of Warwick. Available online at: https://warwick.ac.uk/fac/soc/law/research/events/conferences/beyond_development (accessed 11 February 2019).

East African Royal Commission, 1955. *Report of the East African Royal Commission 1953–1955*. Her Majesty's Stationery Office.

Freire, P., 1970/2018. *The Pedagogy of the Oppressed* (50th anniversary volume). Bloomsbury Publishing.

German, L., Schoneveld, G. and Mwangi, E., 2013. Contemporary Processes of Large-Scale Land Acquisition in Sub-Saharan Africa: Legal Deficiency or Elite Capture of the Rule of Law? *World Development*, *48*, 1–18.

Ghai, Y., 1986. Legal Radicalism, Professionalism and Social Action: Reflections on Teaching Law in Dar es Salaam. In I.G. Shivji (ed.), *The Limits of Legal Radicalism*. University of Dar es Salaam, p. 83.

Hirji, K.F. (ed.), 2010. *Cheche: Reminiscences of a Radical Magazine*. Mkuki na Nyota Publishers.

Kusiluka, M., Kongela, S., Kusiluka, M.A., Lughano, D.K. and Kusiluka, J.M., 2011. The Negative Impact of Land Acquisition on Indigenous Communities' Livelihood and Environment in Tanzania. *Habitat International*, *35* (*1*), 66–73.

Lenin, Vladimir I., 1965. *Collected Works*, Vol. *XXXII*. Progress Publishers.

Lofchie, Michael, 1975. The Political and Economic Origins of African Hunger. The *Journal of Modern African Studies*, *13* (*4*), 551–567.

Manji, A., 2006. *The Politics of Land Reform in Africa: From Communal Tenure to Free Markets*. Zed Books.

Mao Zedong, 1966. *Where Do Correct Ideas Come From? In Selected Works of Mao Tse-tung*, Vol. *III*. Foreign Languages Press.

Mao Zedong, 1967. *Some Questions Concerning Leadership. In Selected Works of Mao Tse-tung*, Vol. *III*. p. 117. Foreign Languages Press.

Massay, G., 2016. Tanzania's Village Land Act: 15 Years On. *Rural 21*. Available online at: https://www.tnrf.org/files/pubs/land_act.pdf (accessed 10 May 2019).
McAuslan, P., 1996. *Making Law Work: Restructuring Land Relations in Africa*. Third Alistair Berkeley Memorial Lecture. 30 May. London School of Economics.
Mwami, A. and Kamata, N., 2011. *Land Grabbing in a Postinvestment Period And Popular Reaction in the Rufiji River Basin 1: A Research Report*. Hakiardhi. Available online at: https://www.farmlandgrab.org/uploads/attachment/LAND%20GRABBING%20IN%20A%20POST%20INVESTMENT%20PERIOD%20AND%20POPULAR%20REACTIONS%20IN%20THE%20RUFIJI%20RIVER%20BASIN.pdf (accessed 10 August 2017).
Neocosmas, M., 1993. *The Agrarian Question in Southern Africa and "Accumulation from Below": Economics and Politics in the Struggle for Democracy*. Research Report No. 93. Nordiska Afrikaninstitutet.
Paliwala, A., 2017. Context, Political Economy and Good Governance: Avatars of Dar Legal Education. In T. Zartaloudis (ed.), *Land Law and Urban Policy in Context: Essays in Honour of Patrick McAuslan*. Routledge, p. 56.
Picciotto, S., 1986. In I. Shivji (ed.), *The Limits of Legal Radicalism*. University of Dar es Salaam. pp. 36–47.
Polanyi, K., 1944. *The Great Transformation*. Farrar & Rinehart.
Sawyerr, A., 1988. *The Politics of Adjustment Policy International Conference on The Human Dimension of Africa's Economic Recovery and Development*. Available online at: http://pdfproc.lib.msu.edu/?file=/DMC/African%20Journals/pdfs/Journal%20of%20Political%20Economy/ajpev2n4/ajpe002004002.pdf (accessed 11 February 2019).
Seidman, Robert, 1969. The Reception of English Law in Colonial Africa Revisited. *Eastern Africa Law Review*, *2* (*1*), 47–85.
Seidman, A. and Seidman, R., 1978. *The State, Law and Development*. St Martin's Press.
Shivji, I.G., 1972. Introduction: From the Analysis of Forms to the Exposition of Substance – the Tasks of a Lawyer Intellectual. *Eastern Africa Law Review*, *5* (*5*), 1.
Shivji, I.G. (ed.), 1986. *Limits of Legal Radicalism*. Faculty of Law, University of Dar es Salaam.
Shivji, I.G., 1998. *Not Yet Democracy: Reforming Land Tenure in Tanzania*. International Institute for Environment and Development/Haki Ardhi: Land Rights Research and Resources Institute.
Shivji, I.G., 2006. *Let the People Speak: Tanzania Down the Road to Neo-liberalism*. CODESRIA.
Shivji, I.G., 2009. *Where is Uhuru? Reflections on the Struggle for Democracy in Africa*. Fahamu/Pambazuka.
Shivji, I.G., Majamba, H., Peter, C. and Makaramba, R., 2005. *Constitutional and Legal System of Tanzania*. Mkuki na Nyota Publishers.
Sundet, G., 1997. *'The Politics of Land in Tanzania'*. DPhil dissertation, University of Oxford.
Tanzania, Ministry of Lands, 1995, *National Land Policy*. Ministry of Lands.
Tanzania, United Republic, 1994. *Report of the Presidential Commission of Inquiry into Land Matters, Volumes I and II*. Ministry of Lands, Housing and Urban Development in co-operation with the Scandinavian Institute of African Studies, Stockholm.

Twining, W., 1997. *Law in Context: Enlarging a Discipline*. Oxford University Press.
Twining, W., 2017. McAuslan in Context: Early Days in Dar and Warwick. In T. Zartaloudis (ed.), *Land Law and Urban Policy in Context: Essays in Honour of Patrick McAuslan*. Routledge, p. 35.
Worsley, Peter, 1976. Proletarians, Sub-Proletarians, Lumpenproletarians, Marginalidados, Migrants, Urban Peasants and Urban Poor. *Sociology*, *10* (*1*): 133–142.

Chapter 7

Academia, activism and the new global governance

Sol Picciotto

The world and the academy

It is not surprising that international economic law, and particularly the regulation of transnational corporations (TNCs), has been such an important focus of both politics and policy-making. For the past century the world's political-economy has been marked by interacting international processes that have transformed national economies increasingly dominated by large TNCs, and states gradually torn apart by the contending forces of nationalism and globalisation. The study of these processes is fascinating, yet understanding them has posed challenges both to orthodox disciplinary perspectives and to the formulation of progressive political and policy responses.

In the traditional law curriculum both international law and economic law were ill-adapted to understanding this reality because each was separated into public and private law spheres. The international economy was considered a realm of private markets and so was dealt with generally in terms of international commercial law, which largely ignored both state economic regulation and the dominant role of large corporations. Other disciplines were equally unsuited, as politics, economics and even sociology focused on the national state, treating international relations as those exclusively between governments, while international economics dealt with flows of goods and money. Indeed, formal economics still treats TNCs in terms of 'foreign direct investment', and the study of TNCs has moved to business schools, which treat them predominantly from an organisational and managerial perspective.

However, I was fortunate that my first academic job was in Dar es Salaam, in the post-colonial ferment of the mid-1960s.[1] There, the stark contrast between the nationalist and socialist rhetoric of radical politicians such as Nkrumah and Nyerere and the realities of 'underdeveloped' socio-economic structures and a

1 Founded in 1961 as a University College, part of the University of East Africa, in Tanganyika; I was there 1964–8, and during that period the revolution in Zanzibar was followed by its union with Tanganyika to form the United Republic of Tanzania.

world economy dominated by TNCs were pointed out by analysts such as Giovanni Arrighi and John Saul (Arrighi and Saul, 1968; 1973). I have continued to find the most relevant writings on international political economy to come from Marxist, developmentalist and other eclectic perspectives, such as Robin Murray (1971), Edith Penrose (1951), John Dunning (1988) and Grazia Letto-Gillies (2012), and economic sociologists such as Kristensen and Zeitlin (2005).

Hence, I have found that an adequate understanding of important realities requires a critical perspective which challenges orthodox viewpoints. Furthermore, since academic analysis was stuck in old orthodoxies, there was need for some practical engagement with the real world. Interestingly, this seemed easiest in the legal field, perhaps because the interactions of economic and political activities are centrally mediated by law. Indeed, the field of 'transnational law' was delineated as early as 1956 by a lawyer-diplomat, Philip C. Jessup.[2] This concept quickly invaded US law schools, resulting in a proliferation of law reviews and courses which provided a grounding for generations of lawyers who spread around the world, facilitating the expansion of TNCs as well as building the regulatory infrastructures of what later became known as global governance. Initially unorthodox concepts such as transnationalism helped to mould the emergence of these new forms of business and government since the 1970s.

So, it was clear that practical engagement did not necessarily produce a critical perspective in policy or political terms but tended mainly to serve politically and economically emergent or dominant interests. Perhaps for that reason, many in academia have been reticent or hostile towards such engagement, considering it as contaminating (Sarat and Silbey, 1988). This can also lead to suspicion of concepts or discourses emerging from the world of practice. Consequently, some academics prefer to stick to orthodoxies, while others develop more radical alternative frameworks aimed at escaping the grip of power, sometimes by protecting themselves behind abstruse academic jargon. Probably the dominant tendency has been to take refuge in technical expertise, separating policy from politics, aiming at a 'policy audience' essentially consisting of those with power, which in turn blunts the critical edge of the research agenda (Sarat and Silbey, 1988).

It is essential for academic inquiry to be independent and to some extent insulated from social conflicts and power struggles. This enables longer-term analysis, abstracting from day-to-day professional practice or the hurly burly of

2 Jessup was in the secretariat of the United Nations Relief and Rehabilitation Administration (UNRRA) conference in 1943, at Bretton Woods in 1944, and a technical adviser to the American delegation to the San Francisco United Nations charter conference in 1945; but his nomination by Truman as US delegate to the UN was blocked in the Senate following accusations by Senator McCarthy of 'unusual affinity for Communist causes'.

politics, with the aim of understanding and depicting the contours and ecology of the forest as a whole beyond the particularities of specific trees. I have often been surprised and intrigued to find, in interactions with practitioners or policy-makers that in some ways I had a better grasp of the general policy issues in their field, although they were obviously more immersed in and skilled at its practical detail. This detachment also means that an academic can appreciate the positions of the various participants in the debates or conflicts in a field, and is able to discern that each person sees and understands it in terms which are valid from their own perspective. That appreciation in turn tends to strengthen the preference for detachment. Is it possible to retain that important detachment if one takes a position in the field?

My view is that some engagement is inevitable, because academic detachment itself involves taking a position. The analyses put forward by academics of an issue themselves contribute to shaping those phenomena. Certainly, a purely sociological study can avoid becoming embroiled in the substance of the processes, and some detachment can be created by framing the issues using a 'reflexive' research methodology, based on analysing the positions and interests of the various actors in the field. Such an approach has been ably applied by sociologists of law inspired by Pierre Bourdieu, notably Yves Dezalay and his various collaborators and followers (Dezalay and Madsen, 2012). I have found this work very insightful and helpful in facilitating more dispassionate analysis that discounts preconceptions and emphasises the investigation of social practices and structures. Viewing the processes of construction of transnational fields or networks of global governance as strategies of competition between different professionals deliberately avoids taking any position about what is at stake. However, as Madsen suggests, claims of detachment or objectivity give the opinions of academics a power that can be used by them and other actors to legitimise their disciplinary practices (Madsen, 2006: 33). Hence, it seems preferable for academics to make their policy preferences explicit rather than lay claim to a spurious objectivity.

Further, it seems to me that analysing these processes from a pure sociological perspective generally misses out their substance, perhaps fearing to become too embroiled and adopting a legal perspective. Since law mediates power relations between the political and economic spheres, I find that it is essential to analyse specific legal forms and concepts to understand adequately the dynamics of particular power relations. A 'pure' sociological analysis which holds back from engaging with these details can usually only demonstrate that legal practices reproduce structures of domination. This does not help to understand the social conflicts involved, or to provide any theory of change (De Sousa Santos and Rodriguez-Garavito, 2005: 12).

The necessity for increased and more direct involvement of academics seems to me to be due to the emergence of the very phenomenon that is now central to international economic law: global governance. This form of rule rests to an unprecedented extent on knowledge, especially that of specialised professionals including academics, and gives the latter a responsibility we cannot and should not avoid.

Changing interactions

Perhaps this is best explained by reflecting on my own experience, which spans the whole period of emergence of this phenomenon. I was fortunate to have been in Dar es Salaam in the 1960s, in a period of great political ferment marked by post-colonial nationalism. Politics was very much in the air, and there were many urgent policy issues, but in the university our main concern was the revision of its educational approach, especially in relation to the curriculum. We saw our role as ensuring that teaching and research should be relevant to the new country, but politics and policy formation were regarded as matters for the local people and their legislature and government.

The university became a focus of lively political and intellectual debates and, interestingly, the Law Faculty led the way in the process of change. Debates within the faculty stressed the 'limits of the law' (Shivji, 1986) taking a critical view of instrumental conceptions which assumed that economic and social change could be produced by state power through legal mechanisms. Many placed their hopes in the nationalisation of foreign-owned assets especially of raw materials (Bolton, 1985), and in the field of international economic law this conception of economic development was expressed in the UN General Assembly's New International Economic Order Declaration of 1974 and related documents (UNITAR, 1984). Although I supported strategies aimed at reversing the legacies of colonialism and under-development, my academic work took a critical view of both nationalist politics and state ownership policies and pointed to their limitations and difficulties (Faundez and Picciotto, 1978).

The reticence of academics to become directly involved in politics was partly because we were mostly expatriates; yet, there were other non-Tanzanians who were closely connected with policy formulation as government advisers. When I returned to the UK in 1968, I retained a similar perspective on the relationship between academics and politics. I was once again plunged into campus politics, but the central concern was reform of universities; any wider political impact was understood to entail alliances with other social forces. In the 1970s, this meant working with community groups and workers' organisations, with my role being one of providing expertise and research services. It was very rewarding that critical theory and practice could interact, nurturing and strengthening each other, but nevertheless my academic work remained quite separate from my broader political engagement.

The academic and policy or political spheres have quite different dynamics and timescales. Those engaged in the latter generally begin from a teleological perspective: they know their objectives and seek proof for their beliefs and justifications for their actions. The academic also has pre-formed views and preferences, but academic inquiry, especially if it is critical, should entail adopting a sceptical stance, challenging received opinion, and treating initial ideas as hypotheses to be tested. It also has a longer time horizon: a research programme lasts many years, sometimes a lifetime, and even the shortest project is rarely completed in less than a year or two.[3] The policy world is much more fleeting, a news item disappears in hours or days at most, and while broader policy issues are not quickly resolved, proposals and campaigns usually demand papers to be written within days and to produce effects within months. Thus, from the policy perspective academic work often seems irrelevant, even utopian; so, it may remain neglected outside (or even inside) academia, although it may turn out later to have been prescient and find its moment.[4]

During the 1970s, my academic work on TNCs came into closer conjuncture with my wider political activities, including helping to provide research services to workplace trade union organisations. In 1974, the election of a Labour government, with Tony Benn as Minister for Trade and Industry (formerly the Board of Trade), sparked an attempt to introduce continental European-style co-determination in the UK through the Industry Act of 1975. The historical strength of shop stewards in the auto industry of Coventry appeared to put them in a good position to take advantage of this, and it seemed that a more structured form of research support could help them engage with corporate strategies, especially those involving internationalisation, the central challenge to the British auto industry at that time. It was also during that period that sources of research funding began to stress relevance to policy and to users. This justifiably aroused academic suspicions, and continues to do so, as disfavouring longer-term research, especially that which is critical and anti-establishment. Nevertheless, a colleague (Richard Hyman, a specialist on industrial relations) and I decided it was worth submitting an application for funding to the Social Science Research Council (SSRC). Somewhat to our surprise we received a letter announcing that we had been successful. However, the sting in the tail was a requirement to

3 There are of course significant differences for full-time researchers and those who also have teaching and other responsibilities, but even a full-time PhD is rarely completed within the three years it is supposed to take. The longest I have supervised took a dozen years, but this was Yao Graham, who was drawn into direct political involvement for several years when Fl. Lt Rawlings came to power while Yao was doing field work in his country, Ghana; happily, he survived a serious injury and a spell in jail to return and complete his thesis.

4 Among many examples I may single out Ronald Coase, whose main work was in the left-wing intellectual context of the London School of Economics in the 1930s, but was taken up some three decades later in Chicago, resulting in the award of a Nobel prize in 1991. Although his work probed the limits of both market-based coordination (due to 'transaction costs') and of corporate management or public planning, in the policy climate of the 1980s it sparked enormous outputs of free-market oriented work. Coase himself, however, sharply criticised the version of his views put forward especially by Richard Posner, the dominant figure in law-and-economics (his mildest comment was that it was 'highly inaccurate': Coase (1993: 96; see Campbell and Klaes, 2005).

confirm that we had the necessary 'research access', which meant a letter of approval from the company management. Needless to say, this was not forthcoming, despite the shop-floor power of our trade unionist sponsors.

In the 1980s, as my teaching and research on international economic law expanded, I planned to write a book covering some of the main issues. I decided to focus on TNCs analysed in the wider context of their historical development and changes in the international state system. I decided to include a chapter on international tax, a topic I had not much studied till then, but which was clearly central to the operation of both states and TNCs, and to their interaction. Immersion in the topic resulted in the intended chapter growing into a separate book entitled *International Business Taxation*.[5] Since the book adopted a wider political-economy and critical legal approach, it received little attention from tax specialists; at the same time, it was too technical and detailed for many of those in the policy communities so that its most receptive audience was in the emerging field of international political economy, pioneered especially by Susan Strange (1984) and Robert Cox (1981).

Once it was published, I moved on or rather back to a wider range of issues, especially trade, which was merging with investment regulation with the establishment of the World Trade Organization (WTO) in 1995. Understanding the complexity of this phenomenon took several years of teaching and research, mixed with other duties and a change of university. I also conducted some research into regulation of financial markets. As part of this, a colleague and I wrote a paper warning of the dangers of financial derivatives (Campbell and Picciotto, 2000), which we had difficulty getting published, and which was duly ignored by policy-makers, as were similar warnings by a few others, some with more influence than we had.[6] Only towards the end of my formal academic career was I able to resume work on a more comprehensive book entitled *Regulating Global Corporate Capitalism* (Picciotto, 2011).

In the meantime, I had taken another plunge into policy arenas. In 1997, a colleague and friend, Jane Kelsey, drew my attention to the draft of the Multilateral Agreement on Investment (MAI), which had been leaked to and then publicised by activist groups. This was during the 1990s period of academic debates about 'globalisation' and activist 'anti-globalisation' campaigns.[7] I was

5 Picciotto (1992) now enjoying a second life at: http://taxjustice.blogspot.be/2013/06/international-business-taxation.html (accessed 14 August 2015).

6 Notably, Frank Partnoy pointed to the specific dangers of credit derivatives (Partnoy and Skeel, 2007); heterodox economists Ann Pettifor, Steve Keen and Nouriel Roubini warned that the private debt bubble especially in housing would lead to a crash (Cooper, 2015), and Raghuram Rajan, then at the IMF, gave the unwelcome message to disbelieving bank regulators in August 2005 (Tooze, 2018: 67).

7 See, for example, the conflicting perspectives of Held (Held, 1995; Held et al., 1999), and Hirst and Thompson (1992), and a thoughtful comment by Sivanandan and Wood (1997); and for a retrospective evaluation Rosenberg (2005).

critical of the prevailing academic debate, much of which seemed shallow and apparently unaware of the earlier work on the internationalisation of capital and the state, and I found difficulty identifying with the activists since I regarded myself as an internationalist and progressive, and they seemed to be defending nostalgic statist models.

However, the text of the MAI proved fascinating and drew me into studying its policy and political contexts. It created broad obligations on states for protection of property rights, derived from investment treaties, as well as the non-discrimination principles of national treatment and most-favoured-nation treatment modelled on those in trade agreements. It applied to 'investors' and 'investments', very broadly defined to include contractual as well as property rights, but made no mention of TNCs. It seemed based on a simplistic understanding of both international political-economy and legal regulation. Interviews with some participants in the negotiations suggested that they were driven by short-term political considerations and the ideology of 'free trade', and had little understanding of the implications of the legal instruments they were designing. Campaigners seemed correct in their opposition, even though this seemed to be based more on gut reactions than intellectual objections. Even an academic economist, called in as a consultant by the UK Department for International Development to evaluate the campaigners' criticisms, produced what seemed to me to be a very superficial analysis based on macro-economic assumptions about the benefits of 'open markets'. Working with researchers in civil society organisations, especially Oxfam, we produced a volume of research-based analyses aimed at strengthening the debate (Picciotto and Mayne, 1999). I also published a more academic paper analyzing the MAI in terms of the emergence of networks of international economic regulation (Picciotto, 1998).

Academics and global governance

Involvement with the MAI campaigns brought home the realisation that my academic work in economic law was unavoidably part of the policy arena. More than that, engagement with this arena seemed a responsibility arising from the nature of the phenomena I was studying. The policy debate was dominated by ideologies favouring 'free' markets, privatisation and reduced state intervention. Opponents of these ideas also understood projects such as the creation of the WTO, and the proposal for the MAI, in a similar way and denounced them as 'neoliberal'. Yet it seemed clear on closer examination that the process was resulting in an enormous growth of regulation in many fields, from technical and health or safety standards for products to regulation of banks and other financial institutions. As Stephen Vogel pointed out, the creation of so-called free markets actually involved many more detailed and formalised rules (Vogel, 1996). On the other hand, what was generally described as a 'market' economy, dominated as it was by corporate behemoths, seemed quite different from my conception of a market. Liberalisation was not a 'retreat of the state', but its transformation into a new type of public–private corporatocracy. At the apex of these complex structures was a rapidly growing kleptocracy, enriching themselves by operating in the grey areas of semi-legality where state and corporate power intersect.

I found it impossible simply to describe these phenomena in a detached way. Academics, as technical experts, had become direct participants in the creation of what now began to be described as global governance. International lawyers were enlisting as WTO panellists and investment arbitrators, just as scientists were active in debates about biotechnology patenting, food safety or environmental protection. My attempts to describe the outlines of the emerging multi-level or networked system were attacked during an academic conference by some critical academics for having adopted the techno-speak of its protagonists. Yet it seemed impossible either to ignore or reject these processes, which were changing the world whether we liked it or not.

The world of nation-states and national economies has been dissolving, or fragmenting, and been restructured around intertwined public-corporate bureaucracies (Picciotto, 2010, 2011). This has weakened already fragile traditional forms of democratic accountability or checks on power within states. In the political sphere, representation through class-based political parties has given way to what Bernard Manin describes as 'audience democracy', based on the 'construction of vague images prominently featuring the personality of the leader' (Manin, 1994, 1997). This has been greatly exacerbated as digital communication has reduced debate to slogans and insults. At the same time, policy arenas now depend much more heavily on knowledge and expertise, largely because the world and its governance have become much more complex and interconnected. Following the great financial crisis, which the experts in thrall to neo-liberal dogma had facilitated, these political failures enabled demagogues to pave the way for populist nationalism.

The economic sphere continues to be dominated by the large corporations which emerged in the late nineteenth and twentieth centuries, but rather than growing ever larger they have tended to become 'lean and mean', focusing on their core business while extending their tentacles through international supply chains of subcontractors (Gereffi, 2014; Gereffi and Korzeniewicz, 1994), or systems of franchising and licensing (Ritzer, 2008). Their cadres have become ever more expert at managing the business itself, but increasingly myopic, driven by the short-term pressures of capital markets resulting from the 'financialisation' of capitalism and the fleeting attention-spans of a highly mediatised politics. The corporate and public policy spheres have become highly intertwined, as the competitiveness and sometimes the very survival of business have become highly dependent on regulatory decisions. For their part, politicians want access to corporate funds for campaign finance, not to speak of personal enrichment. At lower levels, regulatory officials and corporate managers also interact closely in 'epistemic communities' created by 'responsive regulation'. These arenas have become highly technicised, a process which their academic study has reinforced (Picciotto, 2017), yet they have also been a seed bed for corruption.

This new world of 'governance' has spawned new organisational forms of producing, managing and deploying policy expertise. On the one hand, in older professions such as law and accountancy, large corporate firms which had already diverged from traditional family businesses and partnerships have expanded their provision of policy advice and lobbying services to both business and governments. Among the firms involved, the broadest and largest are the accountancy Big Four (Deloitte, EY, KPMG and PwC); followed by large global business consultancy and law firms (Accenture, Baker & McKenzie etc.); a number of smaller public policy advice and public relations firms; and an array of smaller boutique firms focusing on specific issues such as taxation. Business or industry associations range from chambers of commerce, which have a wide scope and a long history, coordinated by the globally powerful International Chamber of Commerce, to more specific groupings such as the Chemicals Industry Association, which set up a global system of chemicals plant safety regulation following the Bhopal disaster in 1984 (King and Lenox, 2000).

Set against these is a motley range of international campaigning organisations. Some, such as Oxfam and Friends of the Earth in the fields of 'development' and the environment, are large, international, and quite well resourced. Although their resources are mainly geared to raising funds and disbursing assistance, they have increasingly focused on campaigns around policy issues backed by research departments. It was with researchers from Oxfam, the Worldwide Fund for Nature and others that I had worked on the MAI campaign. Other international NGOs are focused on more specific issues and are therefore generally smaller. Transnational political activism of course has a longer history, but in the recent period has become dominated by various kinds of international 'activist networks' (Keck and Sikkink, 1998). In countries of the global South in particular they have come to play a role in governance, their reliance on external funding creating an uneasy basis for policy advocacy (Morris-Suzuki, 2000). Some trade union organisations have also developed policy roles, especially international sectoral federations such as Public Services International. The scope of their activities has been somewhat limited because of reduced resources due to declining union membership and their reluctance to expand their concerns beyond the traditional ambit of employment conditions and national politics. Nevertheless, some public sector union organisations have taken up wider issues that affect their members, for example Education International on liberalisation of services, and the International Transport Federation on flags of convenience. Outside economic questions, campaigning organisations such as Amnesty International have been joined by others working on broader issues of human rights and 'security', which often includes ostensibly economic aspects such as corruption, money laundering and capital flight. Some position themselves less as campaigners and more like the think tanks, which have a longer history in many countries, sometimes linked to political parties (even officially, as in Germany), and many acting as a bridge between politics and big business (such as Chatham House in London, and the Council on Foreign Relations in the US).

Inevitably, all these organisations are dependent upon, and therefore more or less beholden to, their sources of funding. This is more direct and explicit for organisations emanating from or linked with business which unabashedly represent the specific interests and concerns of their constituencies. Hence, although all such policy-oriented bodies have been very generally referred to as nongovernmental organisations (NGOs), those which regard themselves as working from a public interest perspective have preferred to be described as civil society organisations (CSOs). They are generally less well-resourced than business or professional organisations, and their need to raise funds can affect their choices of campaigning issues and strategies. However, their staff are generally driven by ideological commitment more than career considerations and are therefore more likely to take independent positions, even though this may result in partisanship or fervent advocacy.

Although I have always been interested in business and economic issues, my focus on understanding and analysis led me away from professional practice into an academic career, and my concerns for emancipatory social change prompted a preference for working with CSOs. Surprisingly, this choice has not been unproblematic. Such engagement seems to be viewed by some as an abandonment of independence and of academic standards of 'objectivity', somehow undermining the integrity and reliability of analytical arguments. This is curious, since it seems generally acceptable for academics to have a parallel professional practice or to work as consultants for business or professional firms. It has also become increasingly normal for large corporations to finance academic research – particularly on business and economic matters – in institutions which organise conferences and symposia with the combined participation of academics and practitioners, usually from business. These seem to me to foster shared perspectives which become accepted as common sense, so that the academic's commitment to critical inquiry is threatened and corrupted in many ways. Close interactions between academics and business professionals and managers seem to be more threatening of academic integrity than work with CSOs, but are rarely criticised.

At the same time, the relationship between academics and activists is also challenging. In choosing this option it may be tempting to become a campaigner, but I have not seen this as my primary role. It seems more important, valuable and rewarding to prioritise critical research, since this is what is most lacking in policy arenas, yet is essential for their effective functioning. Academics are in a unique and privileged position that allows them the time and independence for longer-term research from a critical perspective. During my career, however, the intensification of academic work and the shift towards private sources of funding has led to the reduction of both the amount of time and the degree of independence. On the other hand, there has been some encouragement to engage in research which is relevant to policy although, as my experience in the 1970s with the SSRC showed, this tends to be interpreted to mean work with business and government rather than social movements, but at least it allows a space for such work. The reluctance of many academics to move into this space is often due to a preference for an easier and more financially rewarding path, or conversely an inclination to abandon research for activism. I have preferred to maintain my focus on academic research while trying to contribute to policy debates through supporting social movement organisations.

International tax research and activism

Following my formal retirement from the academy, I was fortunate to have been able to engage more fully in policy work to a degree that would be hard or impossible for most academics with substantial teaching, research and administrative responsibilities. This experience has brought home more directly to me the issues explored in this paper. As already mentioned, after the publication of the book on international tax in 1992, my research interests broadened to include work on the WTO and the MAI, and later on financial markets. However, I remained interested in corporate taxation, especially the ways in which international tax avoidance led to the creation of the tax haven and 'offshore' finance system (Picciotto, 1999). While working with Oxfam on the MAI, I suggested that this should be an area on which they should focus, and although they had too much invested in other issues to redirect their main efforts, short-term funding did result in a report on *Tax Havens: Releasing the Hidden Billions for Poverty Eradication* (Mayne and Kimmis, 2000), for which I was an adviser.

Although Oxfam did not immediately follow this with any campaigning work on tax, other organisations did, notably War on Want. This was the period of the World Social Forums and the anti-globalisation movement about which I had reservations, as mentioned above. Nevertheless, the Forums provided an arena in which international tax could be debated by activists and researchers. The Tax Justice Network (TJN) was launched following a discussion at the European Social Forum at Florence in 2002, mainly through the efforts of John Christensen. An economist originating from Jersey, John had worked there as economic adviser before quitting in 1998 following a disagreement with its government's policy of fostering the island's status as a tax haven and offshore finance centre (Warren, 2014). Christensen had contributed a chapter to an edited book in which I also wrote about the offshore system (Hampton and Abbott, 1999) and had also helped with Oxfam's *Tax Havens* report (Mayne and Kimmis, 2000). John has been the main driving force of TJN ever since, an organisation that spawned a global network of tax justice groups and organisations, resulting in the Global Alliance for Tax Justice in 2013. I helped organise TJN's first conference at the University of Essex in 2003 and, in light of my role of research more than activism, was described as a Senior Adviser (along with several others). I was glad to participate in the meeting in Nairobi, at the time of the World Social Forum there, which led to the foundation of TJN-Africa, renewing my connections with Africa.

The issue of international taxation became increasingly politicised following the great financial crisis, so TJN rode the crest of a wave it helped create. International tax evasion and avoidance had already been taken up by the G7 world leaders. The communiqué from their meeting in Lyon in 1996 stated that '[t)ax schemes aimed at attracting financial and other geographically mobile activities can create harmful tax competition between States',[8] and it supported action through the Organisation for Economic Co-operation and Development (OECD), the main international tax reform body. This resulted in the OECD report on *Harmful Tax Competition* (OECD, 1998) which was relatively timid and further weakened by a US volte-face in 2001 following lobbying of the George W. Bush administration by the far-right Centre for Freedom and Prosperity. The OECD initiative became focused on the negotiation of bilateral treaties for exchange of information on tax matters, which was a very slow process, and was in any case limited to the provision of information on request, which facilitated secrecy in tax havens.

From its formation, the TJN called for a comprehensive multilateral system for the automatic exchange of information, which we suggested could be based on the OECD-Council of Europe multilateral convention for administrative assistance in taxation, published in 1988 but ratified by only a handful of states at that time.[9] Although our stance was considered politically utopian then, it became the global standard following renewed political pressures after the financial crisis of 2008. The convention was amended in 2010 and thrown open to all states, and in 2013 both the G8 and the G20 finally agreed to support multilateral automatic exchange of information for tax purposes. The OECD's Global Forum on Tax Transparency initiated implementation based upon a Global Reporting Standard published in 2014. The TJN continues to track tax transparency through a small team that compiles the Financial Secrecy Index,[10] the design of which resulted from the earlier research and analyses discussed above.

My main interest was international corporate taxation, which seemed to have further deteriorated since publication of my 1992 book. Basic tax treaty rules were little changed since they were first devised under the League of Nations in 1928, and attempts to patch them up through the OECD had worsened the situation. Regulations on transfer pricing drawn up by the US in 1968 and exported to other countries through the OECD had resulted only in entrenching the 'independent entity' principle. This requires the attribution of profits (and hence tax) by national tax authorities to the local affiliates of a TNC by treating them as if they were independent, instead of in accordance with the economic reality that a TNC is a corporate group under common ownership and control, and hence centrally

8 G7 documentation is available online through the G7 Information Centre at: http://www.g7.utoronto.ca/ (accessed 13 May 2019).

9 See: http://www.oecd.org/ctp/exchange-of-tax-information (accessed 26 October 2019) for details on the Convention, and the other actions mentioned in this paragraph.

10 Available online at: https://financialsecrecyindex.com (accessed 10 April 2019).

directed. Based on a fundamentally faulty assumption, the approach proved ineffective in practice, as had become increasingly apparent in the 1980s.[11] The response of the US authorities was to develop more sophisticated methods, leading to conflicts within the OECD, and further elaborations, embodied in the OECD Transfer Pricing Guidelines of 1995.[12] Although formally only soft law, in practice these Guidelines have come to be treated as global norms which are often referred to by courts[13] and incorporated into domestic legislation,[14] even in non-OECD countries.[15] International taxation, and transfer pricing in particular, quickly emerged as an important field, and its practitioners exploited its broad principles to devise ever more elaborate corporate structures. These generally take advantage of the encouragement provided by the independent entity principle to form affiliates in convenient jurisdictions with responsibility for specific functions, with the aim of reducing overall effective tax liability (Picciotto, 2013; Corporate Reform Collective, 2014: chs 1 and 10). The regulations introduced in response by tax

11 For a more detailed account and analysis of the issues discussed in this paragraph see Picciotto (2018).

12 Available online at: https://www.scribd.com/document/362145411/Oecd-1995-Transfer-Pricing-Guidelines-PDF (accessed 10 April 2019). Current Guidelines are available online at: https://www.oecd-ilibrary.org/taxation/oecd-transfer-pricing-guidelines-for-multinational-enterprises-and-tax-administrations-2017_tpg-2017-en (accessed 10 April 2019).

13 In 2005, the Kenya High Court allowed a company to use a transfer pricing method relying on the Guidelines even though they were at that time not mentioned anywhere in Kenyan law. 'We live in what is now referred to as a 'global village'. We cannot overlook or sideline what has come out of the collective wisdom of tax payers and tax collectors in other countries. And especially because of the absence of any such guidelines in Kenya, we must look elsewhere' (Judge Alnashir Visram, *Unilever Kenya v. KRA* 2005, 12). Similarly, a Malaysian court upheld a transfer pricing method based on the Guidelines when rejecting an adjustment made by the tax authority under local law, which it held to be invalid: *MM Sdn Berhad v Ketua Pengarah Hasil Dalam Negeri* Appeal No. PKCP(R) 55/2009 (2013) MSTC ~10–046 (2013).

14 For example, as authoritative guidance for interpretation of tax treaty provisions. In the UK, the Taxation (International and Other Provisions) Act 2010 s.164 provides that treaties based on the OECD Model should be interpreted 'in accordance with' the Guidelines and with any documents published by the OECD as part of the Guidelines prior to May 1998, and any documents designated in an Order made by the Treasury after that date as comprised in the Guidelines. This is a good example of global lawmaking, in which soft and hard law become intertwined, see Picciotto (2011: 20–2).

15 The Nigerian Income Tax (Transfer Pricing) Regulations No. 1 (2012) specify that they shall be 'applied in a manner consistent with' the OECD Guidelines 'as supplemented and updated from time to time' (s.11); there is identical language in the Tanzania Income Tax (Transfer Pricing) Regulations 2014, s.9; the boilerplate provisions suggests a systematic process of ensuring adoption of these norms, presumably resulting from 'capacity building' through the World Bank or the OECD itself. Even where countries enact their own regulations, the Guidelines are relied on in practice, and referred to by courts, e.g. in India a Tax Tribunal even recently referred to a draft report proposing changes to the Guidelines although it had not yet been approved: Income Tax Appellate Tribunal, Mumbai, ITA No. 1565/Mum/2014, *Watson Pharma Pvt Ltd vs. DCIT* (9 January 2015), para. 61.

authorities still begin from the independent entity assumption and have therefore been largely ineffective, except to create a field of complex technical rules. While some tax officials were frustrated by this, for others it provided an opportunity to invest in expertise, and many took advantage of the revolving door into private practice after a period in public service. Private practitioners flooded into the field, offering a range of specialisations and services, and corporate tax departments grew from a handful to a hundred or more people. In the case of General Electric, which built tax minimisation into its management structure from the early 1990s and set up its own finance affiliate, GE Capital, there were as many as one thousand (Kocieniewski, 2011).

As international tax avoidance intensified, the 2000 Oxfam report was followed by occasional exposés from other CSOs, often explaining the avoidance strategies of specific companies and estimating the tax losses, especially in poor countries (ActionAid, 2010; Curtis et al., 2012). Investigative journalism followed, initially in the more liberal press and later, especially after the fiscal crises resulting from the financial crash of 2008–9, in business media channels such as Reuters and Bloomberg (e.g. Bergin, 2012). Parliamentary inquiries in many countries also highlighted the issue, focusing in particular on the very low taxes paid on non-US profits by internet companies such as Apple, Amazon and Google (US Senate, 2012; UK Parliament, 2012). Discussion of the 'Dutch Sandwich' and the 'Double Irish' moved from specialist tax publications to mainstream media (e.g. Drucker, 2010).

These political concerns generated new pressures on OECD tax experts. An opportunity for a new approach came with the retirement in 2012 of Jeffrey Owens, who had built the OECD's Centre for Tax Policy and Administration over two decades (Picciotto et al., 2017). During his tenure, the OECD had continued to prioritise the role of tax treaties as the primary means of preventing double taxation to facilitate international investment. His replacement, Pascal Saint-Amans, arrived in February 2012 and quickly developed a new agenda to redirect attention to 'double non-taxation',[16] through an initially low-key project on 'base erosion and profit shifting'. The acronym BEPS gained high visibility after the publication in January 2013 by the OECD of a 30-month, 15-point BEPS Action Plan, and its endorsement in the G20's St Petersburg Declaration of September 2013.[17]

Work on analysing the defects of international tax rules had also taken place in parallel through the TJN and other organisations. Funding from the government of Finland enabled the TJN to organise a seminar in Helsinki in June 2012. The conclusions of the seminar were clear that the separate entity principle created a fundamental flaw in the system, and most of those participating advocated a shift

16 Double non-taxation refers to situations where the tax rules of two countries combined lead to non-taxation in either.

17 BEPS refers to 'shifting' profits from higher-tax jurisdictions to lower-tax jurisdictions, thus 'eroding' the tax base of the higher-tax jurisdictions. The BEPS project is discussed in greater detail, with citations to documents and other sources, in Picciotto et al., 2017.

towards treating TNCs as unitary firms. I followed up the event by drafting a paper arguing for 'unitary taxation' of TNCs, discussing how a transition to such a system could be achieved, by building on work by others (Picciotto, 2011). I had some helpful comments on the draft, but another TJN senior adviser tried to stop publication of the paper, and then ended his link with TJN acrimoniously.

This highlighted one of the problems of working with an organisation like the TJN that combines research with campaigning. For me, it is important to find ways to debate different views if they fall within the general aims of the organisation, but this can be difficult. People invest a lot in developing their understanding of issues and thus tend to become committed to their own perspective, making them resistant to different ideas. Organisations need to adopt a clear position and campaign for specific policies, leading advisers who feel their views have been disregarded to feel slighted. Such organisations also may attract forceful personalities with large egos, which can make it difficult to sustain open debate and team work. Tensions may also arise over competition for access to scarce funds, researchers dependent on grant funding may feel resentful of academics in secure jobs, and academics may be conscious of the risk to their careers from engagement with activist organisations. These problems are not unique to such organisations, and academia itself is also rife with conflicts and feuds arising from clashing opinions and personal hostility. Interpersonal conflicts can be dealt with to some extent by flexibility in organisational affiliation, as individuals move between different institutions, but this can result in serious loss to research capacity if knowledgeable people are replaced with neophyte newcomers. The more important issue is to decide the appropriate balance in each organisation between campaigning and research.

My view is that research should be a high priority. A central characteristic of global governance today is the importance of a detailed technical grasp of the salient issues and there is too often a wide gap between such understanding and the broad-brush terms in which policy debates are generally conducted (Picciotto, 2015). This is the main reason why academics and researchers generally have a crucial part to play in helping to ensure that such debates are better informed. It is especially important for critical views to be presented and given a fair hearing in policy fora, which can otherwise become mired in a stultifying consensus based on received opinions that generally supports dominant corporatist perspectives. This again suggests the importance of contributions from academics, who can choose to be more independent from big business interests.

Conclusion

I hope that these very personal reflections help to map some of the tangled terrain of policy formation in global governance. In conclusion, I draw out a few general analytical points.

The first concerns the concept of critique. For me being critical does not mean being oppositional or subjecting ideas to criticism from the outside, or only from an alternative criterion of value. I apply a Marxian approach of immanent critique, which begins from a thorough historical examination of the social practices and institutions concerned, and their associated ideologies (Stahl, 2013). The critique emerges from contrasting the self-understanding of practitioners in a field with a detailed examination of their actual practices, and demonstrating the contradictions between the two. The aim is not to denounce hypocrisy, but to understand how and why these understandings developed and how they may be transformed. I did not begin with such a worked-out methodological strategy or theory but have groped towards it through actual practice.

Second, the special position of academics gives them both a responsibility and a unique opportunity, not only because they have a degree of independence. This is certainly important, especially in relation to business and economic law and regulation, which is so dominated by corporate and pro-business views that a counterweight is essential to ensure a genuine debate. However, academics are also subject to pressures, especially from career concerns. Research funding can also create restrictions, not only when it derives from business sources, as my experience in the 1970s with the SSRC showed. More importantly, an academic position offers the chance to take a long-term view, and engage in proper research. Policy fields today are teeming with pressure groups and lobbyists, often with their own policy departments or consultants. However, the research which they carry out tends to be geared to the short-term agendas and the timescales of campaigning and policy advocacy. Its aim is often to buttress arguments for existing policy positions rather than to evaluate evidence or identify and study alternative approaches. Likewise, policy research institutes and think tanks are also driven by short-term agendas. The impetus for the emergence of TJN and its agenda came from researchers and practitioners such as John Christensen and Richard Murphy,[18] who came to campaigning with a wealth of knowledge and experience of the issues.

Hence, my call is not for academics to become campaigners, far from it. I consider it to be much more important that they remain rooted in a commitment to research, especially from a critical perspective. There are many specialists at designing media campaigns and crafting snappy sound-bites, and other professionals, including lawyers and accountants making lucrative careers in fields such as international economic law. In my experience it is much more rewarding to aim to combine critical theory with some form of critical practice in this field.

These factors are even more crucial from the perspective of the global South. Regrettably, the challenges there are far greater. The impoverishment of universities drives their staff to take on outside work, often in the private sector, while many emigrate. Those who resist these temptations can get short-term

18 See his popular and influential blog, available online at: https://www.taxresearch.org.uk/Blog (accessed 13 May 2019).

funding for consultancies, but they must work to the agenda set by the funders (Faria, 2001). Indeed, those who build an expertise regarded as relevant to global policy concerns may even find themselves inundated with invitations 1to speak at meetings and conferences, but this hinders rather than helps their ability to continue sustained research work. A few outstanding institutions have endured, notably the Council for the Development of Social Science Research in Africa (CODESRIA), founded by Samir Amin in 1973. There are also outstanding public intellectuals and committed scholars, some of whom, such as Issa Shivji and Aki Sawyerr, have been my colleagues and friends, who are beacons for succeeding generations.

References

ActionAid, 2010. *Calling Time: Why SAB-Miller Should Stop Dodging Taxes in Africa.* ActionAID UK. Available online at: https://www.actionaid.org.uk/sites/default/files/doc_lib/calling_time_on_tax_avoidance.pdf (accessed 13 May 2019).

Arrighi, G. and Saul, J., 1968. Socialism and Economic Development in Tropical Africa. *Journal of Modern African Studies*, *6* (*2*), 141–169.

Arrighi, G. and Saul, J. (eds), 1973. *Essays on the Political Economy of Africa.* Monthly Review Press.

Bergin, T., 2012. Special Report: How Starbucks Avoids UK Taxes. Reuters. Available online at: http://uk.reuters.com/article/2012/10/15/us-britain-starbucks-tax-idUKBRE89E0EX20121015 (accessed 13 May 2019).

Bolton, D., 1985. *Nationalization – A Road to Socialism? The Lessons of Tanzania.* Zed Books.

Campbell, D. and Klaes, M., 2005. The Principle of Institutional Direction: Coase's Regulatory Critique of Intervention. *Cambridge Journal of Economics*, *29* (*2*), 263–288.

Campbell, D. and Picciotto, S., 2000. The Justification of Financial Futures Exchanges. In A. Hudson (ed.), *Modern Financial Techniques, Derivatives, and Law*, 16th edition. Kluwer Law International, pp. 121–133.

Coase, R., 1993. Coase on Posner on Coase and Concluding Comment. *Journal of Institutional and Theoretical Economics/Zeitschrift für die gesamte Staatswissenschaft*, *149* (*1*), 96–98.

Cooper, C., 2015. 6 Economists Who Predicted the Global Financial Crisis. *InTheBlack*. Available online at: http://www.intheblack.com/articles/2015/07/07/6-economists-who-predicted-the-global-financial-crisis-and-why-we-should-listen-to-them-from-now-on (accessed 13 May 2019).

Corporate Reform Collective, 2014. *Fighting Corporate Abuse: Beyond Predatory Capitalism.* Pluto Press.

Cox, R.W., 1981. Social Forces, States and World Orders: Beyond International Relations Theory. *Millennium*, *10* (*2*), 126–155.

Curtis, M., Ngowi, P., Waris, A., 2012. *The One Billion Dollar Question. How Can Tanzania Stop Losing So Much Tax Revenue?* Christian Council of Tanzania.

De Sousa Santos, B. and Rodriguez-Garavito, C.A., 2005. *Law and Globalization from Below: Towards a Cosmopolitan Legality.* Cambridge University Press.

Dezalay, Y. and Madsen, M.R., 2012. The Force of Law and Lawyers: Pierre Bourdieu and the Reflexive Sociology of Law. *Annual Review of Law and Social Science*, *8*, 433–452.

Drucker, J., 2010. Google 2.4% Rate Shows How $60 Billion Lost to Tax Loopholes. Bloomberg. Available online at: https://www.bloomberg.com/news/articles/2010-10-21/google-2-4-rate-shows-how-60-billion-u-s-revenue-lost-to-tax-loopholes (accessed 3 October 2019).

Dunning, J.H., 1988. *Explaining International Production*. Unwin Hyman.

Faria, J, 2001. Rent Seeking in Academia: The Consultancy Disease. *American Journal of Economics*, *45* (*2*), 69–74.

Faundez, J. and Picciotto, S., 1978. *The nationalization of multinationals in peripheral economies*. Macmillan.

Gereffi, G., 2014. Global Value-Chains in a Post-Washington-Consensus World. *Review of International Political Economy*, *21* (*1*), 9–37.

Gereffi, G. and Korzeniewicz, M. (eds), 1994. *Commodity Chains and Global Capitalism*. Praeger.

Hampton, M. and Abbott, J. (eds), 1999. *Offshore Finance Centres and Tax Havens: the Rise of Global Capital*. Palgrave Macmillan.

Held, D. 1995. *Democracy and the Global Order: From the Modern State to Cosmopolitan Governance*. Polity Press.

Held, D., McGrew, A., Goldblatt, D. and Perraton, J., 1999. *Global Transformations: Politics and Culture*. Polity Press.

Hirst, P. and Thompson, G., 1992. The Problem of 'Globalization': International Economic Relations, National Economic Management and the Formation of Trading Blocs. *Economy and Society*, *21*, 357–396.

Keck, M.E. and Sikkink, K., 1998. *Activists Beyond Borders. Advocacy Networks in International Politics*. Cornell University Press.

King, A. and Lenox, M., 2000. Industry Self-Regulation without Sanctions: The Chemical Industry's Responsible Care Program. *Academy of Management Journal*, *43* (*4*), 698–716.

Kocieniewski, D., 2011. G.E.'s Strategies Let It Avoid Taxes Altogether. *The New York Times*. Available online at: https://familyassetslegacy.com/wp-content/uploads/2012/09/G.E.s-Strategies-Let-It-Avoid-Taxes-Altogether-NYTimes.pdf (accessed 13 May 2019).

Kristensen, H. and Zeitlin, J., 2005. *Local Players in Global Games: The Strategic Constitution of a Multinational Corporation*. Oxford University Press.

Letto-Gillies, G., 2012. *Transnational Corporations and International Production: Concepts, Theories and Effects*. Edward Elgar.

Madsen, M., 2006. Transnational Fields: Elements of a Reflexive Sociology of the Internationalisation of Law. *Retfærd*, *29* (*3/114*), 23–41. Available online at: http://retfaerd.org/retfaerd-nr-114-20063/transnational-fields-elements-of-a-reflexive-sociology-of-the-internationalisation-of-law (accessed 21 August 2015).

Manin, B., 1994. The metamorphoses of representative government. *Economy & Society*, *23* (*2*), 133–171.

Manin, B., 1997. *The Principles of Representative Government*. Cambridge University Press.

Mayne, R. and Kimmis, J., 2000. *Tax Havens: Releasing the Hidden Billions for Poverty Eradication*. Briefing Paper. Oxfam.

Morris-Suzuki, T., 2000. For and Against NGOs. *New Left Review*, *2*, 63–84.

Murray, R., 1971. The Internationalization of Capital and the Nation State. *New Left Review*, *67*, 84–109.

OECD, 1998. *Harmful Tax Competition: An Emerging Global Issue*. Organisation for Economic Co-operation and Development. Available online at: http://www.oecd.org/tax/transparency/44430243.pdf (accessed 13 July 2015).

Partnoy, F. and Skeel Jr, D.A., 2007. The Promise and Perils of Credit Derivatives. *University of Cincinnati Law Review*, *75*, 1019–1051.

Penrose, E.T., 1951. *The Economics of the International Patent System*. Greenwood Press.

Picciotto, S., 1992. *International Business Taxation: A Study of the Internationalization of Business Regulation*. Quorum Books. Available online at: http://taxjustice.blogspot.be/2013/06/international-business-taxation.html (accessed 14 August 2015).

Picciotto, S., 1998. *Linkages in International Investment Regulation: The Antinomies of the Draft Multilateral Agreement on Investment. University of Pennsylvania Journal of International Economic Law*, *19* (*3*), 731–768.

Picciotto, S., 1999. Offshore: The State as Legal Fiction. In M. Hampton and J. Abbott (eds), *Offshore Finance Centres and Tax Havens: The Rise of Global Capital*. Palgrave Macmillan, p. 43.

Picciotto, S., 2010. International Transformations of the Capitalist State. *Antipode*, *43* (*1*), 87–107.

Picciotto, S., 2011. *Regulating Global Corporate Capitalism*. Cambridge University Press.

Picciotto, S., 2013. *Is the International Tax System Fit for Purpose, Especially for Developing Countries?* ICTD Working Paper 13. Available online at: http://www.ictd.ac/en/publications/international-tax-system-fit-purpose-especially-developing-countries (accessed 14 August 2015).

Picciotto, S., 2015. Indeterminacy, Complexity, Technocracy and the Reform of International Corporate Taxation. *Social & Legal Studies*, *24* (*2*), 165–184.

Picciotto, S., 2017. Regulation: Managing the Antinomies of Economic Vice and Virtue. *Social & Legal Studies*, *26* (*6*), 676–699.

Picciotto, S., 2018. International Tax, Regulatory Arbitrage and the Growth of Transnational Corporations. *Transnational Corporations*, *25* (*3*), 27–53.

Picciotto, S. and Mayne, R. (eds), 1999. *Regulating International Business. Beyond Liberalization*. Macmillan.

Picciotto, S., Gallardo, A., Kadet, J., Henn, M. and Villanueva, M., 2017. *The G20 and the 'Base Erosion and Profit Shifting (BEPS) Project'*. German Development Institute/Deutsches Institut für Entwicklungspolitik (DIE).

Ritzer, G., 2008. *The McDonaldization of Society*. Pine Forge.

Rosenberg, J., 2005. Globalization Theory: A Post Mortem. *International Politics*, *42* (*1*), 2–74.

Sarat, A. and Silbey, S., 1988. The Pull of the Policy Audience. *Law & Policy*, *10* (2–3): 97–166.

Shivji, I., 1986. *Limits of Legal Radicalism: Reflections on Teaching Law at the University of Dar es Salaam*. University of Dar es Salaam.

Sivanandan, A. and Wood, E., 1997. Capitalism, Globalization and Epochal Shifts: An Exchange. *Monthly Review*, *48* (*9*), 19–33.
Stahl, T., 2013. What is Immanent Critique? SSRN. Available online at: http://ssrn.com/abstract=2357957 (accessed 13 July 2015).
Strange, S. (ed.), 1984. *Paths to International Political Economy.* Allen & Unwin.
Tooze, A., 2018., *Crashed: How a Decade of Financial Crises Changed the World.* Penguin
UK Parliament, 2012. *Report on HMRC's 2011–2012 Accounts.* HC 716. Public Accounts Committee.
UNITAR, 1984. *Progressive Development of the Principles and Norms of International Law Relating to the New International Economic Order.* United Nations Institute for Training and Research.
US Senate, 2012. *Offshore Profit Shifting and the U.S. Tax Code.* Committee on Homeland Security & Governmental Affairs, Permanent Subcommittee on Investigations. Available online at: http://www.hsgac.senate.gov/subcommittees/investigations/hearings/offshore-profit-shifting-and-the-us-tax-code (accessed 13 May 2019).
Vogel, S., 1996. *Freer Markets, More Rules.* Cornell University Press.
Warren, J.N., 2014. Tax is the Lifeblood of Democracy: An Interview with John Christensen of the Tax Justice Network. *Spirit of Contradiction.* Available online at: http://spiritofcontradiction.eu/niebuhr/2014/08/18/interview-with-john-christensen-of-the-tax-justice-network (accessed 13 July 2015).

Part III

Global governance and justice

Chapter 8

Between Bandung and Doha

International economic law and developing countries

Julio Faundez[*]

Introduction

The Bandung Conference of 1955 is generally regarded as the beginning of a period when developing countries, through concerted action, began to make their presence felt in the international arena, reaffirming their political independence and demanding more effective international assistance for their development objectives. Their efforts were rewarded when, in 1974, the United Nations General Assembly adopted a series of resolutions calling for the establishment of a new international economic order. That success, however, was short-lived. Not long after the approval of these resolutions, the spirit that animated the Bandung process was swept aside by the unstoppable energy of the emerging neoliberal economic orthodoxy. Today, after more than three decades of neoliberal globalisation, the Bandung process seems anachronistic and of little interest, other than as a reminder of the quaint state-centric approach to development prevailing in the aftermath of the Second World War. Lawyers with a critical inclination might also dismiss the Bandung process as a misguided belief in the capacity of International law to address the problems of developing countries. From the perspective of neoliberal globalisation, it is easy to dismiss the demands made by developing countries in the 1970s as ludicrously impractical. Today, who can realistically expect that multinationals should be legally liable for their activities in developing countries or to pay a fair share of taxes to the countries where they extract natural resources? Such demands are likely to be promptly dismissed as imprudent on the basis that they would scare foreign investors. Likewise, the notion that multinationals should transfer technology to developing countries to help them develop capacity to compete with foreign investors would be regarded as equally unrealistic. It thus seems that neoliberalism has forever buried the spirit that animated the Bandung process. Despite

[*]A slightly different version of this chapter was published by Cambridge University Press in 2017 in *Bandung, Global History and International Law*, a collection edited by Luis Eslava, Michael Fakhri and Vasuki Nesiah.

claims about the benefits of liberal globalisation, the underlying issues that prompted the Bandung process persist and even moderate voices such as United Nations Conference on Trade and Development (UNCTAD), the United Nations Department of Social Development and the International Labour Office (ILO) have expressed concern about the negative consequences of the current global governance framework on the economic growth prospects of developing countries (UNCTAD, 2011; United Nations, 2010; ILO, 2008). It is also a matter of concern that the institutions of neoliberal globalisation such as the WTO, the World Bank and IMF seem unable to act to arrest the impact of climate change, especially among the most vulnerable people in the developing world. Despite the strength and validity of these concerns, promoters of neoliberal globalisation have little reason to fear that the spirit that animated the Bandung process will re-emerge as a destabilising factor in the global economy, not least because other political and economic events are doing that anyway.

From an academic perspective, however, to dismiss the Bandung process as the product of naïve or misguided nationalism is short-sighted because it ignores the then prevailing historical conditions. It is mistaken to attribute the failure of the process to the ideology of modernisation (Amin, 2011; Berger, 2004) or to the action of left-wing political movements which pushed governments into making unreasonable demands, especially on matters concerning sovereignty over natural resources (Johnson, 1976; Sacerdoti, 2011; Schrijver, 2009). To understand the Bandung process, it is necessary to take into account the international context during the Cold War, when issues of international security between the two superpowers took precedence over all other matters. As a consequence, as I explain below, developing countries had some flexibility to determine the content and direction of their economic policies. This flexibility did not directly challenge the interests of multinationals, which were few in number and whose activities were largely confined to mining and agriculture (Dunning and Lundan, 2008: 145–97). The UN also provided developing countries with a platform to voice their aspirations and press for the adoption of resolutions that reflected their interests. Between the end of the Second World War and the mid-1970s, developing countries consequently had considerable influence in shaping important areas of international law. This influence is unsurprising, since UN membership trebled, from 51 states in 1945 to 152 in 1979, and all but a handful of these new members had been colonial territories. By 1960, the Afro-Asian bloc, together with Latin American countries, had a clear majority in the General Assembly and made use of their voting power (Emerson, 1965). They strongly supported decolonisation and made an important contribution to the process that brought to an end the colonial rule of recalcitrant powers such as Portugal and the apartheid regime in South Africa. They also managed to introduce important changes to the rules governing international trade. These gains, though modest, were aimed at preventing principles of free trade from undermining their economic development objectives. After successfully lobbying for the establishment of the UNCTAD in 1964, developing countries secured the passage of a series of General

Assembly resolutions on economic development, culminating in 1974 with the adoption of a UN Declaration calling for the establishment of a New International Economic Order. This declaration is based on the following principles: (1) the right of states to choose their own economic and social system on the basis of sovereign equality; (2) full and effective participation in solving world economic problems on the basis of the equality of all countries; (3) the right of every country to adopt economic and social systems it deems appropriate for its own development; (4) full and permanent sovereignty over natural resources and economic activities free from external coercion; (5) just and equitable relationship between the prices of raw materials exported by developing countries and primary commodities, manufactures, capital goods and equipment imported by them; (6) extension of assistance to developing countries free of political or military conditions; (7) preferential and non-reciprocal treatment for developing countries in all fields of international economic co- operation; and (8) access to the achievements of modern science and technology, and the promotion of technology transfer (UN General Assembly, 1974b).

This chapter explains the legal and political dilemmas facing developing countries during the Cold War and contrasts them with the international position today. The first part, covering the period between the Bandung Conference and the adoption of the UN General Assembly resolutions on the New International Economic Order, shows how developing countries managed to come together and influence the development of international law. The second part, which focuses on the legal framework of economic globalisation, identifies the main factors responsible for the demise of the Bandung spirit among developing countries. In particular, it focuses on the legal strategies employed by developed countries to deepen the process of globalisation and on the divisive consequences of global economic integration on developing countries.

International law and policy space during the Cold War

The main concern of the 29 countries represented at the Bandung Conference (23 Asian and six African countries) was to ensure that the superpowers and their former colonial powers would respect their sovereignty and political independence (Heuser, 1986). They reaffirmed their adherence to the principle of collective security but rejected military alliances that served the interests of the superpowers. Although the Bandung countries were unable to organise a follow-up conference, the Bandung spirit was taken up by the non-aligned movement (NAM), a larger group of developing countries established in 1961 (Bedjaoui, 1986). The NAM was a diffuse group of developing countries linked by their concern with economic development and their desire to distance themselves from the ideological and political rifts between the superpowers. They therefore insisted that greater attention should be paid to the division between rich and poor countries and that industrialised countries should firmly commit to reform rules governing international trade, investment and finance to facilitate growth and development for all (Fatouros, 1964). A defining moment in the Bandung process was the Cairo Conference on the Problems of Developing Countries held outside the framework of the UN, which brought Afro-Asian and Latin American countries together for the first time. The Conference called for comprehensive restructuring of the rules governing international trade and economic relations between developed and developing countries (Toye, 2014: 1760). This plea was especially appealing to Latin American countries, which shared the same frustration as the Afro-Asian countries, but had endured these rules for much longer and were still trying to find successful paths to economic development more than a century after independence.

A common complaint about the consequences of contemporary globalisation is that the flood of international rules generated by the imperatives of deregulation and liberalisation has significantly restricted the policy space of developing countries. If this assessment is correct, it would paradoxically appear that the position of developing countries during the Cold War was more auspicious. During that period, the economic model followed by developing countries outside the Soviet bloc was import substitution – a model that was largely inward looking and without major international repercussions since developing countries were not fully integrated into the world economy. Thus, they had room for manoeuvre in the design of their economic policies. This space might explain why they could establish relatively durable coalitions in support of their common economic demands. Indeed, they were all trying to modernise their agricultural sectors and to establish a manufacturing base to consolidate and expand their national markets, their demands were similar and therefore not divisive. They wanted fair prices for their natural resources and agricultural exports, preferential access to developed country markets for their manufactures, technology transfer, greater voice in international financial decisions, sound investment regimes that would generate sufficient resources to invest in other sectors of the economy, and more effective technical mechanisms for the disbursement of economic aid. The similarity and relative simplicity of their economic aspirations during this period explains the durability of their coalitions. Developing countries, however, had to lobby hard within the UN and other international organisations to persuade rich countries that development deserved a place on the international agenda (UNCTAD, 2004). The tortuous diplomatic relations between Latin America and the US illustrates this point.

Latin American countries requested economic assistance from the US from the beginning of the Cold War. In 1947, during negotiations leading to the signature of the Rio Treaty of Reciprocal Assistance, Latin American countries asked US Secretary of State George Marshall to establish a 'Marshall Plan' for Latin America similar to the famous reconstruction programme he had recently launched for Europe. Marshall rejected the request, arguing that security not development was the priority for the region (Keesing's, 1946–8). Two years later, when President Truman launched a development aid programme – the so-called Point IV Programme – the amount allocated by the US Congress for the rest of the world amounted to 1 per cent of the sum allocated to Europe under the Marshall Plan (Maier, 2010: 49). Latin American countries did not give up. In 1948, a year after Marshall dismissed their request for comprehensive economic support, they persuaded the US to accept the Economic Agreement of Bogota, a multilateral treaty that set out their economic aspirations in considerable detail (Connell-Smith, 1960: 454). The US signed this treaty but did not take it seriously. Throughout the 1950s, Latin American states repeatedly requested financial and technical support for development, and the US continued to invoke security considerations to deflect their requests. It was not until after the Cuban Revolution of 1959 and the CIA's botched attempt to overthrow Fidel Castro in 1961 that the US government, through John Kennedy's Alliance for Progress Programme, began to show signs that it understood that left-wing political movements were not instigated by the Soviet Union but were instead prompted by the grossly unequal prevailing distribution of economic and political power (Dunne, 2011; 2013). The Alliance for Progress was an attempt by the US to discourage Latin American countries from establishing closer links with Afro-Asian countries in the Bandung process (Toye, 2014: 1760).

By the early 1960s, as membership of the UN expanded, developing countries voiced their economic demands in the General Assembly and other international fora. The two main points that brought developing countries together in relation to international trade were their lack of access to the markets of industrialised countries and unfair terms of trade reflected in the persistent decline in the prices of their primary product exports compared with the prices of their manufactured product imports (Kunibert and Singer, 2001: 16–31). In 1964, developing countries therefore established the Group of 77 (G-77) and persuaded the UN to establish the UN Conference on Trade and Development (UNCTAD). These events provided the impetus for the movement that led to the series of General Assembly resolutions on the NIEO, which culminated in 1974 in the adoption of the Charter of Economic Rights of States (UN General Assembly, 1974a). This resolution, adopted by an overwhelming majority, was firmly rejected by the leading industrialised countries. Afterwards, developing country activism declined and gave way as they capitulated to neoliberalism as the dominant ideology in the global economy.

Although the argument that the Cold War was kind to developing countries because it allowed them a degree of flexibility to choose and implement economic policies might be appealing, it is also misleading. During the Cold War the principle of multilateralism was widely proclaimed as the foundation of the post-war settlement. The UN Security Council was entrusted with responsibility for managing collective security and formally entrusted with the monopoly of the use of force to repel acts of aggression. Under the UN Charter, the use of force by states or regional blocks was prohibited unless authorised by the Security Council (Hoffmann, 1970; Tsagourias and White, 2013). However, this ideal was never realised because the rift between the US and the Soviet Union paralysed the Council. Consequently, regional security pacts controlled by either of the superpowers emerged as alternative mechanisms used by the superpowers to protect their respective interests. Regional pacts protected the external security of their members and were used to ensure that the political regime of these states was aligned with the economic interests and ideology of the respective superpower (Fenwick, 1949; Miller, 1967). In the West, under the sway of import substitution, developing countries were allowed to design their own economic policies on condition that this did not upset the prevailing alignment of forces at the international level. Real or alleged socialist policies were thus ruled out of order on the basis that they were incompatible with regional peace and security. The situation was far stricter within the Soviet bloc, where countries were required to implement policies based on the USSR model. They were not allowed to open their economy to market mechanisms, and those that defied this rule were promptly and forcefully disciplined, as happened in Hungary in 1956 and Czechoslovakia in 1968. Similarly, the US forcefully suppressed any attempt to establish a political regime deemed to pose a threat to its political values or economic interests. Although the US preferred to assert its power through the Organization of American States (such as the political crises in Guatemala in 1954, and the Dominican Republic in 1965), it resorted to unilateral use of force (Bay of Pigs in 1961) and covert action (Chile in 1973) when other mechanisms were unavailable (Fenwick, 1966; Organization of American States, 1965; Schmeltzer, 1970; Slater, 1964).

To protect their interests, the superpowers stretched the concept of region beyond its ordinary geographical meaning, transforming it into a flexible political concept that created frontiers defined by the reach of their respective ideologies. This approach, which was blatantly inconsistent with the collective security ideal in the UN Charter, prevailed over the rule that prohibited enforcement measures unless authorised by the Security Council. Self-defence and containment through regional political pacts were regularly invoked to protect their spheres of influence (Wright, 1957). The legal arguments used by the US in defence of its ill-fated intervention in Vietnam provide an eloquent illustration of the manipulation of international law during the Cold War (Meeker, 1966; Falk, 1966; Friedmann, 1967, 1969). At least the US attempted to justify its actions in legal terms, unlike the Soviet Union. In 1968, in a speech at the United Nations, Soviet Foreign Minister Andrei Gromyko justified the invasion of Czechoslovakia by arguing that: '[T]he Soviet Union and other socialist countries have on many occasions warned those who are tempted to try and roll back the socialist commonwealth, to snatch at least one link from it, that we will neither tolerate nor allow this to happen' (cited in Jackson, 1969: 111; see also Goodman 1969).

At Bandung in 1955, the question of regional alliances with the superpowers was firmly rejected on the ground that such alliances were inconsistent with the principle of collective security in the UN Charter. In 1954, a few months before the Conference, India's prime minister Jawaharlal Nehru categorically declined an invitation to participate in the establishment of the South-East Treaty Organization (SEATO) because, in his view, it was a military alliance rather than a genuine collective security agreement (Acharya, 2011: 106). Nehru's concern proved accurate, as contemporaneous developments in Latin America demonstrated. In that region, the 1947 Rio Treaty of Reciprocal Assistance provided the US with a convenient legal mechanism to safeguard its economic and political interests and to intervene with impunity in regional political affairs (Connell-Smith, 1960; García-Amador, 1985). Coincidentally, just as Nehru was denouncing SEATO, the US was using the Rio Treaty to justify the overthrow of the democratically elected government of Guatemala that was attempting to introduce agrarian reform. The land distribution proposed by the Guatemalan government affected land owned by notorious US-owned United Fruit Company. Prior to organising the overthrow of the elected government, the US persuaded Latin American countries in the OAS to adopt a resolution at the Tenth Inter-American Conference declaring the influence of international communism in the region to be a threat to the integrity of Latin American states and incompatible with American notion of freedom. The Guatemalan delegate noted that the alleged threat of communism was a ploy to justify the suppression of the legitimate aspirations of Latin American people. He predicted that the resolution would place the Inter-American system at the service of US political and economic interests (Unión Panamericana, 1954). Sadly, this prediction proved accurate. Three months after it was passed, a group of exiled 'freedom fighters' sponsored and organised by the US overthrew the Guatemalan government and installed a dictatorship which promptly restored the expropriated land to United Fruit and violently repressed and killed supporters of the deposed government and trade union leaders (Cullather, 1999).

Throughout the Cold War the US continued to use the Inter-American system to oppose and, if necessary, overthrow left-leaning governments that posed a real or imaginary threat to their interests or to the interests of local elites. The attempt by the US to overthrow Fidel Castro in 1961 (Bay of Pigs invasion), which was modelled on the Guatemala episode, further discredited US foreign policy among some of the progressive Governments in the region, but did not prevent Washington from intervening directly (Grenada in 1983) or indirectly (Chile in 1970–3; Nicaragua in 1981) to rid the continent of even the remote possibility of left-wing groups taking power in the region. Thus, although superficially the Cold War seemed to provide developing countries with ample room to pursue their economic and political objectives, this was not the case. During this period the two superpowers defined their security interests so broadly that regional collective security arrangements became powerful devices that enabled them to impose political and economic policies consistent with their own conception of security, giving them licence to override any political or economic choice that, in their view, might pose a threat to their interests. Thus, from this perspective, the policy prescriptions of the Washington Consensus seem positively mild, even progressive.

The paradox of globalisation: economic integration and political fragmentation

Contemporary neoliberal globalisation demands a drastic reduction of the role of the state on the assumption that the private sector is the main engine of economic growth. Thus, while deregulation and liberalisation substantially reduce the size and functions of the state, the role of contract law and property rights in economic growth has increased. Private sector development and improvements to the contents and enforcement of private law are long-standing priorities for the World Bank and IMF. This focus is justified on the basis that states are the main obstacle to successful integration of the global economy. In the early 1980s, at a time when World Bank economists were beginning to develop the current model of globalisation, they concluded that economic stagnation in developing countries and the endless succession of financial crises were caused by flawed domestic policies, rather than by the inadequacy of the institutions of global governance (Yusuf, 2009: 24). This analysis prompted the launch of the renowned structural adjustment loans, which required developing countries to introduce radical changes to public institutions to reduce state involvement in the economy. This policy objective is reflected in the new rules governing international trade, investment and finance. The combined effect of these reforms has been to transfer power over key economic decisions from nation states to the international sphere. This shift, which has brought about a fundamental transformation to the foundations of international law, has disconcerted developing countries since, from their perspective, globalisation seems to have covertly seized a massive slice of their hitherto much valued economic sovereignty. While it is true that globalisation has reduced the economic sovereignty of all countries, rich and poor, large and small, its impact on developing countries is magnified because, with the exception of the so-called emerging economies, these countries have little or no influence in the design or implementation of these rules.

Discontent among developing countries over current rules of international economic law is expressed in the demand for greater policy space, with the argument that policy space has shrunk because of WTO agreements and bilateral investment treaties' prevalence over domestic policy concerns. Within the WTO the principle of free trade generally overrides any domestic policy that might, even indirectly, restrict the flow of trade. Likewise, bilateral investment treaties offer such sweeping protection to the property rights of foreign investors that states can no longer be certain whether the exercise of ordinary regulatory powers might constitute a breach of international law.

The call to enhance the policy space of developing countries is endorsed, albeit very generally, by UNCTAD and the UN Department for Social Affairs (UNCTAD, 2008, 2011; United Nations, 2010). Development economists and governance specialists have also support developing countries' demand for greater policy flexibility (Akyuz, 2010; Amsden, 2003; Montes, 2014; Nayyar, 2013; Wade, 2003). Prominent among these scholars is Ha-Joon Chang, who argues that restricting the policy space of developing countries through the new rules of international economic law amounts to kicking away the ladder so that the others are unable to make use of the policy instruments that enabled rich countries to achieve their current status (Chang, 2002, 2012).

Fragile coalitions

In recent years, developing countries have been engaged in important multilateral negotiations on a range of issues relating to trade, climate change, regional integration, and intellectual property. These negotiations, mainly those under the umbrella of the WTO Doha round, have provided developing countries with numerous opportunities to establish coalitions, which they have readily taken. Most of these coalitions, however, have been short-lived and their efficacy has been uncertain. The fragility of these coalitions can be explained by the complexity and scope of the international agenda, which has contributed to uncovering countless policy divisions among developing countries. These policy divisions, a consequence of their diverse economic structures and different levels of development, are undoubtedly welcomed by the promoters of neoliberal globalisation as they serve to reassure them that the type of concerted action that led to the call for a new international economic order will never again resurface. Thus, ironically, while global integration brings national economies closer together, it also generates widespread and unexpected divisions that pull developing countries apart. I illustrate this point by reference to the current Doha Development Round.

The failure to conclude the Doha Development Round cannot be attributed to the reluctance of developing countries seriously to engage in negotiations or to seek solutions through the establishment of coalitions. Indeed, the Doha process brought about the establishment of 26 negotiating coalitions, of which 16 consist entirely of developing countries (Narlikar, 2013: 863; Tussie, 2013). Thus, the problem is not that developing countries have been uninvolved in coalitions, but rather that the complexity and breadth of the negotiations creates divisions among them. During the GATT years, solidarity among developing countries was easy to nourish since their demands were relatively simple. In 1965, Part IV of the GATT introduced the concept of non-reciprocity, according to which developing countries were not expected to reciprocate to tariff concessions made by developed countries. In 1971, the GATT approved the Generalized System of Preferences, a waiver of the Most Favored Nation (MFN) clause that later became a permanent fixture of the GATT under the so-called Enabling Clause. These were important mechanisms that clearly favoured the trading interests of developing countries. Compared to the simplicity of the development agenda of the 1960s, the complexity of the current Doha Round is astonishing. It consists of more than 30 items, including longstanding difficult topics such as agriculture, dumping, subsidies, intellectual property, services and environment. It is therefore unsurprising that the negotiations have encountered serious obstacles. From the point of view of developing countries, these obstacles are caused by the sheer breadth of an agenda that encompasses a range of conflicting economic and political interests – which did not arise when trade negotiations largely involved exchanging tariff concessions on a limited number of products. As a consequence, developing countries now often find themselves in alliance with developed countries: in coalitions with exporters of agricultural products (the Cairns Group) or, as part of the Friends of Fish, in coalitions with developed countries that export fish (Najam et al., 2007: 13).

An unexpectedly high level of solidarity among developing countries was displayed at the Cancún Ministerial Meeting in 2003, at which developing countries formed the G 20+ coalition, led by influential countries such as Brazil, South Africa, India, Argentina and China (Matthews, 2007). The G20+ was instrumental in rejecting a compromise proposal on agriculture prepared by the USA and the EU (Najam et al., 2007: 31). At Cancún, developing countries also successfully managed to remove from the Doha agenda three of the four issues introduced at the 1996 Ministerial meeting in Singapore – the so-called Singapore issues of investment, competition and procurement. Trade facilitation remained on the agenda and an agreement on this issue was concluded at the ministerial meeting in Bali in 2013 and entered into force on 22 February 2017. It should also be noted that in 2003 African countries achieved an important victory on public health when they persuaded the WTO to approve a temporary waiver allowing poor countries that do not have manufacturing capacity to import generic drugs made under compulsory licensing (Hoekman and Mavroidis, 2007: 72–6). In 2005, the waiver was transformed into an amendment of the TRIPS Agreement and thus made permanent.

Some observers have considered the possibility that India, Brazil and South Africa (the so-called IBSA countries) might become leaders of a coalition of developing countries as they are important global economic players. Their combined population is more than 1.2 billion and GDP more than $1.3 trillion (Cheru, 2011: 46). Nevertheless, there is justified scepticism as to whether the IBSA countries can effectively represent the interests of all developing countries. Because of their size and level of development, their interests are markedly different from those of the majority of developing countries, especially Least Developed Countries (LDCs), making it unlikely that they could faithfully champion the latter's interests. Even among themselves IBSA countries have divergent trading interests. Brazil, as a member of the Cairns Group, is a strong proponent of market access for agriculture, while India is less enthusiastic, since it has a large subsistence farming sector. South Africa, a food exporter, has conflicting interests with many African countries dependent on food imports (Cheru, 2011: 48). The IBSA countries, plus China and Russia, form the so-called BRICS. They have constituted themselves as a group and are seeking to play a role in reforming global economic relations. In terms of the Doha negotiations, however, the BRICS, for reasons similar to the IBSA countries, do not represent the interests of the vast majority of developing countries. As John Toye explains, the BRICS are more interested in building links between themselves than in leading a coalition of developing countries (2014: 1772).

Even leading developing countries, such as Brazil and India, seem unable or unwilling to provide the required leadership, as evidenced by the failure of the so-called G4 group. In 2007, the Director General of the WTO, along with the USA and the EU, invited India and Brazil to establish an informal group to break the deadlock in the negotiations on agriculture. The negotiations failed, and India and Brazil were strongly criticised by the Africa, Caribbean and Pacific (ACP) countries on the familiar ground that the negotiations had not been transparent and that neither India nor Brazil could effectively represent the interests of developing countries (Odofile, 2011: 92). An ACP Minister stated that '[A]lthough two developing countries are part of the G4, we cannot expect them to carry the responsibility of representing the views and positions of all developing countries. We have been told that the Geneva multilateral process is central, but without knowledge of the political or technical aspects of the G4 negotiations, it is not possible for the majority of members to prepare themselves or provide inputs' (cited in Odofile, 2011: 92). Similar views were expressed by African Ministers in 2009, who acknowledged the value of informal consultations but warned that they were not 'a substitute for a genuine multilateral process, nor should they affect the consensus reached within the multilateral context. We also stress the need for Africa's full participation in all negotiating processes based on balanced and consensually agreed agendas' (Odofile, 2011: 93).

The complexity of the Doha negotiations thus exposed divisions and conflicting interests between developing countries. Although they seem to prefer multilateral rather than bilateral negotiations, the Doha process is a strong reminder that under current conditions the multilateral route does not guarantee outcomes acceptable to all developing countries. It is possible, as some argue, that the label "developing country" is rapidly becoming meaningless (Sumner and Vásquez, 2014; Pauwelyn, 2013). Though not entirely unfounded, this is an overstatement.

Bilateralism and regionalism revived

The failure to complete the Doha Round undermined the status of the WTO, but did not reduce the determination of the promoters of neoliberalism to pursue their objectives. Indeed, though proclaiming adherence to the ideal of multilateralism, they shifted their approach and began to rely on bilateral treaties and regional arrangements. This approach proved useful during the Cold War because the two superpowers had to protect their respective spheres of influence. Today, however, bilateral and regional agreements are used to further the neoliberal agenda, despite contradicting the principle of multilateralism.

Bilateralism was successful in strengthening the rules on the protection of foreign investment. Indeed, the current prominence of bilateral investment treaties (BITs) is, undoubtedly, one of the most remarkable legal developments of the past decades. Since their inception in the 1970s, BITs have spread at a rapid pace. Today there are nearly 3,000 BITs and most countries regard them as indispensable for attracting foreign investment. BITs are similarly structured and, superficially, seemingly innocuous. By signing BITs, states agree to provide fair and equitable treatment to investors and to protect them against arbitrary expropriation. What transformed BITs into a powerful and practically autonomous international mechanism is the clause – common to all BITs – that allows private investors to bring claims against the state before international arbitral tribunals. In recent years investors have made prolific use of this clause, giving rise to hundreds of claims against states, most of which are developing countries. The arbitration awards resulting from these claims have further strengthened and enhanced the scope of investors' rights, since arbitrators are generally commercial lawyers with little understanding or interest in development issues. The literature on BITs arbitration is vast and need not detain us here (see Muchlinski, 2010; Schill, 2011; Tung, 2010; Vandevelde, 2009).

It is important to note, however, that the remarkable changes brought about by BITs would probably not have been achieved through multilateral negotiations. Since the end of the Second World War, there have been two attempts to set up a multilateral mechanism to protect and promote foreign investment. The first attempt was during the negotiations leading to the adoption of the Charter of the International Trade Organization (ITO). As Robert Drache (2000) argues, the distinctive feature of the ITO was that it sought to integrate traditional trade topics with investment, employment and business topics. The second attempt was in the mid-1990s, following the successful conclusion of the Uruguay round that led to the creation of the WTO. The OECD attempted to build on the growing consensus on investment by opening up negotiations among its members with a view to establishing a Multilateral Agreement on Investment (MAI). Although developing countries were not involved in the MAI negotiations, the initiative failed largely because of divisions among OECD members, but also because of pressure by international NGOs (Picciotto, 1999; Sornarajah, 2010: 25).

The failure of the MAI negotiations highlights the shortcomings of multilateral negotiations. Indeed, one of the reasons why they failed is that the multilateral framework encouraged parties to bring into the agenda a variety of issues, such as human rights, environmental protection and the safeguard of cultural values, which diverted attention from the main purpose of the negotiations. By contrast, in a bilateral context, it is easier, through a combination of incentives and threats, to persuade partners, especially developing countries, to accept rules that they would be reluctant to accept in multilateral negotiations (Guzman, 2009).

The GATT Agreement embraced multilateralism in international trade in 1948. Under GATT, the expectation was that trade liberalisation would be progressively achieved through centralised and non-discriminatory trading concessions based upon the most favoured-nation and the national treatment principles. Article XXIV of the GATT, however, allowed departures from these principles in cases where the Contracting Parties decided to establish a closer economic union through regional trade agreements (RTAs), which GATT describes as either free trade areas or customs unions. Parties to RTAs agree either to eliminate duties on specified products or to impose lower duties than those applied on these products to third States. RTAs are, thus, inconsistent with the principle of non-discrimination. Departure from this principle is justified, however, because RTAs are regarded as 'building blocks' in establishing a fully comprehensive multilateral trading system (OECD, 2003). According to this argument, countries are likely to make more generous concessions in bilateral than in multilateral contexts, but once they make these concessions, they will, in due course, extend them to other GATT members, thus reinforcing the principle of multilateralism (Baldwin, 2014; Bhagwati, 2008). In the past the validity of this argument was not questioned because, before the establishment of the WTO, RTAs were not extensively used and, as such, were not regarded as a threat to multilateralism.

Since the establishment of the WTO, however, RTAs assumed enormous importance, both as a means of securing preferential market access and as a device to secure compliance with regulatory standards not traditionally associated with free trade agreements (Lester and Mercurio, 2009). Thus, while in 1990, internal trade of RTAs accounted for only 18% of world trade in goods, in 2008 it accounted for more than 35% (WTO, 2011: 7). Taking into account intra-EU trade, these percentages increased to 28% in 1990 and 50% in 2008 (Bhagwati et al., 2014: 11). Since tariffs across the board have been greatly reduced, the scope for further tariff reduction through RTAs is limited. As a consequence, today RTAs are used as mechanisms to bring about 'deep integration' (Lejárraga, 2014). The WTO identifies two types of deep integration provisions: WTO +, in areas covered by the WTO, and WTO X, in areas not covered by the WTO. WTO + provisions include tariffs, technical barriers to trade, services, intellectual property and trade-related investment measures. WTO X provisions cover areas such as competition policy, investment and capital movement. RTAs thus enable developed countries to persuade developing countries to accept obligations that they rejected during the Doha negotiations (United Nations, 2010: 89).

In recent years, and partly in response to the collapse of the Doha process, the United States, Japan and the European Union have launched more ambitious negotiations to achieve mega trade deals involving large developed countries and important middle income countries from Asia and Latin America (Lewis, 2017; Velut et al., 2018). One of these initiatives was the Trans-Pacific Partnership (TPP), launched by President Obama, which involved twelve countries from the Asia-Pacific region (Australia, Brunei, Chile, Canada, Japan, Malaysia, Mexico, New Zealand, Peru, Singapore, the United States and Vietnam). Although the Trump administration rejected the TPP, the remaining 11 members concluded the agreement, now called the Comprehensive and Progressive Agreement for

Trans-Pacific Partnership, often described as the TPP-11. This Agreement entered into force in December 2018. Another mega trade deal, also negotiated outside the framework of the WTO, is the Trade in Services Agreement (TISA). TISA negotiations include the European Union plus 23 other countries, both developed and developing countries (Australia, Canada, Chile, Chinese Taipei, Colombia, Costa Rica, the EU, Hong Kong China, Iceland, Israel, Japan, Korea, Liechtenstein, Mauritius, Mexico, New Zealand, Norway, Pakistan, Panama, Peru, Switzerland, Turkey and the United States). The expectation is that once concluded the TISA Agreement will be embraced by the WTO and its members.

The foregoing shows that the WTO's failure to conclude the Doha round did not prevent attempts by leading developed countries to further the process of globalisation through deeper economic integration. The objective of mega trade deals, such as the Comprehensive and Progressive Agreement for Trans-Pacific Partnership and TISA, is to cover all trade-related areas, going beyond those covered by the WTO and beyond most bilateral free-trade agreements currently in force (Bhagwati, 2013). Thus, in content, these agreements are undoubtedly WTO X. In terms of their ambition they could be described as open regionalism agreements, because the intention is that, in due course, other countries will embrace their rules and practices. Interestingly, the proponents of the ill-fated MAI Agreement had a similar aspiration. They expected the MAI Agreement to codify the state-of-the-art investment rules, which non-MAI members would be obliged to follow. It is, of course, too early to ascertain whether the aim of the mega trade deals will materialise. What is clear, however, is that if it does, the majority of developing countries that are currently not parties to these trade deals will have to accept international rules and disciplines that they did not make. This is regrettable, but, unfortunately, neither surprising nor novel. Thus, it is difficult to disagree with Jagdish Bhagwati's conclusion that developed countries, which set international rules to serve their economic interests, are making use of trade negotiations to harvest developing country markets (Bhagwati et al., 2014: 23). This process is slowly but surely burying the ideal of a level playing field within a multilateral legal framework. It is also making it increasingly difficult for developing countries to have a say, let alone establish viable coalitions, in the international field.

Conclusion

The Bandung Conference of 1955 marked the beginning of a 20-year period of concerted international action by developing countries, in which they succeeded in placing development firmly on the international agenda. They also made a significant contribution towards securing United Nations' support for the process of decolonisation. During this period, however, the conflicting interpretations of international security by the two superpowers took precedence over matters relating to international economic cooperation. The relative disregard of economic issues provided developing countries with space to engage in collective action in support of their demands for a more equitable international economic order. An important feature of this period was that the rules and principles of international economic law were mainly concerned with procedural rather than substantive aspects of economic policies.

The end of the Cold War and the inception of economic globalisation brought about a remarkable reversal of international priorities. Since politics and security considerations were no longer an obstacle to the expansion of markets, international organisations, led by the World Bank and the IMF, required states in developing countries to adapt their institutions to the expanding international markets. As deregulation and liberalisation were implemented at the national level, a proliferation of new principles, rules and disciplines consolidated the process of economic globalisation at the international level. As noted above, the expansion of international economic law had two important consequences for developing countries: first, it diminished their capacity to formulate economic policies, since key areas of national economic policy fell within the scope of international disciplines; and second, it highlighted important divisions among them because of the breadth of the matters covered by international disciplines. Thus, one of the unintended consequences of economic globalisation is that, as developing countries become more closely integrated into the global economy, they become more fragmented and find it more difficult to form durable alliances.

Although conditions for developing countries are today radically different from 60 years ago, at the time of the Bandung Conference, globalisation's evolution is rapidly exposing the simplistic assumptions held by its political promoters. The expansion of markets across the world is not only reducing the capacity of developing countries to act in unison, it is also exposing divisions among rich countries, empowering new actors (China), reopening old rivalries (US/EU/Russia), revealing the weakness of seemingly strong emergent powers (India and Brazil) and exposing the international community's inability to manage conflict. It is doubtful whether today's worldwide intractable political scenario will benefit many developing countries. Unfortunately, most of the underlying economic and political issues that prompted the unity of developing countries in the 1950s and 1960s have yet to be addressed by the international community.

References

Acharya, A., 2011. Norm Subsidiarity and Regional Orders: Sovereignty, Regionalism, and Rule-Making in the Third World. *International Studies Quarterly*, 55, 95–123.

Akyuz, Y., 2010. Multilateral Disciplines and the Question of Policy Space. In J. Faundez and C. Tan (eds), *International Economic Law, Globalization and Developing Countries*. Edward Elgar, ch. 3.

Amin, S., 2011. *Beyond US Hegemony*. Zed Books.

Amsden, A.H., 2003. Industrialization Under New WTO Law. In J. Toye (ed.), *Trade and Development Directions for the 21st Century*. Edward Elgar, ch. 5.
Baldwin, R., 2014. *Multilateralising 21st Century Regionalism*. Global Forum on Trade. OECD.
Bedjaoui, M., 1986. Non-Aligned States. *Encyclopedia of International Law*. Vol. *9*. Elsevier, pp. 270–276.
Berger, Mark, 2004. After the Third World? History, Destiny and the Fate of Third Worldism. *Third World Quarterly*, *25* (*1*), 9–39.
Bhagwati, J., 2008. *Termites in the Trading System*. Oxford University Press.
Bhagwati, J., 2013. Dawn of a New System. *Finance and Development*, *50* (*4*), 9–13. Available online at: https://www.imf.org/external/pubs/ft/fandd/2013/12/bhagwati.htm (accessed 15 April 2019).
Bhagwati, J., Krishna, P. and Panagariya, A., 2014. *The World Trade System: Trends and Challenges*. Columbia University. Available online at: http://www.columbia.edu/~jb38/papers/pdf/paper1-the_world_trading_system.pdf (accessed 17 February 2019).
Chang, H.-J., 2002. *Kicking Away the Ladder: Development Strategy in Historical Perspective*. Anthem Press.
Chang, H.-J., 2012. Kicking Away the Ladder: Neoliberalism and the Real History of Capitalism. In C. Kyung-Sup, B. Fine, and L. Weiss (eds), *Developmental Politics in Transition: The Neoliberal Era and Beyond*. Palgrave, p. 43.
Cheru, F., 2011. South-South Cooperation: What Prospects for another Bandung Consensus? In R. Modi (ed.), *South-South Cooperation, Africa on the Centre Stage*. Palgrave, p. 19.
Connell-Smith, G., 1960. The Organization of American States. *The World Today*, *16* (*10*), 447–456.
Cullather, N., 1999. *Secret History: The CIA's Classified Account of its Operations in Guatemala 1952–1954*. Stanford University Press.
Drache, D., 2000. *The Short but Significant Life of the International Trade Organization: Lessons for Our Time*. CSGR Working Paper No. 62/00. University of Warwick.
Dunne, M., 2011. Perfect Failure: the USA, Cuba and the Bay of Pigs, 1961. *Political Quarterly*, *82* (*3*), 448–458.
Dunne, M., 2013. Kennedy's Alliance for Progress: Countering Revolution in Latin America. *International Affairs*, *89* (*6*), 1389–1409.
Dunning, J.H. and Lundan, S.M., 2008. *Multinational Enterprises and the Global Economy*. Edward Elgar.
Emerson, R., 1965. Colonialism, Political Development, and the UN. *International Organization*, *19* (*3*), 484–503.
Falk, R., 1966. International Law and the United States Role in the Vietnam War. *Yale Law Journal*, *75* (*7*), 1122–1160.
Fatouros, A.A., 1964. International Law and the Third World. *Virginia Law Review*, *50* (*5*), 783–823.
Fenwick, C., 1966. The Dominican Republic: Intervention or Collective Self-Defense. *American Journal of International Law*, *60* (*1*), 64–67.
Fenwick, C., 1949. Collective Security: Universal and Regional. *World Affairs*, *112* (*2*), 43–45.

Friedmann, W., 1969. Intervention and the Developing Countries. *Virginia Journal of International Law*, *10* (*2*), 205–222.

Friedmann, W., 1967. United States Policy and the Crisis of International Law. *American Journal of International Law*, *59*, 857–871.

García-Amador, F., 1985. The Rio de Janeiro Treaty: Genesis, *Development, and Decline of a Regional System of Collective Security. University of Miami Inter-American Law Review*, *17* (*1*), 1–42.

Goodman, R., 1969. The Invasion of Czechoslovakia: 1968. *International Lawyer*, *4* (*1*), 42–79.

Guzman, A.T., 2009. Explaining the Popularity of Bilateral Investment Treaties. In K. Sauvant and L. Sachs (eds), *The Effects of Treaties on Foreign Direct Investment: Bilateral Investment Treaties, Double Taxation Treaties, and Investment Flows.* Oxford University Press.

Heuser, R., 1986. Bandung Conference (1955). *Encyclopedia of International Law*, vol. *9*, 12–14.

Hinkle, L. and Schiff, M. 2004. Economic Partnership Agreements Between Sub-Saharan Africa and the EU: A Development Perspective. *World Economy*, *27* (*9*), 1321–1333.

Hoekman, B.M. and Mavroidis, P.C., 2007. *The World Trade Organization: Law, Economics and Politics.* Routledge.

Hoffmann, S., 1970. International Organization and the International System. *International Organization*, *24* (*3*), 389–413.

ILO (International Labour Organization), 2008. *ILO Declaration on Social Justice for a Fair Globalization.* International Labour Conference, Ninety-Seventh Session. ILO.

Jackson, H., 1969. The Soviet Invasion of Czechoslovakia and its Impact on NATO: Does the Leopard Change his Spots? *Cornell International Law Journal*, *2* (*1*), 108–115.

Jamison, E, 1980. Cuba and the Inter-American System: Exclusion of the Castro Regime from the Organization of American States. *The Americas*, *36* (*3*), 317–346.

Johnson, H.G., 1976. *The New International Economic Order.* Selected Papers No. 49. University of Chicago Business School.

Keesing's, 1946–8. *Keesing's Contemporary Archives*, vol. *VI.* Keesing's Publications Limited, p. 8881.

Kunibert, R., and Singer, H.W., 2001. *The Economic North–South Divide: Six Decades of Unequal Development.* Edward Elgar Publishing.

Lejárraga, I., 2014. *Deep Provisions in Regional Trade Agreements: How Multilateral-friendly? An Overview of OECD Findings.* Trade Policy Papers, No. 168. OECD.

Lester, S. and Mercurio, B. (eds), 2009. *Bilateral and Regional Trade Agreements.* Cambridge University Press.

Lewis, M.K., 2017. Mega-FTAs and Plurilateral Trade Agreements: Implications for the Asia-Pacific. In J. Chaisse, H. Gao and C.-F. Lo (eds), *Paradigm Shift in International Economic Law Rule-Making.* Springer Nature, p. 419.

Maier, C., 2010. The World Economy and the Cold War in the Middle of the Twentieth Century. In M.P. Leffler and O.A. Westad (eds), *The Cambridge History of the Cold War, Vol. I: Origins.* Cambridge University Press, p. 44.

Mastanduno, M., 2009. System Maker and Privilege Taker: U.S. Power and the International Political Economy. *World Politics*, *61* (*1*), 121–154.
Matthews, A., 2007. Agriculture after Cancun. In S. Griller (ed.), *At the Crossroads: The World Trading System and the Doha Round*. Springer, p. 315.
Meeker, L., 1966. The Legality of United States Participation in the Defense of Viet-Nam. *Department of State Bulletin*, 28 March, p. 474.
Miller, L., 1967. Regional Organization and the Regulation of Internal Conflict. *World Politics*, *19* (*4*), 582–600.
Montes, M.F., 2014. *Obstacles to Development in the Global Economic System*. Research Paper No. 51. South Centre.
Muchlinski, P., 2010. Holistic Approaches to Development and International Investment Law: The Role of International Investment Agreements. In J. Faundez and C. Tan (eds), *International Economic Law, Globalization and Developing Countries*. Edward Elgar, ch. 9.
Najam, A., Halle, M., and Meléndez-Ortiz, R. (eds), 2007. *Trade and Environment: A Resource Book*. International Centre for Trade and Sustainable Development.
Narlikar, A., 2013. The Doha Development Agenda. In A.F. Cooper, J. Heine and R. Thakur (eds), *The Oxford Handbook of Modern Diplomacy*. Oxford University Press.
Nayyar, D., 2013. The Millennium Development Goals Beyond 2015: Old Frameworks and New Constructs. *Journal of Human Development and Capabilities*, *14* (*3*), 371–392.
Ofodile, U.E., 2011. South–South Trade and Investment Relations: Harmony and Disharmony – African Perspectives. In *Proceedings of the ASIL Annual Meeting*, *105*, 521–524. Cambridge University Press.
Organization of American States, 1965. Report of Special Committee on the Dominican Republic. *International Legal Materials*, *4* (*3*), 557–577.
OECD (Organisation for Economic Co-operation and Development), 2003. *Regionalism and the Multilateral Trading System*. OECD.
Pauker, G., 1965. The Rise and Fall of Afro-Asian Solidarity. *Asian Survey*, *5* (*9*), 425–432.
Pauwelyn, J., 2013. The End of Differential Treatment for Developing Countries: Lessons from the Trade and Climate Change Regimes. *Review of European Comparative and International Environmental Law*, *22* (*1*), 29–41.
Picciotto, S., 1999. What Rules the World Economy. In S. Picciotto and R. Mayne (eds), *Regulating International Business*. Palgrave, p. 1.
Raffer, K. and Singer, H.J., 2001. *The Economic North-South Divide: Six Decades of Unequal Development*. Edward Elgar.
Romaniecki, L., 1970. Sources of the Brezhnev Doctrine of Limited Sovereignty and Intervention. *Israel Law Review*, *5* (*4*), 527–541.
Sacerdoti, G., 2011. *New International Economic Order (NIEO)*. Max Planck Encyclopedia of International Law. Available online at: http://opil.ouplaw.com/view/10.1093/law:epil/9780199231690/law-9780199231690-e1542?prd=EPIL (accessed 14 April 2019).
Schill, S.W., 2011. *The Multilateralization of International Investment Law*. Cambridge University Press.

Schmeltzer, K., 1970. Soviet and American Attitudes Toward Intervention: The Dominican Republic, Hungary and Czechoslovakia. *Virginia Journal of International Law, 11 (1)*, 97–124.
Schrijver, N., 2009. Natural Resource Management and Sustainable Development. In S. Daws and T. Weiss (eds), *The Oxford Handbook of the United Nations*. Oxford Handbooks Online.
Slater, J., 1964. The United States, the Organization of American States, and the Dominican Republic, 1961–1963. *International Organization, 18 (2)*, 268–291.
Sornarajah, M., 2010. *The International Law on Foreign Investment*. Cambridge University Press.
Sumner, A. and Vázquez, S.T., 2014. *How Has the Developing World Changed since the Late 1990s? A Dynamic and Multidimensional Taxonomy of Developing Countries*. Working Paper No. 375. Centre for Global Development.
Toye, J., 2014. Assessing the G77: 50 Years after UNCTAD and 40 Years after the NIEO. *Third World Quarterly, 35 (10)*, 1759–1774.
Tsagourias, N. and White, N., 2013. *Collective Security*. Cambridge University Press.
Tung, K.-Y., 2010. Foreign Investors versus Sovereign States: Towards a Global Framework, BIT by BIT. In M.K. Lewis and S. Frankel (eds), *International Economic Law and National Autonomy*. Cambridge University Press.
Tussie, D., 2013. Trade Diplomacy. In A. Cooper, J. Heine, and R. Thakur (eds), *The Oxford Handbook of Modern Diplomacy*. Oxford University Press.
UN General Assembly, 1974a. *Charter of Economic Rights and Duties of States*. GA Res. 3281(xxix), 29th Sess., Supp. No. 31. UN General Assembly Official Records.
UN General Assembly, 1974b. *Declaration on the Establishment of a New International Economic Order*. Official Records: Sixth Special Session, Supplement No. 1 (A/9559). United Nations.
United Nations, 2010. *World Economic and Social Survey 2010: Retooling Global Development*. E/2010/50/Rev.1ST/ESA/330. UN Department for Social & Economic Affairs.
UNCTAD (United Nations Conference on Trade and Development), 2004. *Beyond Conventional Wisdom in Development Policy: An Intellectual History of UNCTAD 1964–2004*. UNCTAD.
UNCTAD (United Nations Conference on Trade and Development), 2008. *The Accra Declaration*. Twelfth Session. TD/L.413. UNCTAD.
UNCTAD (United Nations Conference on Trade and Development), 2011. *Development-Led Globalization: Towards Sustainable and Inclusive Development Paths (Report of the Secretary-General of UNCTAD to UNCTAD XIII)*. XIII/1. UNCTAD.
Unión Panamericana, 1954. *Décima Conferencia Interamericana: Actas y Documentos*, vol. *I*, tercera sesión plenaria, 5 de Marzo, pp. 121–122.
Vandevelde, K., 2009. A Brief History of International Investment Agreements. In K.P. Sauvant and L.E. Sachs (eds), *The Effects of Treaties on Foreign Direct Investment: Bilateral Investment Treaties, Double Taxation Treaties, and Investment Flows*. Oxford University Press.
Velut, J.-B., Dalingwater, V. and Peyronel, V. (eds), 2018. *Understanding Mega Free Trade Agreements*. Routledge.

Wade, R., 2003. What Strategies are Viable for Developing Countries Today? The World Trade Organization and the Shrinking of 'Development Space'. *Review of International Political Economy*, *10* (*4*), 621–644.
Wright, Q., 1957. Intervention, 1956. *American Journal of International Law*, *51* (*2*), 257–276.
World Trade Organization, 2011. *World Trade Report 2011 – The WTO and Preferential Trade Agreements: From Coexistence to Coherence*. World Trade Organization.
Yusuf, S., 2009. *Development Economics through the Decades: A Critical Look at 30 Years of the World Development Report*. World Bank.

Chapter 9

International law and development

From 'company raj' to global governance via indirect rule

Radha D'Souza

Law and development: the diffusion thesis

In his essay *Three Globalizations of Law and Legal Thought: 1850–2000* Duncan Kennedy argues that the study of law and development (L&D) began with 'a particular positioning of its two terms "law" in relation to "development"' (Kennedy, 2006: 19) by 'those with access to the legal, administrative, and judicial processes in the colonies and states' to influence economic activity (20). The struggles to reposition the two terms at different times have produced different legal regimes. Regardless of the differences in the legal frameworks, L&D has always been 'a project for influencing economic activity' (20). Since 1850 three waves of globalisations have diffused certain sets of ideas and concepts about 'law' in relation to 'development' from the core European states to the peripheral Third World. Each wave produced certain dominant ideas about the positioning of law to development in the 'core' which were later diffused to the 'periphery' producing a linear outward movement of legal history that has brought us to the contemporary world where legal concepts, systems and institutions have become internationalised.

'Classical Legal Thought' (1850–1914), the first wave of legal thought, produced and diffused a 'mode of legal consciousness' or a way of thinking about law (20, 25, 36). 'Socially Oriented Legal Thought' (1900–1914), the second wave of legal thought, brought up the concept of 'the social' and expanded the legal consciousness of the first wave to economic development (38) which viewed law as a 'regulatory mechanism to facilitate social life' (22). The third wave of global diffusion of law between 1945 and 2000 focused on institutional and theoretical developments that viewed law as pragmatic administrative techniques to balance human and property rights. The dominant concepts in each wave were challenged by new ideas which produced the next wave.

Kennedy avoids the political and philosophical underpinnings implicit in his diffusion thesis and the geo-historical drivers of L&D. He abstracts legal consciousness from social consciousness and transformations in real social relations. In one stroke, by dating L&D from 1850, Kennedy's diffusion thesis draws the curtain on the period from 1500 to 1850 AD, when European trading corporations played a pivotal role in establishing 'a particular positioning of "law" in relation to "development" in the Third World – in reality, the two-thirds world. In all the three waves of legal diffusion, the agents of change for Kennedy are the elites – jurists, lawyers and administrators including Third World elites. Voluntarism is inherent in this approach. Moreover, elites as agents of change presents people as passive objects of history open to manipulation. Kennedy's self-evolving diffusion thesis abstracts legal forms and essences from the substance and context of L&D (20, 22). Consequently, the ghost of law roams a borderless world and for inexplicable reasons the L&D regime invariably brings prosperity to the capitalist 'North' and misery to the (neo)colonial 'South'. What might L&D look like if it were explicitly grounded in radical philosophy and political theory and anchored to colonial history and geography? How might such an approach alter our conceptions of the diffusion of law and economic governance?

This chapter provides a snapshot of what the elements of a radical L&D, that is grounded in radical philosophy, politics and geo-history might look like. It takes as its point of departure the field of L&D studies as it exists and asks: how did it come to be what it is today? L&D as a legal field comprises several contradictory elements where the stated aims and discourses diverge from the institutional architectures that position 'law' in relation to 'development' in particular ways. Contemporary L&D studies are embedded within a world order that stands on a *de facto* hierarchy of states. In economics, classifications of 'developed', 'developing' 'underdeveloped' countries determine entitlements and claims of states. In politics, the veto powers, victors in the World Wars, have the last word, whereas the powers of the General Assembly, of which all states are members, are limited to making recommendations. Within international economic organisations like the World Bank or International Monetary Fund, five largest capital subscribing countries control the votes. Powerful military alliances like NATO make decisions about war and peace. At the heart of the hierarchy of states is the paradox of sovereignty where formal equality of states coexists with the institutionalisation of unequal relations of economic, political and ideological power between former colonial powers and colonised nations. Taking South Asia to exemplify wider arguments, I argue that contemporary L&D under the United Nations (UN) system is a geo-historically constituted regime where law and legal norms are institutionalised in ways that sustain unequal relations between states and privilege transnational corporations. The legal-institutional regime builds on principles of colonial governance developed within the British Empire and continues to reproduce colonial relations in new forms. More specifically the system of governance known as Indirect Rule developed by the British colonial jurists, administrators and legal scholars provide the conceptual building blocks for L&D under the UN system today.

Indirect Rule: from Company Raj to the UN system

Indirect Rule is a system of colonial governance founded upon a hierarchy of states, rules of recognition and conditional devolution that emerged after the First War of Independence.[1] The war brought about the collapse of the British East India Company (EIC) and ended 'liberal imperialism', the ideological foundations of the EIC's rule popularly known as Company Raj in South Asia (Mantena, 2010). Company Raj was a particular type of relationship between European trading corporations, capitalist states and native rulers formed by public-contracting, profit-sharing and public–private partnerships. Unlike the Dutch, French, Spanish and Portuguese trading corporations, where the colonial enterprise was either state-owned or founded on delegated sovereignty, British colonialism was from its inception a private enterprise embedded in public contracts in Asia and chartered as public-private partnerships in North America (Egerton, 1918; Osgood, 1902; Robins, 2012; Stern, 2011). Contracting out colonial governance to a trading corporation entailed extended legal relationships between the crown and the corporation on the one hand and the corporation and native rulers on the other.

Contracts embody an inherent tension between and among the contracting parties and third parties. Besides, being time-bound, contracting parties must address insecurities associated with failure, renewal and competition from others. The three-way contracts between the British crown, the EIC and the native rulers created opportunities for legal innovation and adaptations of English law for colonial rule. Most notably innovations under Company Raj included changes to European concepts of sovereignty, trusteeship, paramountcy and subsidiarity. Company Raj legalised unequal contractual relations between Britain, the EIC and native Indian states.

The imperatives of the transition from 'liberal imperialism' under Company Raj to Indirect Rule forced the colonial administration to further advance existing jurisprudence developed under Company Raj on sovereignty, trusteeship, paramountcy and subsidiarity. Indirect Rule transformed unequal relations based on contracts into public law principles as argued below. The British Empire collapsed under the weight of the First World War (Gerwarth and Manela, 2014) and brought down the ideological and legal authority of Britain. Nevertheless, the legal frameworks and principles of colonial governance under Indirect Rule in the British Empire provided the conceptual resources for the international order after the Second World War as the rest of this chapter will argue. Kennedy's 'diffusion thesis' seeks to explain the globalisation of law and the continuities and changes in legal ideas from 1850s onwards when legal ideas were

1 The First War of Independence, also known as the Indian Sepoy Mutiny in British historiography, is so-called because it came very close to defeating British rule in the subcontinent and became a reference point for successive waves of freedom struggles leading to independence in 1947 (D'Souza, 2014).

diffused from the core to the periphery. The British Empire offers a radically different way of understanding the globalisation of law and the continuities and changes in the ideological and legal frameworks for colonial governance under the Company Raj, Indirect Rule and global governance under the UN system.

Within the British Empire, India was a separate administrative category, distinct from self-governing dominions, crown colonies, directly administered by Britain and agency states where native rulers ruled as crown-agents (Voigt, 1987). India became a crucible for innovation of law and colonial governance. It was, as J.S Mill saw it, a great experimental laboratory for the British Empire (Bell, 2010). British India was also a sub-empire within the British Empire with jurisdiction over several African, Middle Eastern, central, eastern and south-east Asian territories (Onley, 2009). The principles of colonial governance developed in India were exported throughout the British Empire, adopted and adapted by other imperial powers and universalised as international law in the League of Nations and later in the UN as elaborated further on. Of the different European empires in the 17th and 18th centuries, only the British adopted a form of governance based upon the complex maze of legal arrangements that characterised Indirect Rule. Indirect Rule laid the groundwork for the League and the UN systems. Fisher (1984: 395) states that 'many would argue that the neocolonialism of multi-national corporations is only the latest, most sophisticated form of indirect rule.' A variety of models of indirect rule were trialled under Company Raj and the insights led to jurisprudential innovations that systematised colonial governance of the vast British Empire in the 19th century (Fisher, 1984; Mantena, 2010; Onley, 2009).

The metamorphosis of English legal ideas and concepts impelled by imperatives of colonial governance, far from being the benign 'diffusion' that Kennedy describes, shows continued application of principles of colonial governance that call into question the claims of the UN system after the Second World War to be constituted by equal and sovereign states. Colonial rule as the reason for global diffusion of European law and economic governance is precisely what Kennedy's diffusion thesis fetishises.

Sovereignty and the Company Raj

The field of L&D reflects the interplay of two types of sovereignty: the territorialised sovereignty of states and the trans-territorial sovereignty of corporations. With the exception of a small nascent body of scholarship on corporate sovereignty, the vast literature on sovereignty focuses overwhelmingly on the sovereignty of nation-states. States and corporations are both legal entities with authority and control within the limits established by law, one territorial, the other organisational. Throughout the history of modern capitalism the two legal entities have always been interdependent, mutually contingent and co-constituted (Barkan, 2013; Chandler and Mazlish, 2005; Ericson et al., 2003; Stern, 2011). The public/private divide in modern law establishes distinct legal domains for corporations and states. In the private domain state intervention is, ideally, minimal and in the public domain corporate interventions ought to be minimal at least in theory. This structure of modern law fetishises the interdependent and contingent nature of the two sovereignties and obscures the interplay of the two sovereignties in the colonial enterprises of the past and the continued exploitation of natures and labours of peoples in the Third World in the present. It therefore becomes essential to deconstruct this interplay.

Historically, corporations and nation-states coevolved during the transformations in Europe from feudal societies founded on land-relations to capitalist societies founded on commodity-relations. In the capitalist West, modern ideas of sovereignty emerged in the course of establishment of the modern nation-state as a centralised institution, a legal entity without the person of the sovereign. The very same processes also institutionalised the modern corporation as a legal entity independent of the state. These processes institutionalised the separation of economy and polity as distinct domains. The EIC, the first modern corporation, was founded in 1600 under a Royal Charter 'as one body corporate and politick' (Robins, 2012: 24). The English Civil War (1642–51) and the Glorious Revolution (1688–9) established the foundations of modern 'bourgeois democratic' state in England founded on constitutional principles of parliamentary sovereignty and representative democracy (Hobsbawm, 1962/2010; Stern, 2011). Private corporations of the mercantile era were modelled on the public corporations of the feudal era: the church, universities and municipalities, each with their own constitutions, legal personalities, internal administration with one qualitative difference (Barkan, 2013; Osgood, 1896a; Osgood, 1896b; Osgood, 1896c; Stern, 2011). The feudal public corporations were established to achieve public goals, whereas the new private corporations were established to achieve the private goals (profits) of traders, entrepreneurs and merchants. Indeed, the 'advancement of trade' became a public purpose in the Royal Charter that established the EIC (Robins, 2012: 45). In contrast, the trajectory of ideas of sovereignty and the social and political imperatives for it in the colonies developed through radically different processes.

In India, the corporation was simultaneously also the state – hence 'Company Raj'. Successive royal charters issued under the British crown's prerogative powers gave the EIC the rights to establish armies to defend their trading posts, make laws for their employees - native, British and European - and dispense justice within its jurisdiction (Stern, 2011: ch. 2). During the early mercantile era the EIC recognised the sovereignty of native rulers, signed treaties with them to secure trading concessions, customs and tariff exemptions, trading rights and rights to establish trading posts (Robins, 2012; Stern, 2011). The contemporaneous incorporation of trading companies by several European states unleashed trade wars around the world between European corporations for trade routes, trade concessions, trading posts and alliances with native rulers and peoples. These trade wars were often resolved through military conflicts fought by corporations outside Europe. Of all European trading companies, the EIC enjoyed most autonomy including in military affairs (Stern, 2011: ch. 3). The corporate wars opened the pathway for corporate interventions in the politics, societies and cultures of the colonies (Dodwell, 1920/1967). Company Raj emerged from these interventions.

By 1757, the EIC had established a complex maze of treaties on trade with native rulers in south, south-east and east Asia (Bakshi, 1967; Ferrier, 1970; Ramachandran, 1980). The battle of Plassey in 1757 – after which the EIC acquired the wealthy province of Bengal – is considered to be the formal beginning of the Company Raj with the EIC's takeover of the governance of a large and wealthy kingdom (Robins, 2012; Stern, 2011). The idea that a trading company should behave like a sovereign was novel for many Enlightenment thinkers. Adam Smith called it a 'strange absurdity', Edmund Burke ridiculed it as a 'state in the disguise of a merchant', and Thomas Macaulay thought 'it is strange, very strange' that a joint stock company should have sovereignty 'of a larger population, the disposal of a larger clear revenue, the command of a larger army, than are under the direct management of the Executive Government of the United Kingdom' (quoted in Stern, 2011: 3).

The acquisition of territory by the EIC presented a new set of constitutional questions for which there was no precedent, the most important being the nature of sovereignty in India and the extent of parliament's powers to regulate the EIC (Cohn, 1989, 1997). The debates of the time included questions like whether sovereignty could be sub-contracted, and did the Royal Charters 'lend' the British state's sovereignty to the corporation? Did Parliament's interventions in company affairs violate the sovereignty of native rulers? (Cohn, 1997). If the parties to the treaties were the EIC and the native rulers, did the British parliament have the authority to intervene in the enforcement or otherwise of those treaties to which it was not a party? (Wilbur, 1945).

In 1773 the British parliament seized the opportunity presented by the EIC's financial difficulties to assert its authority to regulate the EIC for the first time. The Regulating Act of 1773 provided for the appointment of a five-member council headed by the Governor General, three of whom were nominees of the parliament, to oversee the EIC's India operations (Robins, 2012: 111–12). The attempts were minimal and ineffective. In 1783 a parliamentary bill to give the EIC a new constitution was passed by a big majority in the Commons but defeated in the House of Lords (Wilbur, 1945: 295). By the 1790s the relations between the British parliament and the EIC reversed. Until then, parliament depended on the EIC for capital and war-financing but thereafter the EIC, in financial difficulties due to its own wars, turned to the crown for war-financing. This reversal of financial dependence gave the British parliament reasons to become involved in the administration of India. The Charter Acts from 1793 to 1853, renewed every ten years, formalised a hierarchy of governance where the EIC was overseen by the British parliament without challenging the EIC's authority to govern India (Wilbur, 1945). The hierarchy of governance triggered continuous infighting between parliament's nominees and the EIC officials

(Robins, 2012: 111–12; Wilbur, 1945: 298–300). Notably, parliament stopped short of claiming sovereign authority over the EIC.

In the struggle between the parliament and the EIC, both invoked doctrines of private and public trusteeship to justify their actions. Parliament claimed that the EIC was established under royal prerogative and was therefore an agent of the crown. The crown as sovereign trustee owed a duty of care to the EIC's Indian subjects by ensuring that the terms of the treaties were honoured (Court of Directors, 1833b). In the impeachment proceedings for corruption against Warren Hastings, the Governor-General of EIC appointed under the 1773 Act, which began in 1787, the core of the 22 charges against him was that he breached the trust of Indian rulers and people and that out of the misery of Indian peasants 'is derived the wealth and subsistence of the East India Company, who use funds thus procured to buy the China tea served on English breakfast tables' (quoted in Wilbur, 1945: 299).

In response, the EIC claimed that the native kingdoms were tantamount to private estates of landlords comparable to the estates of manorial lords in feudal Europe. The treaties gave the EIC authority to collect revenues and manage the native estates as the private trustee of native rulers. In theory, the EIC was merely a revenue collector and manager under the treaties and its activities were consistent with those of a trading corporation over which the legislature had no authority (Court of Directors, 1833a; Court of Directors, 1833c). The Permanent Settlement Act 1793 enacted by the EIC for the governance of Bengal established a Court of Wards within the remit of the Board of Revenue (Court of Directors, 1833c). The Court of Wards borrowed principles of guardianship from English family law and applied them to the management of the so-called native estates. Land could be confiscated or managed by the EIC if native rulers did not pay revenues, were of unsound mind, committed gross misconduct, or their behaviour was considered depraved (Court of Directors, 1833c). The infamous 'doctrine of lapse' extended to Indian estates/kingdoms the private law principle that estates of wards who died without heirs 'lapsed' to the trustees (Choudhary, 2009; Fisher, 1993). Similar four-way conflicts between the crown, the trading corporations, the native rulers and rival companies resulted from the activities of other British corporations such as the Virginia Company incorporated in 1606 with trading rights on the east coast of the Americas, the Royal African Company incorporated in 1660 in partnership with the Stuart monarchy and London merchants for trade in Africa, the Hudson Bay Company incorporated in 1662 by members of the British aristocracy for exclusive trade in what later became Canada (Carlos and Kruse, 1996; Fitzmaurice, 2015; Rich, 1960). The EIC, however, was the first and the most 'private' of the corporations formed exclusively by London merchants.

As the EIC was both a state and a trading company, there was separation neither of economy from polity under Company Raj, nor in their institutionalisation as a modern centralised state and a self-governing corporation. This merger created complexities for a legal system based on a public/private divide. At a time when European states were establishing the modern centralised nation-state by institutionalising the separation of powers within their constitutional frameworks, Company Raj fused legislative, judicial and administrative powers in India. For more than two and half centuries beginning in the 17th century, the historical context for the theories and practices of governance and institution building in India developed in opposite directions to those in Europe. The tendency to project theories developed in the European geo-historical context to India, and the Third World more generally, as Kennedy's diffusion thesis does, has obfuscated understandings of legal and institutional developments.

Legal justifications by the crown and corporations did little to stem popular revolts in the colonies. The doctrine of lapse used by the EIC to justify annexations of large kingdoms as well as the company's convoluted approach to the sovereignty of native states triggered the 1857 war (Fisher, 1993). This was followed by the Morant Bay rebellion in Jamaica in 1865, the Fenian rising in Ireland in 1867, and the Maori Land Wars from 1843 to 1872 (Mantena, 2010). It was in the context of such rebellions that challenges arose to theoretical and doctrinal ideas of sovereignty and governance. These centred on the nature of the relationship between European states, their corporations, native rulers and native peoples. Legal theories of indirect rule addressed those relationships. An elitist account of history that writes out popular resistance obscures the real reasons for continuities and changes in legal frameworks.

Indirect rule: native and European sovereignty under Empire

The 1857 war was started by the EIC but ended with its dissolution. The EIC narrowly won the war with considerable logistical support from the crown including large loans which it was unable to payback (Keith, 1961: 185). The crown relied on its authority as *creditor* to take over the administration of the affairs of the company (ibid.). The end of Company Raj and the structural uncoupling of the colonial trading corporations and the crown occurred in the wake of the epochal transformation of capitalism from mercantile to industrial capitalism in the United States and Europe and the consequent re-casting of the relationship between the corporation and the capitalist states (Chandler, 1990/2004: 1).

Previously, overseas colonial trade and territorial expansion used monopolistic corporate forms of organisation (Stern, 2011). Domestic economic activities were carried on by owner-managed enterprises and 'the number of salaried managers in these enterprises were tiny.' (Chandler, 1990/2004: 1). The innovation of railroad and transport enabled the expansion of the scale and scope of the national enterprises which evolved into national corporations initially and transnational ones after the end of the Second World War (Chandler, 1990/2004). The conceptual and legal resources for corporate governance developed in their most advanced form in the United States, a former colony originally established by monopolistic colonial trading corporations. Both strands of governance: corporate and colonial were internationalised and institutionalised after the Second World War as discussed below. Lord Canning, the first Governor-General of India appointed after the 1857 war made Sir Henry Maine the law member of his council in 1862. Maine, one of the main architects of colonial law and governance, reworked the concept of sovereignty in colonial governance. He used anthropological typologies to critique liberal thinkers like John Locke and Jeremy Bentham arguing that their approaches were inappropriate in the colonies. (Mantena, 2010). Rebellions occurred because Company Raj had introduced drastic changes to traditional systems of governance (Mantena, 2010). Whatever the EIC's claims before the British parliament, recognition of the sovereignty of native rulers over defined territories was implicit in the maze of treaties with them. At the same time establishment of modern nation-states had transformed ideas of sovereignty in Europe.

Whereas the idea of the monarch as the 'sovereign' with authority over subjects within the realm is an older one, Osiander (2001) argues that modern ideas of sovereignty of the Austinian type, as a depersonalised sovereign nation-state with absolute power nationally and internationally, is an invention of the 'great nineteenth- and twentieth-century international lawyers' (281). Challenging dominant understandings of Westphalian treaties as the source of modern ideas of sovereignty, he argues that 'the most significant transition occurred with the French Revolution and the onset of industrialization, not with the Peace of Westphalia' (281). Osiander's challenge to dominant conceptions of Westphalian sovereignty (also see Osiander, 1994) raises interesting questions about Maine's imperative to redefine sovereignty in India. Even as rigid theories of sovereignty as absolute and indivisible authority congealed in the European context, concurrently, Maine developed ideas of 'shared sovereignty' in the context of colonial governance. This is not 'diffusion' of international law from the core to the periphery as Kennedy argues but rather development of opposite conceptions of sovereignty in the core and the periphery. Theories of absolute sovereignty of the Austinian type were incompatible with the maze of treaties that the EIC had signed with the native rulers. Continued governance of India entailed recognising the EIC's treaties with native rulers, the fragility of Britain's authority in India after the 1857 war, the increasing rivalries between European states and the need for rational justifications for the subordinate status of native rulers.

Maine departed from the divide between law and ethics in Austinian legal positivism and replaced it with a sociological and anthropological approach to law, which differentiated between law in modern (i.e. Western) and ancient (i.e. Eastern) societies (Maine, 1909). Maine argued that all societies evolve from status-based relationships in traditional law to modern contract-based relations just as Europe had progressed from Roman law to modern constitutionalism. Imperial governance must recognise historical evolutionary processes and steer colonial societies to modern contract-based statehood (Maine, 1909). Maine's evolutionary legal theory introduced the idea of stages of development, prefiguring the stages of growth theories propounded by development scholars such as Walt Rostow (see Arndt, 1987: chs 2–3). His doctrinal contributions and principles of colonial governance 'regularised' the laws made by the EIC without which their legality and legitimacy would remain suspect following the 1857 war. A semblance of stability arguably became possible after the 1857 war partly with the promise to native rulers incorporated in the Queen's Proclamation of 1858 that 'all Treaties and Engagements made with them by or under the authority of the Honorable East India Company are by Us accepted, and will be scrupulously maintained' (Open University, n.d.).

Maine's lasting legacy to colonial governance and L&D was the divisibility of sovereignty which could be shared between several authorities. (Maine, 1909; also Mantena, 2010). However, he distinguished sovereignty from independence (in Indian States Committee, 1929: 44). Absolute sovereignty between independent sovereigns could operate only between European states as they had advanced to a higher stage of civilisation by evolving from status to contract based social relations (Holdsworth, 1930; Indian States Committee, 1929; Maine, 1909). In India, sovereignty could be shared between the British Crown, native rulers and the Indian people. Company Raj could not guide societies from tradition to modernity as it was premised on the false understanding that European liberalism could be transplanted in India without regard for the historical social processes through which law evolves (Maine, 1909). Any transition from ancient to modern could be neither automatic nor spontaneous and required policy guidance (Mantena, 2010). Divided sovereignty between Britain and native rulers was necessary to establish modern legal systems, a process led by the crown for India's benefit (Holdsworth, 1930). Those sharing power had to develop systems that respected property and trading rights in ways that were compatible with native cultures and traditions (Mantena, 2010).

Maine's reversal of ideas of absolute sovereignty prevalent in Europe was an essential building block in the emergence of indirect rule as a model of British colonial governance. While shared sovereignty provided the basis for distinguishing sovereignty in European and colonial contexts, the doctrine of paramountcy and subsidiarity supplied the justifications for the idea that some sovereigns could be more equal than others.

Indirect rule: paramountcy and subsidiarity

The doctrine of paramountcy and subsidiarity is best synthesised in the 1929 *Report of the Indian States Committee* (the Butler Committee), which reviewed its history and scope. Shared sovereignty is possible where one sovereign is independent (the paramount power) and the other dependent (the subsidiary power). Even as the Queen's Proclamation announced the promise of equal treatment of native rulers and respect for treaties between the EIC and the

Crown, the new British-Indian government with Maine as the law member began the process of systematically codifying the plethora of treaties affecting India. Native states were classified into nine typologies with varying degrees of sovereignty (Holdsworth, 1930).

According to Maine's revisionist doctrine, sovereignty in international law is an assemblage of separate powers and privileges which are divisible between an independent sovereign, the paramount power, and subsidiary sovereigns. He explains:

> A sovereign who possesses the whole of this aggregate of rights is called an independent sovereign; but there is not, nor has there ever been, anything in international law to prevent some of those rights being lodged with one possessor, and some with another. [...] [a]ccording to the more precise language of modern publicists, 'sovereignty' is divisible, but independence is not. Although the expression 'partial independence' may be popularly used, it is technically incorrect. Accordingly there may be found in India every shade and variety of sovereignty but there is only one independent sovereign – the British Government.
>
> (Quoted in Holdsworth, 1930: 420–1)

According to W.S. Holdsworth, a member of the Butler Committee, the doctrine of paramountcy/subsidiarity is a combination of international and municipal law (421) and applied to all protectorates within the British Empire (422–4). For him (i) the source of paramountcy is the treaties and agreements with native sovereigns (419); (ii) the law on the comity of nations 'which exempt a foreign Sovereign from the process of the Courts' such that the actions of the paramount power 'are not cognizable by any municipal Court either in India or in Great Britain' (421); (iii) the principle of international law that treaties are not void because of coercion, applied to treaties with native states (421); and (iv) the people of subsidiary native states are not British subjects protected by British laws (423).

Paramountcy was partly municipal because it was grounded in the exercise of prerogative powers in British constitutional law. Nevertheless, there were important differences between such prerogative powers and paramountcy. Prerogatives were not the source of paramountcy, because the latter was *a new and distinct form of prerogative power.* Whereas prerogative powers extended to all territories governed by the British parliament including the dominions, there were territorial limitations to prerogative powers in the indirectly ruled native states such as limited control of the army and coinage. In addition, native peoples in subsidiary states were not subjects of the crown (423–6). The source of paramount powers, Holdsworth argued, is usage and political practices of successive governments rather than treaties and agreements with native rulers (427–8).

Indeed, paramountcy existed independently of such treaties and agreements as it rested on the historical de facto submission of native rulers to the authority of the company and later the crown (417, 428–9). Treaties notwithstanding, successive EIC governments circumscribed the military and political powers of native rulers (414, 418). As custom and usage are the basis of English common law so also, past practices between the EIC and the native states were regarded as creating valid law (427). The Queen's Proclamation of 1858 agreed to respect treaties with native rulers and recognise their sovereignty. By accepting the Proclamation, native rulers had implicitly acquiesced to their subsidiarity (416). Holdsworth's legal opinion held sway with the Indian States Committee appointed to report on the constitutional status of native Indian states, which became an important issue after the Paris Peace Conference in 1919. Holdsworth's analysis extends Maine's formulations and develops a comprehensive constitutional doctrine of paramountcy and subsidiarity rationalising the EIC's rule.

This doctrine extrapolates a common law principle that pre-existed modernity among the people of England as a historically constituted nation and projects it onto relations between a trading company and foreign states with no common history, nationhood or cultural ties. This extrapolation was a deliberate, ex post-facto development of legal and theoretical rationalisations for colonial governance. In effect, such arguments are based upon 'might is right' rather than the rule of law. Nonetheless, the British colonial doctrine of paramountcy and subsidiarity would have profound influence on the UN system after the dissolution of the Empire system.

Far from being an imperial relic Maine's 'shared sovereignty' and relations of 'paramountcy and subsidiarity' are here to stay. In *Rasul v Bush* (2004), for example, the US Supreme Court held that whereas Cuba has 'ultimate sovereignty' over Guantanamo Bay the US could exercise 'plenary and exclusive jurisdiction' without 'ultimate sovereignty'. In *The Chagos Islanders v The United Kingdom* (2012), the European Court of Human Rights held that native inhabitants of Chagos Islands, a British Indian Ocean Territory, who were expelled from their homelands by the UK, were not entitled to human rights protections even when the 'ultimate decision-making authority' were 'politicians or officials within the United Kingdom' (2012: 19). The reasoning in the two cases have deep antecedents in the history of colonial governance.

The League, the UN, hierarchy of states and global governance

The League of Nations was the first systematic attempt to institutionalise international law (Alvarez, 2006). By the time the First World War ended there was an established body of doctrine, legal precedent, legislation and principles for indirect rule as a form of colonial governance. The body of legal and administrative knowledge on indirect rule was thus available when European empires imploded and anti-colonial revolts for national liberation presented new challenges. The institutionalisation of international law was prompted by the implosion of European empires on the one hand and the anti-colonial movements on the other. Contrary to Kennedy's linear 'diffusion' thesis, during the World Wars legal ideas travelled from the colonies to the League. Jan Smuts, South Africa's prime minister, a member of Britain's Imperial War Cabinet and one of the architects of apartheid played a central role in shaping the League of Nations (Curry, 1961; Dubow, 2008; Hyslop, 2009; Kochanek, 2013).

Smuts was tasked by the British Prime Minister David Lloyd George with writing Britain's policy document for the Peace Conference at Versailles in 1919 (Curry, 1961). Smut's inspiration for his 21 recommendations, most of which were incorporated in the League's statute, was the British Empire which he argued was already a 'small league of nations' (Smuts, 1918: 9). Whereas other European Empires had 'broken down' because they were based on inequality, the British Commonwealth alone remained because it was 'based on the true principles of national freedom and decentralisation' (9). Smuts argued 'the work [of rebuilding the European empire] has to be done all over again on a new basis and an enormous scale' (10). In Smut's view, Europe was 'being liquidated' and 'if there is going to be a scramble among the victors for this loot, the future of Europe must indeed be despaired of' (11). Smut's solution to avoid the 'spoils system' was 'to make the League of Nations the reversionary in the broadest sense of these Empires' (11). In its territorial policy the League should be 'the general heir or successor of the defunct Empires' (12). Smut's vocabulary of 'estates' and 'reversionary' reminds us of the EIC's view of native states as 'estates' and the EIC as reversionary as discussed above. Smuts advocated for the League as the 'successor of the Empires' (26) and modelled the organisation on mechanisms for colonial governance in the British Empire (Smuts, 1918: 29). The League must, however, 'avoid the old legal concepts of Imperialism in the new world of Freedom' (32). The challenge lay in how to acknowledge the equality of states while maintaining the superiority of Western nations. 'We are, in the first place, called upon to decide what we mean by equality in the new system. Will the United States of America count for as much and the same as Guatemala? The question is crucial' (Smuts, 1918: 33).

Smuts's solution was to elevate the idea of hierarchy of states to the League's constitution. The Imperial Cabinet of the British Empire could be the model for the League. Within the British Empire different categories of colonies – i.e. the dominions, the crown colonies, the protectorates, and India, a distinct administrative category – were organised in a hierarchy overseen by the Imperial Cabinet (29). The same hierarchy of governance arrangements could be replicated on an expanded scale in the League. Of specific relevance to L&D, Smuts advocated 'the economic policy of the open door and non-military police policy' for the 'autonomous or underdeveloped territories' that were 'in vogue in the analogous' British colonies (30). Smuts internationalised the racialised hierarchy of states in the British Empire (Dubow, 2008) and ideas of differing stages of development propounded by Maine. Eastern European colonies were entitled to self-determination, but the rest could not because they were inhabited by 'barbarians' 'to whom it would be impracticable to apply any ideas of political self-determination in the European sense' (Smuts, 1918: 15). The main difference between the British Empire and the League, according to Smuts, was that 'whereas peace in the British Empire is ensured by a common allegiance, in the League it would have to be elaborately provided for by special arrangements' (Smuts, 1918: 30).

The institutional architecture of the UN, especially the distribution of power within its organs, is modelled after the League. Smuts recommended that the powers of the General Conference (the precursor to the UN General Assembly) should be limited to making non-binding recommendations (33–5). The powers of the UN General Assembly are similarly limited to making recommendations. In contrast, the great Powers (Britain, France, Austria and Russia after the First World War) should have powers to decide matters affecting Europe (35–6). Outside the UN, organisations like NATO and OECD institutionalise the special arrangements for the dominant nations after the Second World War. The 'real work of the League', Smuts argued, ought to be done by a Council comprising a small group of states with the great powers as permanent members, and four additional members 'to be added in rotation' (35–6). Membership of the UN Security Council is modelled after the League's Council.

Ideas of trusteeship inherited from the EIC and Maine era also found their way into the constitutions of the League and the UN. Smuts was the architect of the mandate system. Instead of annexing the colonies of the Axis powers, the Allied powers would be mandatories of the League and govern the colonies as trustees of the League (21). Recall the foregoing sections, where it was argued that Britain abandoned the EIC's policy of annexations after the war of 1857 and established indirect rule to discharge its obligations to the Indian people as sovereign trustee. Under Article XII of the UN Charter a full-fledged Trusteeship Council was established to oversee the orderly transition from colonialism to the post-war system.

The idea that empires had the authority to 'oversee' subsidiary states, in Smuts's words 'watch over the relations inter se of the new independent States arising from the break-up of those Empires [with a] view to the maintenance of good order and general peace' (26) was also incorporated into the powers of the UN Security Council. The idea of 'watching over' lesser states is older than the League informed by Smuts's recommendations, however. The office of the Resident under Company Raj was established by the EIC precisely to 'watch over' native rulers (Arnold-Baker, 2001; Fisher, 1984).

Globalisation, disaggregated sovereignty and subsidiarity

Neoliberal globalisation, with its push to 'roll back the state' through privatisation, deregulation and the sub-contracting of what were hitherto regarded as state functions led to resistance in large parts of the Third World where many saw it as a new form of Company Raj (e.g. in India; Robins, 2012: 13). Globalisation restructured the relations between states and the transnational corporations that had, since the turn of the 20th century, expanded into global oligarchies. Anne-Marie Slaughter's writings provide a systematic retheorisation of shared sovereignty, trusteeship, paramountcy and subsidiarity in the contemporary globalised neoliberal world order led by the United States (US). Transcending polarised debates on state sovereignty versus globalism, Slaughter's solution to the vexed question of sovereignty when the state is 'rolled back' is much like Maine's: simply redefine the concept.

According to Slaughter, governments, operate through 'networks of officials, police investigators, financial regulators, judges and legislators, finance ministers, central bankers, environmental officials' (Slaughter, 2005a). Each network has a specific aim but they generally 'expand regulatory reach', 'build trust' 'establish relationships' and 'create incentives to establish good reputations and avoid bad ones', 'develop best practices' and much more (Slaughter, 2005a: 38). One way of thinking about sovereignty, Slaughter argues, is to understand it as disaggregated sovereignty (Slaughter, 2004; Slaughter, 2005a; Slaughter, 2005b). The 'principal moving parts' of the contemporary world order comprise global networks of various agencies, institutions and officials who exercise some level of independent rights and are subject to some obligations (Slaughter, 2005a: 68). Together these globalised networks of states are responsible to their sovereign governments. These rights and obligations derive from functional needs of 'effective transgovernmental relations' (Slaughter, 2005a: 68). Whatever the reasons, 'sovereignty of states must become a flexible and practical attribute' (Slaughter, 2005a: 68).

Slaughter and Burke-White (2002: 1) recognise 1945 as an 'international constitutional moment' that established the state-centric '*grundnorm*, of the post-World War II world order'. Nations face a second constitutional moment after the end of the Cold War because in a globalised world, governments operate as interdependent networks and participate in structures of global governance. In order to participate effectively in the global structures, the participants must have 'a basic code that takes account of the rights and interests of *all* peoples' (Slaughter, 2005a: 39, italics added). Slaughter extends the obligations of governments to 'all peoples' beyond their own citizens and subjects them to the supranational authority of international law (Slaughter, 2005a: 39). Whereas under indirect rule native rulers were required to subject themselves to the paramount power, and after the First World War they had to submit to international authorities that became Smuts's 'heirs to the empires', Slaughter extends this idea to international 'rule of law'.

When government agencies participate in international networks on behalf of their states, they exercise some degree of autonomy and therefore a proportion of their state's sovereignty (Slaughter, 2005a: 62). Conceptually, Slaughter's idea of 'disaggregated sovereignty' extends Maine's idea of shared sovereignty for colonial governance without referring to colonial history. To operationalise disaggregated sovereignty, the principle of subsidiarity too returns in new forms under neoliberal globalisation. Drawing on ideas of subsidiarity of James Madison, considered the architect of the US constitution, and later the EU which also uses the concept, Slaughter argues that the idea of subsidiarity should be internationalised as it 'institutionalizes a system or a political process of global governance from bottom up' (Slaughter, 2005a: 61).

Maine argued that treaties were not the only basis for relations between imperial powers and their colonies (Holdsworth, 1930). Slaughter similarly argues that the international order is no longer a system based solely on conventional sources like interstate treaties and includes transnational actors like transnational enterprises and NGOs (Slaughter, 2000b: 242). Like Maine, Slaughter gives weight to contemporary usages and practices like transnational commerce, bilateral commercial agreements, international commercial arbitrations, environmental NGOs, transnational human rights organisations and voluntary codes of conduct as sources of law between states (ibid.). Slaughter prioritises the practices of private transnational actors as being 'ground-up' (ibid.), arguing states, acting in the public domain, should model their own behaviours after private actors (Slaughter, 2000b, 2005b).

Subsidiarity presupposes paramountcy in some form. For Maine the challenge was to constitutionally embed the EIC's principles of colonial governance after it was dissolved. For Smuts the challenge was to expand and entrench the laws and administrative principles of colonial governance of the imploding British Empire in the new international order under the League. For Slaughter, the challenge is to shift the loci of American supremacy in international relations from the state-centred model of the post the Second World War era to a corporate-centred model after the Cold War.

Arguing for 'radical surgery' (Ikenberry and Slaughter, 2006: 7) of the post-Second World War order institutions, Slaughter takes a two-pronged approach to the challenge. The first is to rework theories of sources of power in the UN system in which states are primary units (Slaughter, 2009).The sources of relative powers of states in the international system are not exclusively military and political as international law and international relations theorists have argued, but flow from the strength of their corporations, banks and NGOs. US supremacy rests, not on military prowess but on corporations and diaspora which connect the country to the whole world (Slaughter, 2009). Other states must recognise this and afford similar freedoms to corporations if they wish to become strong states and players in the international order.

The second prong concerns remodelling the UN system. For too long international law and international relations have modelled relations between states on state–citizen relations within liberal democracies (Slaughter, 1994: 388). All states seek investments, borrow money and engage in transnational activities. The national/international divide in international law is a fetter on 'primary actors' within states. The US must take the lead to reform the UN to allow full scope to the 'primacy actors' who may be individuals, corporations or NGOs

(Ikenberry and Slaughter, 2006; Slaughter, 1994, 2000a, 2000b). US diplomats must extend their diplomacy to all sectors to have a 'more "distributed presence", both virtually and physically' among 'a wide range of groups in their host countries' (Slaughter, 2009: 98–9). Third World states must grow up and take responsibility by making choices about their place in a connected world.

More significantly, like Maine and Smuts, Slaughter argues for entrenching a hierarchy of states in the UN system and returns to the vocabulary of European 'concerts' that resonate with the 'Concert of Vienna' in the post-Napoleonic era. The US must establish 'a concert of democracies', as a 'new institution' to 'institutionalize and ratify the "democratic peace"' (Ikenberry and Slaughter, 2006: 7). The Concert would be limited to states that commit to liberal democratic models of governance internally (i.e. electoral democracy, civil and political rights, property rights), and accept the responsibility to protect these internationally. 'If the UN cannot be reformed, the Concert would provide an alternative forum for liberal democracies to authorize collective action, including the use of force, by a supermajority vote' (Slaughter, 2006: 7). Thus, power-sharing between states is a vertical hierarchy between concert and non-concert states as well as horizontal networks between corporations, states and NGOs in liberal democracies.

Horizontal power and connectivity notwithstanding,'[at] their core, both liberty and law must be backed up by force' (Ikenberry and Slaughter, 2006: 8). Instead of the state-centric doctrines of the past, 'the United States should aim to sustain the military predominance' through the concert within the UN General Assembly, 'encourage the development of military capabilities by like-minded democracies' to prevent a return to great power policy and ensure that economic as well as political threats are effectively governed' (Ikenberry and Slaughter, 2006: 8; also Slaughter, 2009). Thus, American paramountcy returns, not sitting at the top of the 'ladder' of power as it did after the Second World War but at the centre of a 'web' where corporate power structures the American state and keeps it connected to a hierarchy of states. 'The twenty-first century looks increasingly like another American century' declares Slaughter (2009: 100).

Slaughter's thinking sits on a continuum with those of J.S Mill, Thomas Macaulay, Maine and Smuts. Mill and Macaulay were employed by the EIC, Maine was the law member of the Governor-General in Council for India, Smuts was a member of the Imperial War cabinet and Slaughter is a prominent member of the Democratic Party in the US who served as director of policy planning for the US state department between 2009 and 2011 and held various positions in influential American foreign policy institutions like the National Endowment for Democracy. She is recognised as one of the most influential US foreign policy experts (Munk Debates). Coming after the Reagan and Bush presidencies when the US was seen to be breaching international law, and US actions were perceived as unilateralism and exceptionalism, Slaughter's work synthesises numerous strands in liberal international law and international politics to rework the theoretical premises for international law and institutions on neoliberal-corporatist lines after the end of the Cold War.

Conclusion

Duncan Kennedy's thesis advances two related propositions. First that L&D is a field of study where lawyers, administrators and judicial processes position and reposition law in relation to development in particular ways. The forgoing sections have shown how the repositioning is impelled by resistances to imperial governance in different periods on the one hand and the transformations in capitalism and imperialism on the other. By abstracting legal consciousness from the wider social consciousness, Kennedy removes the agency of the colonised peoples in the development of L&D. In his second proposition, the diffusion thesis, by dating the history of globalisation of law from 1850, Kennedy cuts adrift the history of the relationship between corporations and capitalist states in the development of L&D as a body of knowledge for colonial/Third World governance. Datelines are important methodological tools for inclusion and exclusion of events and histories. The linear progression of international law from core to peripheries becomes questionable when one considers the extent to which the laws of empires have been incorporated within contemporary international law and institutions.

By abstracting legal relations from the materiality of social relations and side-stepping more fundamental questions about the nature of so-called 'development', Kennedy's thesis does three things. First it obscures the ways in which the economic power of corporations and political powers of capitalist states coalesce in imperial governance during different periods of capitalism and (neo)colonialism. Seen in this light, the present period based on sovereign equality of states is not less imperial than past empires. Second, it obscures the fact that behind the so-called 'development' agenda there are powerful economic and political interests of capitalist states. L&D is an elaborate political, economic, ideological, legal, institutional, scientific and technological regime of imperial governance in the contemporary era. Lastly, the methodological moves that rely on fragmented facts, disciplinary silos and disengagement with the materiality of the world reinforce the ideological power of capitalist/imperialist epistemology. In doing so, they disempower resistances to the corporate-state nexus in L&D scholarship as well as to new forms of imperialism in the contemporary world.

References

Alvarez, J.E., 2006. International Organizations: Then and Now. *American Journal of International Law*, *100*, 324–347.

Arndt, H.W., 1987. *Economic Development: The History of an Idea*. University of Chicago Press.

Arnold-Baker, C., 2001. *Resident, Residency*. Routledge.

Bakshi, S.R., 1967. Early Trade and Expansion of East India Company. *Modern Review, 121* (*4*), 286–293.
Barkan, J.E., 2013. *Corporate Sovereignty: Law and Government under Capitalism.* University of Minnesota Press.
Bell, D., 2010. John Stuart Mill on Colonies. *Political Theory, 38* (*1*), 34–64.
Carlos, A.M. and Kruse, J.B., 1996. The Decline of the Royal African Company: Fringe Firms and the Role of the Charter. *Economic History Review, XLIX* (*2*), 291–313.
Chandler Jr, A.D., 1990/2004. *Scale and Scope: Dynamics of Industrial Capitalism.* Harvard University Press.
Chandler Jr, A.D. and Mazlish, B. (eds), 2005. *Leviathan: Multinational Corporation And The New Global History.* Cambridge University Press.
Choudhary, A., 2009. Doctrine of Lapse – A Frayed Link for the Expansion of the British Empire in India. *Journal of Law and Business, 16*, 41–55.
Cohn, B.S., 1989. Law and the Colonial State in India. In J. Starr and J.F. Collier (eds), *History and Power in the Study of Law: New Directions in Legal Anthropology.* Cornell University Press.
Cohn, B.S., 1997. *Colonialism and Its Forms of Knowledge: The British In India.* Oxford University Press.
Court of Directors, E.I.C., 1833a. *Appendix to the Report from the Select Committee of the House of Commons on the Affairs of the East-India Company 16th August 1832 and Minutes of Evidence Volume IV, Judicial.* J.L. Cox and Son.
Court of Directors, E.I.C., 1833c. *Regulation II Of 1793 in Appendix to the Report from the Select Committee of the House of Commons on the Affaris of the East-India Company 16th August 1832 and Minutes of Evidence Volume IV, Judicial.* J.L. Cox and Son.
Court of Directors, E.I.C., 1833b. *Minutes of Evidence Taken Before the Select Committee of the House of Commons on the Affairs of the East-India Company, February 28th to July 9th, 1832 VI Political or Foreign.* Hathi Trust Digital Library. Available online at: https://catalog.hathitrust.org/Record/102187723 (accessed 1 October 2019).
Curry, G., 1961. Woodrow Wilson, Jan Smuts, and the Versailles Settlement. *The American Historical Review, 66* (*4*), 968–986.
Dodwell, H.H. 1920/1967. *Dupleix and Clive: The Beginning of Empire.* Cass.
Dubow, S., 2008. Smuts, the United Nations and the Rhetoric of Race and Rights. *Journal of Contemporary History, 43* (*1*), 43–72.
D'Souza, R., 2014. Revolt and Reform in South Asia: Ghadar Movement to 9/11 and After. *Economic & Political Weekly (Special Articles), XLIX* (*8*), 59–73.
Egerton, H. 1918. The System of British Colonial Administration of the Crown Colonies in the Seventeenth and Eighteenth Centuries Compared with the System Prevailing in the Nineteenth Century. *Transactions of the Royal Historical Society, 1*, 190–217.
Ericson, R.V., Doyle, A. and Barry, D., 2003. *Insurance as Governance.* University of Toronto Press.
Ferrier, R.W., 1970. The Trade between India and the Persian Gulf and The East India Company in the 17th Century. *Bengal Past and Present, 89* (*2*), 189–198.

Fisher, M.H., 1984. Indirect Rule in the British Empire: The Foundations of the Residency System in India. *Modern Asian Studies, 18* (*3*), 393–428.

Fisher, M.H., 1993. *The Politics of the British Annexation of India 1757–1857.* Oxford University Press India.

Fitzmaurice, A., 2015. Sovereign Trusteeship and Empire. *Theoretical Inquiries in Law, 16* (2), 447–471.

Gerwarth, R. and Manela, E., 2014. *Empires at War: 1911–1923.* Oxford University Press.

Hobsbawm, E., 1962/2010. *The Age of Revolution: 1789–1848.* Abacus.

Holdsworth, W.S., 1930. The Indian States and India. *Law Quarterly Review, 46,* 407–446.

Hyslop, J., 2009. Martial Law and Military Power in the Construction of the South African State: Jan Smuts and the 'Solid Guarantee of Force' 1899–1924. *Journal of Historical Sociology, 22* (2), 234–268.

Ikenberry, G.J. and Slaughter, A.-M., 2006. Forging a World of Liberty Under Law: U.S. National Security in the 21st Century: Final Report of the Princeton Project on National Security. Available online at: https://carma.newcastle.edu.au/jon/Preprints/Oddments/princeton-report.pdf (accessed 10 March 2019).

Indian States Committee, G.B., 1929. *Report of the Indian States Committee, 1928–29.* His Majesty's Stationery Office.

Keith, A.B., 1961. *A Constitutional History of India: 1600–1935,* 2nd edition. Central Book Depot (Allahabad).

Kennedy, D., 2006. Three Globalizations of Law and Legal Thought: 1850–2000. In D.M. Trubek and A. Santos (eds), *The New Economic Law and Development and Economic Development: A Critical Appraisal.* Cambridge University Press, p. 19.

Kochanek, J., 2013. Jan Smuts: Metaphysics and the League of Nations. *History of European Ideas, 39* (2), 267–286.

Maine, H.S., 1909. *Ancient Law: Its Connections with the Early History of Society and Its Relation to Modern Ideas.* Routledge and Kegan Paul.

Mantena, K., 2010. *Alibis of Empire: Henry Maine And The Ends of Liberal Imperialism. Munk Debates.* Princeton University Press. Available online at: https://www.munkdebates.com/debates/obamas-foreign-policy/speakers-con/anne-marie-slaughter (accessed 25 November 2015).

Onley, J., 2009. The Raj Reconsidered: British India's Informal Empire and Spheres Of Influence in Asia and Africa. *Asian Affairs, XL* (*1*), 44–62.

Open University. *Making Britain: Queen Victoria's Proclamation: The Open University, research project, text of Proclamations issued on 01 November 1858.* Centre for South Asian Studies. Available online at: http://www.csas.ed.ac.uk/mutiny/confpapers/Queen'sProclamation.pdf (accessed 1 April 2019).

Osgood, H.L., 1896a. The Corporation as a Form of Colonial Government. I. *Political Science Quarterly, 11* (*2*), 259–277.

Osgood, H.L., 1896b. The Corporation as a Form of Colonial Government. II. *Political Science Quarterly, 11* (*3*), 502–533.

Osgood, H.L., 1896c. The Corporation as a Form of Colonial Government. III. *Political Science Quarterly, 11* (*4*), 694–715.

Osgood, H.L., 1902. England and the American Colonies in the Seventeenth Century. *Political Science Quarterly, 17* (2), 206–222.

Osiander, A., 1994. *The States System of Europe, 1640–1990: Peacemaking and the Conditions of International Stability.* Oxford University Press.

Osiander, A., 2001. Sovereignty, International Relations, and the Westphalian Myth. *International Organization, 55* (2), 251–287.

Ramachandran, C., 1980. *East India Company and South Indian Economy.* New Era Publications.

Rich, E.E., 1960. *Hudson's Bay Company 1670–1870.* Macmillan.

Robins, N., 2012. *The Corporation That Changed the World: How the East India Company Shaped The Modern Multinational.* Pluto Press.

Slaughter, A.-M., 1994. The Liberal Agenda for Peace: International Relations Theory and the Future of the United Nations. *Transnational Law & Contemporary Problems, 4*, 377–419.

Slaughter, A.-M., 2000a. Building Global Democracy. *Chicago Journal of International Law, 1*, 223–229.

Slaughter, A.-M., 2000b. A Liberal Theory of International Law. *American Society of International Law, 94*, 240–249.

Slaughter, A.-M., 2004. Sovereignty and Power in a Networked World Order. *Stanford Journal of International Law, 40*, 283–327.

Slaughter, A.-M., 2005a. Disaggregated Sovereingty: Towards the Public Accountability of Global Government Networks. In D. Held and M. Koenig-Archibugi (eds), *Global Governance and Public Accountability.* Blackwell Publishing.

Slaughter, A.-M., 2005b. *A New World Order.* Princeton University Press.

Slaughter, A.-M., 2006. A New U.N. For A New Century. *Fordham Law Review, 74*, 2961–2970.

Slaughter, A.-M., 2009. America's Edge: Power in the Networked Century. *Foreign Affairs, 88* (*1*), 94–113.

Slaughter, A.-M. and Burke-White, W., 2002. An International Constitutional Moment. *Harvard International Law Journal, 43* (*1*), 1–21.

Smuts, J.C., 1918. *The League of Nations: A Practical Suggestion.* Hodder and Stoughton.

Stern, P.J., 2011. *The Company-State: Corporate Sovereignty and the Early Modern Foundations of the British Empire in India.* Oxford University Press.

Voigt, J.H., 1987. *India in the Second World War: A History with Problems.* Arnold-Heinemann.

Wilbur, M.E., 1945. *The East India Company: And the British Empire in the Far East.* Stanford University Press.

Chapter 10

Multiple enclosures through land concessions

Water, fiscal resources and police power

Tomaso Ferrando

Land concessions as the source of multiple enclosures

Between 2007 and 2008, the Global South was severely affected by famine and subsequent food riots. For some, the link between food scarcity and political instability was central to the so-called 'Arab Spring' (Himenez and Shattuck, 2011). The main causes were identified as the effects of climate change (with droughts in Russia and excessive rains in other productive countries), protectionist policies aimed at guaranteeing national food security in food-exporting countries, and the volatility of grain prices due to financial speculation (Clapp and Isakson, 2018a, 2018b; Clapp, 2014; Russi, 2013; SOMO, 2011; De Schutter, 2010, 2011c; Brobakk and Almås, 2011; Wiggins and Keats, 2009; Burch and Lawrence, 2009).

Many countries with limited food production capacity were suddenly troubled by their dependence on markets and foreign countries for their food security. At the same time, transnational companies, international financial institutions and investors realised that agricultural land represented a crucial (and scarce) resource and an opportunity for economic gains. Moreover, development agencies and international organisations began realising the centrality of land for food and energy production and declared large-scale agricultural projects a new priority.

Soon, the productivist agricultural paradigm,[1] agricultural corridors and global trade in food became the unchallenged strategies to solve food insecurity: a new wave of large scale investment in farmland aimed at mobilizing available and 'idle land' was on its way.[2] Throughout the Global South – but also in some areas of

1 A productivist approach to agriculture focuses on yields and the amount of food that can be grown in a determined space. It is often supported by a Malthusian vision of the world and by the fear of food insecurity due to lack of insufficient production. Therefore, land, water, seeds, labour and all the other elements that are required to grow food are perceived and treated as factors of production to be maximised. Large-scale, industrialised and standardised agriculture is considered to be the most efficient way to fulfil this vision.

2 The discourse of 'idle land' has been crucial to the replacement of small-scale farming and common land by industrialised agriculture, monocropping, export-led agriculture and the

the Global North such as Eastern Europe – private and public actors (including sovereign wealth funds, hedge funds and pension funds) engaged in a new scramble for land fed by the win-win-win rhetoric of feeding an increasing population, generating high revenues and expanding the frontiers of industrialised agriculture. Land in sub-Saharan Africa, which is characterised by a low level of titling and a proprietary system based on the colonial idea of the state as the protector of people through the use of public land, represented a preferred destination for these new projects.

By 2017, around 70 million hectares of publicly owned land had shifted to ownership or control by third parties (Land Matrix, 2017). This massive enclosure of land led to bottom-up movements of resistance to protect communities dependent on that land (Martinez-Alier et al., 2016) as well as considerable academic critique (Peluso and Lund, 2011; White et al., 2012; Fairhead et al., 2011; Sassen, 2013b; Künnemann and Monsalve Suárez, 2013; De Schutter, 2011a, 2011b; Goetz, 2013; Margulis et al., 2013; Berhman, 2011; Chu, 2011). Codes of conduct for responsible investments were promoted by International Financial Institutions that had supported land-related projects, the United Nations, the UN Food and Agriculture Organization (FAO, 2012), along with some transnational corporations. Some national policy makers were forced to consider remedies too, as in the case of the Brazilian moratorium against foreign investments in land.[3] Yet, critical voices from local activists and academia promptly highlighted that these responses were mere quick fixes, flawed in their systemic overlooking of the problems behind the adoption of a capital intensive agricultural model based on homogenisation of production, large-scale and international trade (Borras and Franco, 2010). Similarly, lawyers and legal scholars, exposed the multiple ways in which the enclosure of large tracts of land violate the human rights of the people living on the land and the dramatic consequences for the environment. Posing law as the solution, the focus of international human rights, national legal orders and transnational advocacy has been on the violation of the Free, Prior, Informed Consent, on the displacement of communities and on the way in which legal structures could be deployed to remedy the environmental damages. Because the problem is generally perceived as a lack of

global reallocation of land resources through international food markets. Because of its incompatibility with international human rights law, the impact on traditional land rights, and its consequences for sustainability and the loss of livelihoods, the discourse has been widely criticised (Hall, 2011; Ferrando, 2014).

3 Some countries, especially in Latin America, have introduced moratoriums on the sale or concession of land to foreign capital. This happened, for example, in Brazil in 2010, mainly, as a result of pressure exercised by environmental groups and international public opinion. However, these measures were justified on the desire to keep foreign investors away from land as a strategic asset, but did not question the socio-environmental impact of large-scale agriculture nor the notions of idle land and the desirability of industrialised agricultural development (Coutinho et al., 2018; Advocacia-Geral da União, 2010).

legal protections or a legal gap in the context of otherwise appropriate investment, law is often described as the source of solutions rather than an enabler of the violations.

This chapter looks at law as part of the problem and – in particular – recognises that land concession agreements are legal tools through which new legal frameworks are created by the parties that crystallise the inequality of the state-market-community power dynamics (Santos, 2010). It is through these complex concession agreements, in which representatives of the host state guarantee rights and power to the lessee, that the global enclosure of land takes place. Concessions reveal how 'land grabbing' involves the transfer of power and control from the public/communal to the private enacted through a legal agreement – even though this may be contrary to national or international law (Franco et al., 2013).

By putting the concessions at the centre of the investigation, this chapter reveals that these public-private agreements do much more than privatising land and transforming local territory into a factor of global production (Ferrando, 2017). Concessions are about legalising multiple enclosures within the space of the investment. First, they define how the investors can appropriate water, a crucial 'asset' when it comes to agricultural production; then, they concern taxes and the privatisation of the value extracted from land and water; finally, they transfer to the investor's control the power of policing and securitising the space that has been enclosed.

This chapter relies on a selection of ten agreements out of the 193 land concessions that were publicly available in the Open Land Contracts database at the time of writing.[4] The specific focus is on sub-Saharan African countries, and Ethiopia in particular, because the intensity of the phenomenon in the region and because Ethiopia was the sole country to openly disclose part of the agreements concluded with various investors. Although the deals represent only a fraction of the investments concluded after 2006, they are enough to reveal the multiple enclosures beyond land and – by means of comparison and juxtaposition – offer basis for some critical reflections for further investigation and engagement. Section 2 examines the provisions relating to water in the agreements and especially how these provide investors with full access to this vital resource, which is often exploited with little or no concern for local communities and the environment. Section 3 analyses the creation of Special Fiscal Zones through *ad hoc* sub-systems of law that embed investments into a legal and financial

4 All the agreements utilised in this paper are available at Open Land Contracts, a recently established online database realised with the support of the Columbia Centre for Sustainable Investment. In September 2017, the database contained 193 contracts concerning 14 countries and 45 resources. According to the webpage, 'OpenLandContracts.org is a repository of publicly available investment contracts for land, agriculture, and forestry projects. It features plain language summaries of key provisions and provides tools for searching and comparing contracts.' (http://www.openlandcontracts.org/) (accessed 9 September 2017).

architecture that is similar to tax havens.[5] Section 4 discusses how concessions recognise the right of private investors to exercise traditionally sovereign prerogatives such as arrest and detention, involving the replacement of the public by the private. Concession agreements create 'special legal zones' that generate multiple appropriations and accumulations of resources, and value for the concessionaires. My comparative examination of concessions facilitates an analysis of the diversity and similarities of the agreements and the legal, political, economic and social reasons behind each combination of rights and obligations.

Water grabbing through investment clauses

It is not surprising that stable and continuous access to water is regarded by investors as an essential feature of any large-scale agricultural project. However, it took some years before the link between global land enclosures, the availability of water for local communities and the possible contamination of streams was put at the centre of the research agenda. Water was the hidden treasure in land enclosures, and concessions the hidden tool to satisfy investors' thirst.

In the last few years, an increasing number of studies have highlighted the relationship between the private accumulation of land for agricultural projects and the dispossession of water resources (Mehta et al., 2012; Woodhouse, 2012). During the same period, Franco et al.'s *Primer on Water Grabbing* argued that:

> [l] and and water grabbing are driven by large-scale monoculture production of both food and non-food crops. Premised on the application of industrial production practices, these monocultures gear agriculture towards profit maximisation in which water is seen simply as a raw material to be converted into higher value commodities.
>
> (2014: 8)

Subsequently, a few empirical studies were undertaken, with Rulli et al. (2013) being among the first to seek to calculate the impacts of large-scale investment projects on freshwater resources. Because the industrialised model of agriculture proposed by large-scale land investments cannot rely exclusively on rain, the study showed that the increase in water input needed by new large-scale projects

5 According to Ronen Palan (2009: 1): 'The term "tax haven" has been widely used since the 1950s. Yet there is no consensus as to what it means. The problem is that on the one hand many governments use their sovereign right to enact law in order to help successful sectors within their economies to compete in the world economy or, alternatively, to spur the development of new competitive sectors. They often employ some combination of fiscal subsidies and sweeteners, including reductions in taxation (sometimes by informal or highly opaque set of arrangements) and removal of 'red tape' (i.e. regulation) to attract or retain mobile capital.'

had a negative impact on the availability of irrigation water for ungrabbed neighbouring farmland areas. They concluded that an analysis of 'the top 24 grabbed countries shows that land grabbing is associated with a virtual grabbing of a substantial amount of freshwater resources, including both water supplied by rainfall and irrigation' (Rulli et al., 2013: 893).[6]

Pearce (2013) claimed that the amount of water extracted from its natural cycle and utilised for new industrial projects may not be as high as Rulli et al. claim, nevertheless there is no doubt that the enclosure of land must be studied together with the enclosure of water. While several authors have examined the human rights implications of diverted water resources and much has been written on how law contributes to the transformation of common water into privatised 'blue gold' (Spagnuolo, 2017; D'Odorico et al., 2017; Dell'Angelo et al., 2017), these analyses do not enter into the detail of land concessions and the allocation of rights on water.

Clauses concerning access to water are present in the majority of the concessions analysed. Yet, a comparison between the agreements shows that there are differences in the quality and quantity of water privatisation, even in concessions granted by the same government. Ethiopia provides a good example. The government made public a dozen concessions granted around 2010. These agreements, which are based on a standard contract template that is then adapted to individual projects, contain a water clause that recognises the risk for the environment (but not for the neighbour communities), and thus attempt to strike a balance in relation to the quantity and quality of water usage. For example, Article 3.3 of the Karuturi Agro Products Plc Agreement, a project extending over 100,000 hectares, provides the lessee with the right to: 'use irrigation water from rivers or ground water respecting present and future environmental and water laws and regulations ***without any disturbance to the environment with prior permission from responsible federal and regional institutions***' (Ethiopia–Karuturi Agro, 2010, emphasis added).[7]

However, individual clauses must be read in the broader context of the whole agreement, its enforceability and the possibilities that third parties would have to challenge any breach. For example, Article 3.2 of the same document states that the lessee has the additional right:

6 The authors estimated that global land grabbing is associated with the grabbing of 308 billion cubic metres (m^3) of green water (i.e. rainwater) and an additional grabbing of blue water between 11 billion m^3 (current irrigation practices) and 146 billion m^3 (maximal irrigation) per year.

7 The same disposition is contained in the contracts concluded between the Ministry of Agriculture of the Federal Democratic Republic of Ethiopia (FDRE) with Hunan Dafengyuan Agriculture Co. Ltd (Ethiopia–Hunan, 2010), Saudi Star with Ethiopia (Ethiopia–Saudi Star, 2010), Ruchi Agri PLC Lease (Ethiopia–Ruchi Agri, 2010), and Bho Bio products PLC (Ethiopia–Bho Bio, 2010) despite their difference in size.

> to build infrastructure such as dams, water boreholes, power houses, irrigation systems [...] at the ***discretion of the lessee*** upon consultation and submission of permit request with concerned offices subject to the type and size of the investment project ***whenever it deems so appropriate.***
>
> (Ethiopia–Karuturi Agro, 2010, emphases added)

Thus, although Article 3.3 may appear restrictive, Article 2.2. gives wide discretion to the investors by leaving the whole process in the hands of the lessee and non-specified concerned offices, with no clear procedure nor role for the public authority, the local communities and any third party interested in the protection of the environment. Although a concession is generally interpreted as the binding law between the parties, the content of the clause and its inclusion in a private–public agreement raise three considerations.

First, the investor obtains a discretionary right to alter the geography and hydrology of the land by building permanent infrastructure that can significantly impact the availability of water in neighbouring areas: however, only the environmental impact is recognised and not the consequences that this can have on communities depending on the same waterways. Second, the agreement recognises access to water as a contractual right without any provision for payment for the service nor any grievance procedure for communities whose access to water is reduced or to third parties interested in the preservation of the environment. Third, the agreements are subject to both present and future environmental and water law, suggesting that a tightening of the regulatory framework that negatively affects the right of the investor to access water may not be raised by the investor as a breach of contract.[8] Nevertheless, it is not clear whether an investment arbitral tribunal would consider such a clause sufficient to oust the fair and equitable treatment required by several bilateral investment treaties.

An interesting example is the concession of a tract of Malian land in favour of the Société Malibya Agricole signed in 2008. Although the project never went beyond the first stage of land clearing – mainly because of the political situation in the North of Mali – the agreement is worth mentioning both because of its content and form. As for the latter, the concession was not concluded between Mali and Malibya Agricole, but between Mali and Libya: rather than a public-private deal, the document assumes the characteristics of an international agreement between states for the benefit of a private actor, a sort of *ad hoc* bilateral investment treaty. Second, the agreement goes further than the Ethiopian concession by granting Malibya Agricole access to all the water needed by the project and imposing over the Malian government the obligation:

8 See note 14 below for reference to clause 22.2 of Cameroon–SG (2009) and the recognition that any conflict between future laws – with the exception of the Constitution – and the agreement shall be solved in favour of the agreement (Cameroon–SG, 2009).

> to provide the Société Malibya Agricole all the permits needed to use the water deriving from the Macina channel along with all the water that flows in the subsoil, according to the water needs of the project as determined by the Economic Feasibility Analysis.
>
> (Malibya, 2008)[9]

The fact that the agreement was about water as much as land becomes even more evident when looking at article 8.1, according to which Mali has to 'allow the Société Malibya Agricole to utilise for the project all the water that is needed, with no restriction, in the period between June and December of every year',[10] that is, the dry season in the area of Macina. As constructed, the agreement enclosed land and introduced a clear hierarchy of water use where the project had priority over local communities and other uses and the host state the obligation to uphold it (Malibya, 2008). Unlimited access to water at no cost is also guaranteed in Cameroon–SG (2009), where water is not considered for its environmental and social role, but just as a factor of production.[11]

Compared to the previous cases, the 2009 concession agreement between Sime Darby Plantation (Liberia) Inc. and Liberia (Liberia–Sime Darby, 2009) demonstrates that the tensions between communities and investors' rights can be taken into consideration and made subject to specific arrangements. Although the first part of Article 4 introduces a 'water clause' that recognises the investor's right to free, unlimited access to water, stones, rocks, sand and other resources, the second part of the clause states that the investor's right must be subordinated to the existing 'rights of third parties or with use by Government', which cannot be freely impeded.

More specifically, Article 4.4(e) states:

> Investor may not dam any streams or use amounts of water that could materially interfere with the activities of farmers or residents being conducted on the Effective Date. Prior to damming any streams or other bodies of water, the Investor shall seek approval from the relevant

9 Original document reads: 'La République du Mali s'engage à offrir à la Société Malibya agricole tous les permis d'usage de l'eau du canal de Macina ainsi que les eaux souterraines ou les deux selon les besoins du projet déterminés par l'étude de faisabilité économique du projet, de la manière suivante'.

10 The original document reads: '1. permettre à la Société Malibya agricole d'utiliser la quantité d'eau nécessaire et sans restriction pour le projet pendant le période de mois Juin à Décembre de chaque année; [...] 3. La République du Mali s'engage à assurer la quantité d'eau nécessaire pour les dites cultures à partir du canal de Macina' (Malibya, 2008).

11 Articles 3.3(v) and 3.8 provide the investor with the exclusive right within the Production Area, to take and use, subject to the limitations pursuant to Article 10, free of charge [...], such water [...] as Investor may consider necessary or useful for Investor Activities, without the need to obtain any further authorization or pay any further fees' (Cameroon–SG, 2009).

> governmental authority, which approval shall not be unreasonably withheld unless there is evidence that the construction of such dam or dams would breach this Section.
>
> (Liberia–Sime Darby, 2009)

Instead of legalising water-grabbing and prioritising the investors' rights above everything else, the concession becomes an opportunity to anticipate foreseeable conflicts between communities and private parties and limit the latter's rights over the common resource. However, the Sime Darby agreement may still be ineffective as it does not involve the community in the control or enforcement of the agreement. Similarly to the Ethiopian concessions discussed above, the agreement identifies the host state as the sole party with the power to intervene and sanction a breach of the contract by investors. Local communities' access to water is regulated by a concession in the drafting of which they have had no involvement.

It is thus possible to conclude that access to water represents a central element in large-scale land deals, and that 'water grabbing' regularly occurs under the cover of the law. State-investor concessions are utilised to introduce and protect the private right to access and accumulate 'blue gold', and to impose an obligation on the state to ensure that these rights are not impeded (even during the dry season as in the case of Malibya). However, the differences in the clauses demonstrate that the concessions may also be used to introduce limits to the ways in which dispossession and private accumulation of water takes place. The introduction of limits, authorisation and competing rights does not appear to transform the state-investor relationship into a broader and more inclusive legal space. Without proper participation in the drafting, monitoring and enforcing, local communities are present but voiceless, so that their rights are at continuous risk of being extinguished (Perrone, 2016). If the main problem in relation to water is that land concessions subordinate the rights of local communities to the economic interests of the investors and recognise states' legal obligations to accept exploitative practices, the implications of land concessions for the appropriation of fiscal revenues goes well beyond the local effects of the investment.

Enclosure of fiscal revenues and the contractual construction of Global Wealth Chains

According to a 2015 report of the United Nations Conference on Trade and Development (UNCTAD), countries in the global South lose about $100 billion per year in revenues from tax avoidance, false invoicing and transfer pricing (UNCTAD, 2011). In some cases, fiscal authorities only capture 40 per cent of their tax potential, losing crucial resources for the implementation and expansion of their public policies (International Tax Compact, 2011). This phenomenon has been discussed and analysed from multiple angles.

Along with corruption and insufficient infrastructures, one of the reasons has to be found in host states entrapment in a tax competition that leads to a constant reduction of fiscal restraints (Abbas and Klemm, 2013). Governments are victims of a 'sovereign dilemma' where they have to choose between losing the investment or lowering the amount of value that they can capture. While this loss of value has been studied in the context of mining and transfer pricing (Guj et al., 2017; Christian Aid, 2009), almost nothing has been said with regard to the link between large-scale investments in land and the minimisation of the revenue stream accruing to the state via taxes and royalties. Once more, concessions provide a unique opportunity to cast light on the link between law and the creation of what Seabrooke and Wigan (2017, 2014) define as 'Global Wealth Chains' and that Quentin and Campling (2017) call 'Global Inequality Chains', i.e. combinations of jurisdictions and legal structures that facilitate the private accumulation of the value extracted from exploiting nature and labour.

More concretely, land concessions become the legal space where the competition for foreign investments is translated into the investors' rights to lower taxes and the states' commitment to give out land almost for free. For example, under article 6.2 of the Ethiopia–Hunan concession (2010) the state provides the investor with special investment privileges 'such as exemptions from taxation and import duties of capital goods and repatriation of capital and profits granted under the investment laws of Ethiopia.' The entirety of the rent generated through the exploitation of land, labour and water is thus accumulated by the investor.

Other contracts contain more detailed and extensive dispositions generally involving reductions of or exemptions from corporate and trade taxes, along with favourable foreign exchange rates. Two examples of palm oil agreements illustrate this., Article 11 of the Cameroon–SG (2009) exempts the investor from 'any and all existing and future Taxes and Duties from the Initial Production Date of the Production Area' for ten years and

> upon the expiration of each 10 years period, and continuing throughout the remainder of the Term, the Investor shall continue to enjoy an exemption from any and all existing and future Taxes and Duties, with the exception of a tax on Taxable Profits at a flat rate not exceeding 15%.

This is less than half of the 38.5 per cent standard tax rate in Cameroon at the time of the investment (Trading Economics, 2020). The Sierra Leone–Addax Agreement of 2010 provided for a 13-year exemption from corporate tax, estimated at $100 million a year.

While each case depends on the specificity of negotiation and the particular socio-political-economic and legal context, they have a common thread: states assume the obligation to provide investors with financial conditions that are better than those imposed on the broad population, with the consequence that they will have access to less resources than otherwise required by the law and thus less possibilities to fulfil their human rights obligations towards the citizens subject to the 'normal' tax regime

From the point of view of global wealth chains, the fiscal clauses introduced in the concessions may also have significant repercussions at the international level because of the increase possibility of manipulative transfer pricing (MTP) that arises when states with limited resources to control accounting practices and capital mobility guarantee low or zero fiscal imposition and open their borders to the flow of money. Investors use MTP through complex networks of subsidiaries and branches located in multiple jurisdictions to artificially allocate expenses and revenues to maximise profits for the whole conglomerate. In order to achieve this, high expenses are allocated to jurisdictions with high taxation so that profits are generated in low tax jurisdictions (Bartelsman and Beetsma, 2003; Eden and Smith, 2011; Clausing, 2002; Tomohara, 2004).

In the case of land concessions, it is important to keep in mind that in most cases the concession agreement is concluded between the host state and a subsidiary or affiliate of the investor corporation which is incorporated in the host state.[12] In some cases, this is used to comply with legal requirement that excludes foreign ownership of the land, but in other cases it is done to allocate rent in jurisdictions with more favourable fiscal conditions or to shield wealth from external scrutiny.

When investors are guaranteed low corporate tax, zero trade tax and unlimited currency mobility, they have an incentive to declare all their profit there and then channel the profit to a parent company located in a fiscal haven, without the need to channel payments through an intermediary entity registered in a low or no tax jurisdiction (Picciotto, 2012). The wealth that the investor gains through the use of the land can thus be relatively easily protected from the fiscal scrutiny of other jurisdictions and is likely to be transferred to foreign bank accounts in tax havens (Henry, 2012). In the context of global wealth chains and the protection of rent from public scrutiny, we can thus argue that land concessions are the legal tool through which sovereignty is commercialised and becomes a shield that legitimates avoidance and appropriation (Palan, 2009). With host states wishing to gain whatever crumbs they can from the investment, the consequence is a global race to the bottom and an overall global loss in revenue collection. Instead of an opportunity for development and socio-economic improvement, such investments are legally constructed as sources of increased inequality both locally and globally. When revenues and values are legally extracted and appropriated

12 Chinese investors are an exception. Both the Mali-China Light Industrial Corporation for Foreign Economic and Technical Cooperation (China Light–Mali, 2009) and the Ethiopia–Hunan Dafengyuan Agriculture Co. Ltd (Ethiopia–Hunan, 2010) agreements are directly concluded by private limited company incorporated in China and registered under the national law of both countries. Thus, no national subsidiary was created to receive and manage the public–private concession.

without adequate returns for host countries, government support for large-scale investment projects loses much of its justification.

A critical and expansive approach to the concession reveals, in conclusion, not only that they are about more than land, but that they must be studied as legal connectors between a local act (the conclusion of the agreement that encloses a specific part of territory) and the global economic system. Whereas the appropriation of land and water may be simplistically labelled as a local concern,[13] its fiscal repercussions are global in nature. Thus, any attempt to address the negative externalities produced by these agreements has to be transnational, collective and based upon a systematic redefinition of the legal and economic assumptions that operate in concessions negotiations. A narrow approach that rigidly respects freedom of contract while ignoring the content of private-public concession agreements, reinforces the vicious circles of local and global distributive inequalities.

Enclosure of the use of police power and the right to self-securitisation

A third element that emerges from a comparative consideration of land concessions is the enclosure and privatisation of the right to use force to protect the investments from any form of dissent. When looked at with critical eyes, concessions are the legal tools to allocate land, give priority access to water and limit the value gained by the host state and its citizens. They are also the way in which states formalise the guarantee that dissent and resistance will be prosecuted, either by the use of force by the host state or by carving out spaces of private impunity. This can be done by the state assuming the obligation to use its police or military forces to protect the investment or by the investors receiving the right to protect themselves with the use of powers that are traditionally reserved to the public authority.

An example of provisions that give investors the right to demand the use of public coercion and violence to defend their activities is article 6.6 of Ethiopia–Karuturi (2010). This requires the host government to take police or military action against resistance to the investor's project. More precisely, the government:

> shall ensure during the period of the lease, that the Lessee [Karuturi] shall enjoy peaceful and trouble-free possession of the premises and it shall be provided adequate security, free of cost, for carrying out its entire activities

13 It is erroneous to deny the transnational nature of land and water appropriation. This is both because of the close link between enclosures, urbanisation and migrations and because land that is transformed into a productive investment is also linked to global supply chains (Ferrando, 2017).

in the said premises, against any riot, disturbance or any other turbulent time other than force majeure, *as and when requested by the Lessee*
(Ethiopia–Karuturi, 2010, emphases added)

Similarly, article 14 of the Ethiopian standard contract, 'Covenant of peaceful possession', states that 'the Lessor warrants that it has full ownership and property rights in the leased area for granting this land lease agreement and *shall protect the right of the Lessee to the peaceful possession, use and quiet enjoyment thereof*' (emphasis added).

Such clauses establish clear hierarchical relationships between the rights of investors, the state and the communities. First, the investors are provided with an action for breach of contract in case the state does not deal effectively with communities' resistance; second, investors may action these clauses to deflect allegations of aiding and abetting the state in the commission of human rights violations, by claiming that the intervention to maintain the peaceful enjoyment of the investment is an obligation of the state; third, the investor may claim that the state must indemnify it in respect of any damages awarded against it for torts committed against the resisting communities in order to protect its right of peaceful enjoyment.

As a result, concessions ensure that the cost of protecting the enclosure of land, water and fiscal resources falls on the host state, whether in terms of direct costs occurring to repress 'disruptive behavior' or in the form of compensation for human rights violations committed by the state or by the investor.

Some concessions transfer public functions, including police powers, to the investors. In the case of Cameroon–SG, the concession provides that the investor is authorised to establish and manage their own security system and that such service 'shall have the power to search, apprehend, detain, exclude and evict unauthorised persons from the Production Area, and from such other areas as may be properly restricted for economic, operational or security reasons, subject to applicable Law' (Cameroon–SG, 2009). Similarly, clause 4.6 of the Addax Agreement (Sierra Leone–Addax, 2010) reserves the right of the investor to evict third parties in exceptional circumstances subject to the payment of compensation. Yet, the concession does not outline such exceptional circumstances and does not specify procedural and substantive elements of the compensation.

Although there is no evidence that the clauses have ever been triggered, they must be understood in the context of concessions that claim priority over the national law of the host states (e.g. Cameroon–SG, 2009: Clause 22.2)[14] This is reinforced by provisions for investment arbitration whether in the concession

14 Article 22.2, 'Construction and Interpretation', affirms that' *in the event of a conflict between this Agreement and any Law, except for the Constitution of Cameroon, as in effect as of the date hereof, the rights, obligations and duties of a Party shall be deemed to be those set forth in this Agreement*' (emphasis added).

agreement or in a bilateral treaty.[15] These provisions have contributed to increases in violence against environmental and human rights activists during the last decade – often with state acquiescence (Franklin, 2009; Gartner and Regan, 1996). Land concession agreements are thus used by states and investors to normalise the use of violence against local communities and to establish a legal framework that prioritises the protection of private property over the rights of people to protest, access traditional land or challenge the enclosure. In this context, it appears naïve to try to think of law as part of the solution and, more importantly, it seems reductive to discuss the potential of international human rights and environmental law without embedding the state-investors-community tensions in a pluralist legal framework significantly affected by the content of the concessions.

Conclusion

In her analysis of land grabbing as a de-territorialised phenomenon, Saskia Sassen (2013a: 37) concluded:

> the materiality and visibility of foreign land acquisitions become heuristic: they tell us something about a larger process that is often not as visible and material as land and the direct participation of the executive branch of government in the execution of contracts. This is a very different way of representing economic globalization than the common notion of the whole state as victim. Indeed, to a large extent it is the executive branch of government that is getting aligned with global corporate capital, both in the Global South and in the Global North.

In line with her claim, this chapter has examined land concession agreements with a heuristic purpose, i.e. to demonstrate how public–private legal encounters crystallised in the agreements are central to the realisation of multiple enclosures beyond the privatisation of land. Analysing ten agreements concluded between 2006 and 2009 that were selected from the Open Land Contracts database, I have argued that concessions of public land to private investors not only sanction the transfer of the land value from the public to the investor, but also the control over water, fiscal revenues and police powers. Contrary to the dominant narrative of grabbing as illegal or a-legal, the role of law in public–private concessions shows that the multiple enclosures are not the outcome of hidden processes or inevitable dynamics, but the consequence of political decisions embodied in legal documents.

The juxtaposition of texts and the assessment of their implications has brought to light two aspects that merit detailed future research. First, that state–investor

15 E.g. The United States and Cameroon Bilateral Investment Treaty 1986, which entered into force in 1989.

agreements are about more than land and stretch beyond local communities: they define how wealth and value are extracted locally, but have a domino effect because of their transnational implications for wealth shielding, transfer pricing, migration, social and political unrest, and environmental degradation. Second, although agreements concluded by different countries with different investors may have identical clauses, the comparative approach revealed that a government may sign agreements that differ in terms of substance, rights, obligations and third parties. Although it is not a surprise that public–private contracts differ, a further analysis of the reasons and effects of similarities and differences can lead to a better understanding of the internal and external elements in the wording and operation of concessions. Moreover, mapping the content of large-scale land concessions, their genealogy and their distributive patterns could provide better understanding of their role in the international division of labour and the construction of Global Wealth Chains (Seabrooke and Wigan, 2017, 2014) and the reproduction of structural inequalities in the global political-economy (Quentin and Campling, 2017).

In conclusion, lawyers, legal scholars and activists can use land concessions to engage with law and land grabbing beyond land enclosure and evictions, and abandon the idea that law is part of the solution rather than part of the problem. Linking Sassen's idea of the heuristic materiality of investments in land, a critical approach to land concessions sheds light on the state–capital nexus and the inequalities that it reproduces and crystallises by means of investors' rights and states' obligations (Van Apeldoorn et al., 2012). In the absence of a systematic critique of law and transnational systems of production, legal interventions can offer no more than temporary and provisional solutions.

References

Abbas, S. and Klemm, A., 2013. A Partial Race to the Bottom: Corporate Tax Developments in Emerging and Developing Economies. *International Tax and Public Finance*, *20* (*4*), 596–617.

Advocacia-Geral da União, 2010. *Adams explica parecer que restringe aquisição de terras brasileiras por estrangeiros*. Advocacia-Geral da União. Available online at: https://www.agu.gov.br/noticia/adams-explica-parecer-que-restringe-aquisicao-de-terras-brasileiras-por-estrangeiros–1 (accessed 1 August 2019).

Bartelsman, E. and Beetsma, R., 2003. Why Pay More? Corporate Tax Avoidance through Transfer Pricing in OECD Countries. *Journal of Public Economics*, *87* (*9–10*), 2225–2252.

Berhman, J., Meinzen-Dick, R. and Quisumbing, A.R., 2011. *The Gender Implications of Large-Scale Land Deals*. IFPRI Discussion Paper 01056.

Borras, S. and Franco, J. 2010. From Threat to Opportunity? Problems with the Idea of a 'Code of Conduct' for Land-Grabbing. *Yale Human Rights and Development Law Journal*, *2* (*13*), 507–523.

Brobakk, J. and Almås, R., 2011. Increasing Food and Energy Prices in 2008: What Were the Causes and Who Was to Blame? *International Journal of Sociology of Agriculture & Food*, *18* (*3*), 236–259.

Burch, D. and Lawrence, G., 2009. Towards a Third Food Regime: Behind the Transformation. *Agricultural and Human Values*, *26* (*4*), 267–279.

Cameroon–SG Sustainable Oils Cameroon PLC, 2009. Establishment Convention by and between the Republic of Cameroon and SG Sustainable Oil Cameroon PLC. Openland Contracts: An Online Repository of Open Land Contracts. Available online at: http://openlandcontracts.org/contract/ocds-591adf-9515165470/view#/pdf (accessed 4 September 2017).

China Light–Mali, 2009. China Light Industrial Corporation for Foreign Economic and Technical Cooperation (CLETC), Contrat de Concession Agricole. Openland Contracts: An Online Repository of Open Land Contracts. Available online at: https://openlandcontracts.org/contract/ocds-591adf-6757462987/view#/search/china%20light%20industrial (accessed 3 August 2019).

Christian Aid, 2009. *Breaking the Curse*. Available online at: http://www.christianaid.org.uk/Images/breaking-the-curse.pdf (accessed 4 September 2017).

Chu, J., 2011. Gender and 'Land Grabbing' in Sub-Saharan Africa: Women's Land Rights and Customary Land Tenure. *Development*, *54* (*1*), 35–39.

Clapp, J., 2014. Financialization, Distance and Global Food Politics. *Journal of Peasant Studies*, *41* (*5*), 797–814.

Clapp, J. and Isakson, R., 2018a. Risky Returns: The Implications of Financialization in the Food System. *Development and Change*, *49* (*2*), 437–460.

Clapp, J. and Isakson, R., 2018b. *Speculative Harvests: Financialization, Food and Agriculture*. Fernwood Publishing.

Clausing, K.A., 2002. Tax-Motivated Transfer Pricing and US Intrafirm Trade Prices. *Journal of Public Economics*, *87* (*2003*), 2207–2223.

Coutinho, D., Marques Prol, F. and Almeida de Castro, H., 2018. Brazil for Sale: as Transformaçoes do regime jurídico da Aquisiçao de Terras por Estrangeiros. In D. Ungaretti, M. Rolemberg Lessa, D. Coutinho, F. Marques Prol, I.Z. Miola and T. Ferrando, *Propiedades em Transformação. Abordagens Multidisciplinares Sobre a Propiedade No Brasil*. Blucher.

Dell'Angelo, J., D'Odorico, P. and Rulli M.C., 2017. Threats to Sustainable Development Posed by Water Grabbing. *Current Opinion in Environmental Sustainability*, *26–7*, 120–128.

De Schutter, O., 2010. *Food Commodities Speculation and Food Price Crises: Regulation to Reduce the Risks Of Price Volatility*. Briefing Note 02. United Nations.

De Schutter, O., 2011a. The Green Rush: The Global Race for Farmland and the Rights of Land Users. *Harvard International Law Journal*, *52*, 503.

De Schutter, O., 2011b. How Not to Think of Land-Grabbing: Three Critiques of Large-Scale Investments in Farmland. *Journal of Peasant Studies*, *38* (*2*), 249–279.

De Schutter, O., 2011c. *Observations on the Current Food Price Situation*. Background Note. United Nations.

De Sousa Santos, B., 2010. From the Postmodern to the Postcolonial – and Beyond Both. In E. Gutierrez Rodriguez et al. (eds), *Decolonizing European Sociology. Transdisciplinary Approaches*. Ashgate.

D'Odorico, P., Rulli, M.C., Dell'Angelo, J. and Davis, K.F., 2017. New Frontiers of Land and Water Commodification: Socio-Environmental Controversies of Large-Scale Land Acquisitions. *Land Degradation & Development*, *28* (*7*), 2234–2244.

Eden, L. and Smith, M., 2011. *The Ethics of Transfer Pricing. AOS Workshop on Fraud in Accounting, Organizations and Society. 1–2 April.* Imperial College, London.

Ethiopia–Bho Bio, 2010. Land Rent Contractual Agreement Made Between Ministry of Agriculture and Rural Development and Bho Bio Products Private Limited Company. Openland Contracts: An Online Repository of Open Land Contracts. Available online at: http://openlandcontracts.org/contract/ocds-591adf-7602403637/view#/pdf (accessed 4 September 2017).

Ethiopia–Hunan, 2010. Land Rent Contractual Agreement Made Between Ministry of Agriculture and Rural Development and Hunan Dafengyuan Agriculture Co. Ltd. Openland Contracts: An Online Repository of Open Land Contracts. Available online at: http://openlandcontracts.org/contract/ocds-591adf-3697697327/view#/pdf (accessed 4 September 2017).

Ethiopia–Karuturi Agro, 2010. Land Rent Contractual Agreement Made Between Ministry of Agriculture and Rural Development and Karuturi Agro Products Plc. Openland Contracts: An Online Repository of Open Land Contracts. Available online at: http://openlandcontracts.org/contract/ocds-591adf-3081785170/view#/pdf (accessed 4 September 2017).

Ethiopia–Ruchi Agri, 2010. Ruchi Agri Plc, Lease. Openland Contracts: An Online Repository of Open Land Contracts. Available online at: https://openlandcontracts.org/contract/ocds-591adf-2841169712/view#/pdf (accessed 3 August 2019).

Ethiopia–Saudi Star, 2010. Saudi Star Agricultural Development Plc. Openland Contracts: An Online Repository of Open Land Contracts. Available online at: https://openlandcontracts.org/contract/ocds-591adf-9604461339/view#/search/water (accessed 3 August 2019).

Fairhead, J., Leach, M., and Scoones, I., 2011. Green grabbing: A New Appropriation of Nature? *Journal of Peasant Studies, 39* (*2*), 237–261.

FAO (UN Food and Agriculture Organization), 2012. *Voluntary Guidelines on the Responsible Governance of Tenure of Land, Fisheries and Forests in the Context of National Food Security.* UN FAO. Available online at: http://www.refworld.org/docid/5322b79e4.html (accessed 31 May 2016).

Ferrando, T., 2014. BITing Land Abroad: The anti-distributive impact of Bilateral Investment Treaties. *African Yearbook of International Law, 20* (*39*), 249–287.

Ferrando, T., 2017. Land Rights at the Time of Global Production: Leveraging Multi-Spatiality and 'Legal Chokeholds'. *Business and Human Rights Journal, 2* (*2*), 275–295.

Franco, J., Borras, S., Alonso-Fradejas, A. and Buxton, N., 2013. *The Global Land Grab: A Primer, Revised Edition. TNI Agrarian Justice.* Amsterdam, Transnational Institute.

Franco, J., Kishimoto, S., Kay, S., Feodoroff, T. and Pracucci, G., 2014. *The Global Water Grab: A Primer. TNI Agrarian Justice.* Amsterdam, Transnational Institute.

Franklin, J.C., 2009. Contentious Challenges and Government Responses in Latin America. *Political Research Quarterly, 62* (*4*), 700–714.

Gartner, S.S. and Regan, P.M., 1996. Threat and Repression: The Non-Linear Relationship between Government and Opposition Violence. *Journal of Peace Research, 33* (*3*), 273–287.

Goetz, A., 2013. Private Governance and Land Grabbing: The Equator Principles and the Roundtable on Sustainable Biofuels. *Globalizations*, *10* (*1*), 199–204.

Guj, P., Martin, S. and Readhead, A., 2017. *Transfer Pricing in Mining with a Focus on Africa. A Briefing Note.* World Bank Group, Centre for Exploration Targeting and International Mining for Development Centre.

Guzman, A.T., 1998. Why LDCs Sign Treaties That Hurt Them: Explaining the Popularity of Bilateral Investment Treaties. *Virginia Journal of International Law*, *38*, 639–688.

Guzman, A.T., 2006. Competing for Capital: The Diffusion of Bilateral Investment Treaties, 1960–2000. *International Organization*, *60* (*4*), 811–846.

Hall, R., 2011. Land Grabbing in Southern *Africa: The Many Faces of the Investor Rush. Review of African Political Economy*, *38* (*128*) 193–214.

Harvey, D., 2003. *The New Imperialism.* Oxford University Press.

Henry, J., 2012. The Price of Offshore Revisited New Estimates for Missing Global Private Wealth, Income, Inequality, and Lost Taxes. Tax Justice Network. Available online at: http://www.taxjustice.net/cms/upload/pdf/Price_of_Offshore_Revisited_120722.pdf (accessed 3 September 2017).

Himenez, E. and Shattuck, A., 2011. Food Crises, Food Regimes and Food Movements: Rumblings of Reform or Tides of Transformation? *Journal of Peasants Studies*, *38* (*1*), 109–144.

International Tax Compact, 2011. Benefits of a Computerized Integrated System for Taxation. iTax case study, Bonn, February.

Künnemann, R. and Monsalve Suárez, S., 2013. International Human Rights and Governing Land Grabbing: A View from Global Civil Society. *Globalizations*, *10* (*1*), 123–139.

Land Matrix, 2017. Global Observatory. Available online at: https://landmatrix.org/global (accessed 5 May 2020).

Liberia–Sime Darby, 2009. An Act to Ratify the Amended and Restate Concession Agreement Between the Republic of Liberia and Sime Darby Plantation (Liberia) Inc., Approved July 23, 2009. Openland Contracts: An Online Repository of Open Land Contracts. Available online at: http://openlandcontracts.org/contract/ocds-591adf-3371037354/view#/pdf (accessed 4 September 2017).

Malibya (2008) La Sociétè Malibya, Contrat de Concession Agricole, 2008. Openland Contracts: An Online Repository of Open Land Contracts. Available online at: http://openlandcontracts.org/contract/ocds-591adf-3711703286/view#/pdf (accessed 4 September 2017).

Margulis, M.E. McKeon, N. and Borras, S.M., 2013. Land Grabbing and Global Governance: Critical Perspectives. *Globalizations*, *10* (*1*), 1–23.

Martinez-Alier, J., Temper, L., Del Bene, D. and Scheidel, A., 2016. Is There a Global Environmental Justice Movement? *The Journal of Peasant Studies*, *43* (*3*), 731–755.

Mehta, L., Veldwisch, G.J. and Franco, J., 2012. Introduction to the Special Issue: Water Grabbing? Focus on the (Re)appropriation of Finite Water Resources. *Water Alternatives*, *5* (*2*), 193–207.

Oakland Institute, 2011. *Enough Is Enough: Gambella*, Ethiopia. Oakland Institute.

Palan, R., 2009. History of Tax Havens. History and Policy. Available online at: http://www.historyandpolicy.org/policy-papers/papers/history-of-tax-havens (accessed 6 September 2017).

Palan, R. Murphy, R. and Chavagneux, C., 2009. *Tax Havens: How Globalization Really Works*. Cornell University Press.
Pearce, F., 2013. Splash and Grab: The Global Scramble for Water. *New Scientist*. Available online at: https://www.newscientist.com/article/mg21729066-400-splash-and-grab-the-global-scramble-for-water (accessed 5 September 2019).
Peluso, N.L. and Lund, C., 2011. New Frontiers of Land Control. *Journal of Peasant Studies, 38* (*4*), 667–681.
Perrone, N., 2016. The International Investment Regime and Local Populations: Are the Weakest Voices Unheard? *Transnational Legal Theory, 7* (*3*), 383–405.
Picciotto, S., 2012. *Towards Unitary Taxation of Transnational Corporations*. Tax Justice Network.
Quentin, C. and Campling, L., 2017. Global Inequality Chains: Integrating Mechanisms of Value Distribution into Analyses of Global Production. *Global Networks, 18*, 33–56.
Rulli, M.C., Saviori, A. and D'Odorico, P., 2013. Global Land and Water Grabbing. *Proceedings of the National Academy of Science of the United States of America, 100* (*3*), 892–897.
Russi, L., 2013. *Hungry Capital: The Financialization of Food*. Zero Books.
Sassen, S., 2013a. Land Grabs Today: Feeding the Disassembling of National Territory. *Globalizations, 10* (*1*), 25–46.
Sassen, S., 2013b. When Territory Deborders Territoriality. *Territory, Politics, Governance, 1* (*1*), 21–45.
Seabrooke, L. and Wigan, D., 2014. Global Wealth Chains in the International Political Economy. *Review of International Political Economy, 21* (*1*), 257–263.
Seabrooke, L. and Wigan, D., 2017. The Governance of Global Wealth Chains. *Review of International Political Economy, 24* (*1*), 1–29.
Sierra Leone–Addax, 2010. Memorandum of Understanding and Agreement between The Government of the Republic of Sierra Leone, Addax Bioenergy Sierra Leone Ltd, and Addax & Oryx Holding BV, February 9th, 2010. An Online Repository of Open Land Contracts. Available online at: http://openlandcontracts.org/contract/ocds-591adf-7804618381/view#/pdf (accessed 4 September 2017).
SOMO, 2011. *Building a Coalition against Food Speculation*. SOMO. Available online at: https://www.somo.nl/building-a-coalition-against-food-speculation (accessed 28 February 2017).
Spagnuolo, F., 2017. Global Land Rush, Water Grabbings and the Human Right to Water. In M. Alabrese, M. Brunori, S. Rolandi and A. Saba (eds), *Agricultural Law*. Springer, p. 293.
Tomohara, A., 2004. Inefficiencies of Bilateral Advanced Pricing Agreements (BAPA) in Taxing Multinational Companies, LVII. *National Tax Journal 57* (*4*), 863–873.
Trading Economics, 2020. Cameroon Corporate Tax Rate 2004–2020. Available online at: https://tradingeconomics.com/cameroon/corporate-tax-rate (accessed 5 May 2020).
UNCTAD (United Nations Conference on Trade and Development), 2011. *Tax Incentives and Foreign Direct Investment: A Global Survey*. ASIT Advisory Studies No. 16. United Nations.

Van Apeldoorn, B., de Graaff, N. and Overbeek, H., 2012. The Rebound of the Capitalist State: The Rearticulation of the State–Capital Nexus in the Global Crisis. *Globalizations*, *9* (*4*), 467–470.
Van Gelder, J.W., de Wilde, J., van Koningsveld, J., and Ferwerda, J., 2016. *Tax Avoidance by Mining Companies in Developing Countries – An Analysis of Potential Dutch Policy Initiatives*. Profundo.
White, B., Borras, S., Hall, R., Scoones, I. and Wolford, W., 2012. The New Enclosures: Critical Perspectives on Corporate Land Deals. *Journal of Peasant Studies*, *39* (*3&4*), 619–647.
Wiggins, S. and Keats, S., 2009. *Grain Stocking and Price Spikes*. Overseas Development Institute.
Woodhouse, P., 2012. New Investment, Old Challenges: Land Deals and the Water Constraint in African Agriculture. *Journal of Peasant Studies*, *39* (*3&4*), 777–794.
World Finance, 2012. Transfer Pricing Runs Ragged across Africa. World Finance Online. Available online at: http://www.worldfinance.com/markets/transfer-pricing/transfer-pricing-runs-ragged-across-africa (accessed 25 May 2016).

Chapter 11

Community development agreements and the state's extractive development strategy in Mongolia

Participatory governance or governance participation?

*Jennifer Lander**

Introduction

In this chapter, I analyse the emergence of a new institution of 'accountability' in the socio-political governance of the Mongolian mining sector through Community Development Agreements (CDAs).[1] CDAs in the Mongolian context are part of a global 'explosion in the negotiation of agreements between commercial developers and local communities (O'Faircheallaigh, 2013: 222), and I focus on the particular ways in which this global governance institution functions within the specific juridical-political structure of the Mongolian state, at the local and national level. I argue that the significance of CDAs for Mongolia can only be understood in the context of the opening of the Mongolian mining sector to foreign investment.

CDAs are part of a broader 'toolkit' of global social and environmental governance, which has developed alongside the expansion of global protections for foreign investment. Mongolia opened its economy to 'global' finance and investment in 1997, through its entry into the World Trade Organization (WTO) and national adoption of a liberal framework for foreign investment in minerals, a previously nationalised sector. The World Bank funded the development of the law, with the support of the new government, and organised a foreign investors'

*This chapter is partly drawn from chapter 4 of the author's PhD thesis (Lander 2017), which has been accepted for publication as a monograph with Routledge (Law, Development and Globalization series), entitled *Transnational Law and State Transformation: The Case of Extractive Development in Mongolia* (Lander 2019). The interview material is based on the author's fieldwork (2014–2015).

1 CDAs have also been referred to as 'local development agreements', 'community cooperation agreements', 'local-level agreements' and 'local development agreements' in the Mongolian context. I have chosen to stick with the generic title 'community development agreements' given that the model template adopted in 2014 in official state policy uses this terminology.

conference in the same year to advertise the new framework and stimulate investment into the minerals economy. The 1997 law provided a comprehensive liberal framework for the mining sector, easing conditions for investment and restricting the role of the state. The role of the state within the new legal framework was to facilitate investment by establishing 'procedures for obtaining mineral licenses [which] are clear, simple, and quick' (International Business Publications, 2013). Key characteristics of the 1997 Minerals Law were the prohibition of direct state involvement in the mining sector, the removal of distinction between domestic and international investors, and the right for investors to sell minerals at global market prices. The 1997 Minerals Law was known widely as the most competitive mining regime in Asia, with exceptionally low rates of taxation.

The adoption of this legal framework precipitated a mining boom in the late 1990s and early 2000s, in which foreign companies (both public and private) competed for access to Mongolian mining licences, distributed liberally by the central government's Mineral Resources Authority of Mongolia (MRAM). By 2004, approximately 26% of Mongolian land was covered in mining licences for exploration and extraction (Husband and Songwe, 2004: 7); 50% of these licences were held by only seven companies, the four largest of which were foreign (ibid.). By 2009, the number of licences had almost doubled, to cover 45% of Mongolian territory (Suzuki, 2013: 277). The environmental inputs of mining in terms of land and water created an economic conflict of interest with Mongolian pastoralists (30–40% of the population) over access to limited water and grazing resources, particularly in the South Gobi region where mining was most intensive. Mining also was perceived to undermine the 'material, environmental and cultural bases of the livelihood of local communities' (Byambajav, 2012: 13). Sub-national authorities received little financial benefit from a centralised system of extracting rents from mining companies and faced pressure from disgruntled local communities about the sudden increase in unregulated mining activities. Consequently, since the early 2000s, residents and local authorities in major mining provinces[2] regularly obstructed mining projects through direct action and various forms of political bargaining.

This chapter analyses the central state's response to resistance to mining in rural regions of Mongolia by local communities and sub-national authorities. I argue that CDAs are an institutional solution devised by the central government to remedy the conflict-prone relationship between communities, local authorities and mining companies with the primary aim of mitigating political risk for foreign investors and resurrecting their confidence in Mongolia's investment environment. The crisis of foreign investment confidence in Mongolia's legal and regulatory framework for the mining sector in 2012–2013 created a sense of political urgency for the central government to address the systemic issue of local resistance to mining

2 Major mining provinces include Arkhangai, Overkhangai, Bayankhongor, Selenge, Dundgov, and Umnogov.

(Lander 2019; Lander, 2014). CDAs were thus an integral part of the new State Minerals Policy 2014–2025, adopted to resuscitate foreign investment in the mining sector. In the new Policy, CDAs were intended to 'support local development and protect community interests' (Article 3.5). However, I argue that the provision of economic and social benefits for impacted regions is a *secondary* and subordinate function of CDAs, which have been strategically used by the central government since the crisis of foreign investment (2012–14) to *primarily* constrain anti-extractive resistance and thereby to stabilise the extractive process for mining companies generally. Although CDAs undoubtedly produce some economic benefits for local populations and include limited recognition of the socio-environmental impacts of mining, they have been devised to fragment resistance by co-opting local government into supporting national mining policy. CDAs provide a concrete case study of the ways in which the central government has attempted, using financial mechanisms and legal institutions, to systemically subordinate resistance without the appearance of domination. More generally, the Mongolian case points to the need to understand the political context in which CDAs are introduced to determine whether they are beneficial to the democratisation of industrial projects. It is crucial to understand the subtle distinction between 'participatory governance' – driven by and for communities impacted by mining – and 'governance participation' in the form of nominal participation in pre-determined governance structures.

The chapter introduces the global origins of CDAs as an institutional mechanism to address the local socio-economic impacts of mining projects in Mongolia. I argue that understanding the national socio-political environment and the driving impetus behind their introduction is essential for an adequate assessment of their value as participation-enhancing governance instruments, particularly given the serious risk that CDAs may introduce modes of participation and recognition which narrow rather than deepen democratisation. I conclude by reflecting on the importance of recognising the actors and rationalities that energise CDAs and consider their long-term benefit. I argue that CDAs should contribute to the democratisation of mining projects rather than simply operate as tools for global and national elites to guarantee stable conditions for investment. In this sense, the underlying impetus of the chapter is to challenge the way that global governance norms and institutions tend to depoliticise high-impact forms of industrial 'development'[3] like mining.

3 In this chapter, I use the term 'development' in a descriptive rather than normative sense. While I am currently unconvinced that Mongolia's emergence as a mineral-exporting economy truly constitutes 'development' in the sense of social and economic progress, the Mongolian government and international financial institutions have framed mining as a national development strategy, which is part of the legitimising discourse of mining in Mongolia. I hope by using the term and critiquing its governance vis-à-vis CDAs that it will be clear to the reader that the political and legal ramifications of extractive 'economic development' are deeply problematic.

Community development agreements in global context

Environmental degradation and social displacement caused by mining is not unique to Mongolia. Globally, extractive industries provoke high levels of social conflict, despite the apparent fact that 'the extractive sector has embraced social responsibility' (Harvey and Bice, 2014: 327). Conflict between miners and communities occur particularly around the environmental impacts of mining projects and in the marginalisation of citizen access to decision-making processes (Davis and Franks 2014; Bebbington et al., 2008; Bebbington 2011). The social conflict generated by extraction has become a global governance concern, because of both transnational activism on the side of impacted communities and industry pressure to reduce the financial and reputational costs of delayed projects (Franks et al., 2014; IIED, 2002; Chatham House, 2013). In its 2002 Toronto Declaration, the International Council of Mining and Metals affirmed the industry's 'commitment to work collaboratively with other stakeholders' to 'contribute to the social, economic and institutional development of the communities in which we operate' (ICMM, 2012: 7). Increasingly, the business case for sharing benefits more widely with local communities has been promoted as a means of guaranteeing the smooth running of development projects, particularly those involving extractive industries (Chatham House, 2013). Objections from local communities to mining projects can lead to delays or the cancellation of projects. CDAs are discursively supported in global governance as a 'win-win-win' for local communities, the extractive industry and national governments: mining companies formalise their contributions to local development, which ostensibly benefits communities and smoothes their relationships with local authorities. However, CDAs also *limit* what can be demanded of mining companies by communities.

According to a recent study, approximately half of all 'risk factors' associated with extractive development projects are 'non-technical in nature, with 'stakeholder-related' risks being the single biggest issue' (Chatham House, 2013: 2, citing Davis and Franks, 2011). Mitigating political risks posed by local protests is explicitly stated as a goal of the World Bank Group's International Finance Corporation (IFC) and Multilateral Investment Guarantee Agency (MIGA) (Hatcher, 2014: 15–16). CDAs are thus not just a social add-on to the global governance agenda, but are core to global financial regulation and governance. CDAs have been thoroughly integrated into global governance of extractive industries, reinforced by the Equator Principles – a 'risk management framework, adopted by financial institutions, for determining, assessing and managing environmental and social risk in projects' (Equator Principles, 2017) – and the Community Development Toolkit, a collaborative publication of the World Bank and the International Council of Mining and Metals (ICMM, 2012). The Equator Principles are part of a wider infrastructure for global finance which seeks to harmonise risk management strategies for investors and corporations, as well as developing minimum standards for addressing social and environmental impacts of infrastructure and industrial projects. There are ten principles for socio-environmental risk mitigation: 1) review and categorise the scale of risk and due diligence required, 2) carry out environmental and social risk assessments, 3) evaluate compliance with host country and/or IFC Performance Standards, 4) develop and maintain an Environment and Social Management System, 5) demonstrate stakeholder engagement with the affected community, 6) establish a grievance mechanism, 7) undergo an independent review, 8) covenant to comply with all relevant host country environmental and social laws, regulations and permits, 9) ensure ongoing independent monitoring and review, 10) submit to transparency and reporting requirements. Because the IFC and MIGA have significant influence over foreign direct investment in emerging markets and frontier economies such as Mongolia (Hatcher, 2014: 12–16), CDAs are fast becoming a core element of global mining governance.

Despite their integration into the corporate social responsibility framework around mining projects, CDAs are a flexible institution that has appeared in various forms, albeit with substantive similarities (O'Faircheallaigh, 2013: 222–3):

> They involve formal agreements between developers (public or private) and community representatives or organisations. They are designed to minimise negative project impacts and ensure that local communities obtain benefits from development they otherwise would not enjoy in the absence of agreements, thus helping to reduce or eliminate conflict surrounding development.[4]

O'Faircheallaigh argues that CDAs can be understood as a *juridical* response to conflicts about the recognition of project impacts and local entitlements, with an associated mechanism for redistribution. The juridical nature of CDAs sets them apart from more informal mechanisms of corporate social responsibility, such as voluntary community support programmes offered by a company; they have a 'law-like' nature based on principles of contract for negotiation and enforcement. When a CDA is breached, the dispute may be settled informally, or it will be subject to a specified dispute resolution process. CDAs are thus a powerful institutional mechanism in development projects with direct impact upon local populations. They have the potential to equalise the negotiating power of local communities and developers, but they are more likely to institutionalise unequal power dynamics and *limit* rather than *enable* community claims. There are three factors that affect the success of CDAs as social justice-enhancing institutions:

4 O'Faircheallaigh discusses Community Benefits Agreements between real estate developers and locals in major Western cities, Impact and Benefit Agreements for mines and oil pipelines in northern Canada, Native Title Agreements in Australia, Consent Agreements in Peru and Development Forum Agreements in Papua New Guinea as cases of CDAs.

'the effect of unequal bargaining relationships ... on the content and impact of CDAs; equity and social justice issues involved in the distribution of benefits from CDAs; and the enforceability and implementation of agreements' (O'Faircheallaigh, 2013: 223).

The way in which these factors affect the implementation of CDAs is extremely context dependent and particularly influenced by the nature of community representation and the extent to which any individual company is committed to delivering substantial community benefits. Two additional variables may be added to this list. Which actors drive the introduction of CDAs and for what rationales? How does a CDA fit within existing governance arrangements? In Mongolia, these two factors are critical in establishing whether CDAs function primarily as social justice-promoting mechanisms or as stability mechanisms for companies to insulate them from 'political risks' from discontented communities.

Community development agreements in Mongolia: 'cooperation agreements'

Mongolia is a unitary state, with its capital in Ulaanbaatar, and is comprised of 21 provinces (*aimags)* and 329 districts (*soum),* and over 1,500 sub-districts (*baghs*). Each *aimag* and *soum* has an executive branch (governor's office) and a local assembly (*khural*) with legislative jurisdiction over some socio-economic issues, local development priorities and land disputes between herders. While representatives in the local *khural* are directly elected, *soum* governors gain their positions through nomination by the *soum khurals* and then appointment by the *aimag* governor. The *aimag* governor is nominated by the *aimag khural* and ultimately appointed by the Prime Minister (Enkhbaatar et al., 2015: 59).

Between 1921 and 1990, Mongolia was the first socialist country to 'independently' align with the Soviet Union. Like neighbouring Soviet republics, it underwent a hasty process of democratisation and marketisation during the economic crisis that followed the Soviet Union's collapse in the early 1990s (Rossabi, 2005). During this period of intense political and economic upheaval, Mongolia democratised while retaining aspects of the socialist constitutional framework, especially the structure of territorial administration (i.e. the province/district/sub-district system) (Enkhbaatar et al., 2015: 59). A vast country approximately the size of Western Europe, Mongolia has only 2.8 million people: the lowest land-to-population ratio in the world. One-third of the population live in rural areas. Rural life and livelihoods are still dominated by the pastoral economy, although the mining boom since the late 1990s has introduced competition for land and water. Prior to the mining boom, agriculture dominated national GDP, at almost 39% in 1995 (UNDP, 2007: 62). Mining which now constitutes approximately 20% of GDP has surpassed agriculture (17%) in the last 20 years (World Bank, 2017). The Mongolian system was highly centralised on paper and in practice during the socialist period. Governance of the pastoral economy was central to national economic development, requiring a relatively high level of coordination (see Lander 2019: ch. 2). The formation of pastoral collectives – *negdels* – were central to socialist development planning and the industrialisation of Mongolia's economy from the 1950s onwards (Boikova, 1999; Bawden, 1968/1989: 399). In the socialist period all major positions in sub-national administrations were central appointments, but the 1992 constitution introduced a balance between principles of central state management and self-government. *Khural* seats are now democratically elected, but the nomination of a governor must be approved by the higher level of state administration. The constitutional relationship between provincial and central government has been ambiguous and controversial, being based on conflicting principles of 'self-governance and state management' (Lkhagvadorj, 2010: 79). This constitutional ambiguity has generated conflicts about where the line between these principles should be drawn in practice.

In the post-socialist period, particularly the 1990s, sub-national administrations gained more autonomy not only through constitutional reform but also as a result of the central government's *de facto* abdication of the regulation of the pastoral economy on a national level (Mearns, 2004: 139). As Jackson (2015: 442) puts it, 'as neoliberal austerity policies destabilised economies throughout the Soviet Bloc in the 1990s, *de*collectivisation, *de*industrialisation *and ruralisation* swept across Mongolia.' In this sense, one could concur with Reinert (2000) that the 'development' policies pursued in the 1990s actively underdeveloped the economy. The socialist state had controlled both the mobility of herders and the export of pastoral products but following the privatisation of the herding collectives in the early 1990s, individual herders were ushered into the new 'age of the market' (Sneath, 2003: 42). The post-socialist transition saw the removal of critical state support systems for pastoral production (Upton, 2012: 138), such as tax incentives, repairing winter sheds, providing machines for haymaking, and crucially, getting products on the market for export. The sudden loss of state assistance has led to the atomisation of herders as individual competitors in meat and cashmere markets (Rossabi, 2005: 122; Fernandez-Gimenez, 2006). Consequently, and especially because of the retreat of the central state and land legislation that authorised local regulation of these matters sub-national governments have become the main governing institutions in land disputes, water access and seasonal mobility enforcement (Fernandez-Gimenez, 2006: 33). Prior to the mining boom in the late 1990s, local government took a *laissez-faire* approach to the pastoral economy because there was virtually no economic competition for access to land or water apart from pastoral use. However, the growth of the mining sector since 1997 redirected central state attention to the governance of rural areas and increased the significance of sub-national administration as representative institutions for conflicts between pastoralists and mining companies.

Mongolia entered the World Trade Organization and passed one of the most liberal mining investment laws in 1997 (1997 Minerals Law), as part of the post-socialist shift towards a national development strategy based on attracting foreign investment and exporting minerals. This challenged the balance between local authorities and the central government. The 1997 Minerals Law established a centralised regulatory regime for the mining sector that concentrated decision-making power in the central state, particularly the Mineral Resources Authority of Mongolia (MRAM). However, central institutions did not assume a strong regulatory role beyond the issuance of licences. Subsequently, widespread environmental degradation and social dislocation in the early 2000s catalysed the formation of rural social movements across the country – 11 'River Movements' – which contested the preferential access to land and water given to mining companies through MRAM's lax licensing regime, which led to the dehydration and pollution of rivers, a boom in artisanal mining and the subordination of herders' customary use rights (Byambajav, 2012, 2014). These 11 movements formed a loose coalition – the Homeland and Water Protection Coalition of River Movements – in 2006.

Based in small rural communities, the official members of the River Movements were generally small, with a core of ten to 20 activists. However, these small groups were able to mobilise widespread support from the public for specific petitions, protests and campaigns, such as Ongi River protest march in 2004 and the protests in Sukhbaatar Square in Ulaanbaatar in 2011.[5] Their early successes and political momentum, especially in the case of the Ongi River Movement, were linked to their capacity to forge strong networks at all levels of sub-national administration including local governors and chairs of parliaments (Byambajav 2014). Many local administrations were sympathetic to the groundswell of anti-mining sentiment among rural citizens because they were also largely excluded from central decision-making about mining as well as the redistribution of mineral rents.

Initial lack of regulatory oversight by the central state created a political opportunity for local authorities to cultivate public support, particularly as social movements and NGOs began to lobby for governmental intervention to address the socio-environmental crises caused by irresponsible mining. An underlying provocation for many Mongolians in the early years of the mining boom (1997–2006) was the apparent inability or unwillingness of the central state to protect citizens against the impacts of natural resource extraction. Fear of foreign access to Mongolian resources, dispossession of customary and sacred land, the degradation of land, water and forests, and economic displacement as mining took priority over pastoralism emerged as strong currents in the Mongolian anti-mining discourse (Byambajav, 2012, 2014; Endicott, 2012).

5 Combellick-Bidney (2012: 287) estimates that hundreds, if not thousands, of rural Mongolians participated in direct action protests in local areas and the city between 2004 and 2012. For example, in parallel with the 2004 elections, the leaders of the Ongi River Movement organised a month-long march along the Ongi River 'to persuade local people to vote only for candidates who would work for the protection of the river' (Byambajav, 2014: 3). The River Movements also mobilised thousands of rural Mongolians to protest in front of Parliament about the lack of implementation of environmental legislation in 2011.

Local authorities at provincial and district levels responded to these concerns in a variety of formal and informal ways. In Mongolian land law, provincial authorities have the right to set aside land for 'special use' and to grant 'certificates of possession' to customary land users (i.e. herders) (Endicott, 2012: 97). These provisions were strategically used by sub-national authorities across the country as a formal but indirect intervention to exclude land from mining and to protect herders' land entitlements in the absence of justiciable rights. Informally, governors lobbied mining companies to contribute to rural projects by building infrastructure, schools, financing social events, etc. in return for approving water and land permits for which local authorities' approval is necessary. The threat of delays gave local authorities leverage. These lobbied 'requests' were regularly granted to enable mining operations to continue even though they are perceived by the companies as illegitimate. In some high-profile instances provincial or district parliaments blocked access to water for mining companies.[6] Although these decisions have been overturned by the central government, this has been a slow process because of the distance from the capital. Therefore, they effectively delay projects in the short term and reflect wider social anxieties about the impacts of mining projects on scarce resources. In acting in this way, local authorities challenged the cosy relationship between the central licensing agency and mining companies and the latter's presumption that the receipt of a licence would guarantee stable operating conditions. Conflicts about mining exacerbated tension in the relationship between the central government and sub-national administrations, particularly given low levels of central budgetary support for agriculture, the mainstay of the rural economy (Amponsah and Annor-Frempong, 2014: 1). For example, between 2003 and 2012, agriculture's share of the national budget in terms of government spending was only 2.4% on average (ibid.).

In my fieldwork (see Lander 2019: ch. 4), resistant actions by local governments were typically framed by central policy-makers and mining companies as 'corruption', allegedly on the basis that local authorities were trying to squeeze personal benefits out of mining projects. For example, a foreign CEO of a medium-scale mining company stated that 'obviously, community relations are about risk management' (author interview, January 2015): 'If they see a big mine with hundreds of trucks, obviously generating big revenue, they will say "where's my piece, where's my cut?" They're not going to be satisfied with government royalty and tax' (ibid.).

6 For example, in 2013 a *soum khural* in Umnogov *aimag* (southern province) banned corporate access to groundwater, which would have affected major mining projects in the region. The *khural*'s decision was immediately overturned by the central government, but indicated a strong level of local frustration and discontent with the impacts of mining companies on scarce water resources.

A Mongolian CEO similarly suggested that local authorities were putting onerous and superficial demands upon the companies. He stated, 'local government or local people want many different things', characterising local governments' demands as purely self-seeking: 'They want to travel to London ... [They say] I'm governor of this village, so my wife needs a mink coat, so you can bring me the mink coat' (author interview, November 2015).

Senior officials from the Ministry of Mining reinforced and legitimised the perspectives of mining companies. The Director of the Department of Strategic Policy and Planning in the Ministry of Mining acknowledged openly that 'there have been cases where local governments demanded too much from mining companies' (author interview, October 2015), describing the needs of rural citizens and authorities as 'infinite'. These comments were in the context of a discussion about central state strategies to 'make fences, limitations for local government'.

However, the corruption narrative ignores that local governments were actively responding to the concerns of citizens about foreign access to mineral resources, displacement from customary land and environmental degradation caused by mining. The alleged caricatured corruption cases (i.e. demanding flights and mink coats) ignore the more substantive and systematic responses made by local governments to either limit extraction in their regions in response to pastoral land-use requirements and environmental concerns, or to require companies to invest in local infrastructure (i.e. hospitals, roads and schools).

'Stability in the investment environment' as the driving rationale

Formalised Community Development Agreements were introduced in Mongolia through amendments to minerals legislation and policy in 2014. CDAs were part of a broader programme of law and policy reform to renew capital flows in the mining sector, following a devastating collapse of foreign investment between 2012 and 2014. Low commodity prices contributed to the crisis, but the exodus of investment was mainly provoked by a perception of 'instability' and nationalism in the Mongolian legal environment. This chapter does not deal with this crisis of confidence in the state's governance of the mineral sector. It was caused primarily by a) attempted renegotiation by the central state of the Oyu Tolgoi international investment agreement; b) the revocation of licences due to new environmental legislation and corruption allegations; and c) the 'politicised' screening of investment based on the state's geopolitical anxiety about growing Chinese control of mining projects and export prices (see Lander 2019: ch. 3; Lander, 2014). These factors dovetailed with declining commodity prices and decreasing Chinese demand for mineral commodities to bring the Mongolian economy to the brink of collapse; foreign direct investment almost halved in 2013 and spiralled down a further 64% by the first half of 2014.

While there was a general legal obligation on companies to 'cooperate' with local authorities in relation to local development priorities since 1997, the nature of that obligation shifted from an ad-hoc 'consult and coordinate' model (Article 33.1/1997 Minerals Law), to multiple agreements on specific issues (Article 42.1/2006 Minerals Law) to a single agreement based on a model developed by national policy-makers (Amended Article 42.1/2014 Minerals Law). The 1997 'consult and coordinate' model placed local governments at the centre of local development, with extensive leeway to negotiate without oversight from the central government. The 2006 amendment limited the scope of local governments' demands on mining companies to a narrower range of 'specific issues', although there was still space for a mining impacted region to require agreements at different levels of local government depending on the scale of the project. The 2014 amendment, however, limited the scope of local governments' leverage over the social contribution of mining companies by requiring a *single* agreement. The single agreement was to be limited to 'matters of environmental protection, infrastructure and job creation, *voluntarily* supporting local community development' (Article 42.1, emphasis added), thus placing the corporate partner in the stronger bargaining position.

In 2014, the central government introduced a new State Policy for the Minerals Sector (2014–2025), following the introduction of a new Investment Law in late 2013. The main stated objective of the new policy was

> to establish a *stable investment environment*, to improve the quality of minerals exploration, mining and processing by encouraging advanced equipment, technologies and innovations with low negative impacts on the environment, to produce value-added products and to *strengthen competitiveness in the global market.*
>
> (Government of Mongolia, 2014, Article 1.2, emphasis added)

The new state policy prioritised the *stability of the investment environment* as the primary goal of governance, and entailed a series of amendments to the 2006 Minerals Law. This broad programme of reform was intended by national policy-makers to address gaps in the mining regime that were creating obstacles in the smooth running of mining projects, including local sources of instability. Prior to 2014, the ambiguity of the Minerals Law provisions for local-level agreements with mining companies and the informality of the arrangements had given governors significant political leverage and had created space for local governments to express their dissatisfaction with, or make demands upon mining companies in conflict with the central state's interests in opening up provincial territories for extraction. This leverage became a major 'governance gap' addressed in the 2014 reforms to the mining regime (Lander 2019: ch. 3).

Local governments' dissatisfaction with central government was fuelled by intertwined issues of a lack of local input in licensing and lack of local direct benefit from mining revenue. The 1997 Minerals Law established a centralised regulatory regime for the mining sector that concentrated decision-making power in the central state, particularly in the Mineral Resources Authority of Mongolia. The centralised pattern of decision-making meant that provincial and district governments were not consulted in the issuance of mining licences. Consequently, the mismatch between the centralised licensing process and the 'decentralised' approach to addressing the environmental and social impacts of mining contributed to an overall sense of local exclusion from decision-making. Furthermore, the fiscal structure governing mining revenues was highly centralised in the first decade of the mining boom. Taxes, mining licence fees and royalties were collected centrally and redistributed through the national budget presented by the Ministry of Finance and approved by Parliament (Lkhagvadorj, 2012: 6). This centralised system excluded local governments from both the 'budget planning and approving process' (ibid.).

The budgetary exclusion and local-national conflicts about mining became an increasing issue of legitimacy for the central government and contributed to negative global perception about investing in Mongolia's mining sector. This led to the Ministry of Mining, in conjunction with the World Bank, to develop a template for CDAs in 2014. Crucially, the model template provides authorities and companies with clear formulae for contract negotiation, which, while not mandatory, provide an approved structure for stakeholders to follow (Hogan Lovells, 2014).[7] It enables MRAM to give mining companies and local governors official guidance about the extent and limits of community development agreements (Head of Mining Division, MRAM, author interview, November 2015). The reason for taking a 'template' approach, according to a former senior mining policy-maker involved in the drafting of the State Policy on the Minerals Sector 2014–2025, was that the 'government wanted to create and approve a long-term model… so the [central] government can say [to local governors] 'you [only] have the right to request certain things within a certain framework'' (author interview, November 2015). Consequently, the model CDA template resembles a complex contractual framework, designed to cover any potential loop-holes so that local authorities and communities can be relied upon to abide by the agreement.

The model establishes firm parameters for the terms and manner of negotiation between local authorities and mining companies, requiring the 'Relationship Committee', a separate public-private institution external to the local administrations to govern the agreement. The Relationship Committee is to be comprised of the governor – either *soum* or *aimag*[8] – and representatives of the

7 The models were developed by Hogan Lovells, the global legal firm which won the bid from the World Bank.

8 The governor may be from the district or province-level of local government, depending on the scope of the CDA.

mining company, with civil associations invited as observers. The Governor is designated as the 'representative of the local community' (CDA Model Template, Article 3.2). The model promotes a *hybridised* governance arrangement, because it incorporates the public and private sector into a relationship that is decidedly public in its ramifications (i.e. affecting local economic development overall) and yet is non-governmental in its structure, with financial and dispute resolution mechanisms that operate outside of governmental controls. CDA-specific financial and dispute resolution mechanisms are supposed to be developed on a case-by-case basis, with the basic guidance being that both are 'independent', that is insulated from public legal and political power. Thus, local development finance is promoted through private development funds accessible only through the CDA governance structure. While the template allows for different forms of legal review (independent mediation, private arbitration, court settlements), private investors are unlikely to opt for the national court system given the choice. As well as the ambiguous notion of the 'community', CDAs introduce a new governance concept in local development: the idea of 'stakeholding'. The parties to the agreement – the *soum* or *aimag* governor and the mining company – have social, cultural and economic responsibilities to 'the local community and other stakeholders' although there is no guidance as to how these so-called stakeholders should be identified or included. Thus, despite its 'community' rhetoric and 'public' connotations, the 2014 CDA model looks like a private contract intended to tightly link the governor as the executive arm of local governments with the mining company, empowering the appointed governor at the expense of elected officials.

The introduction of a Community Development Agreement model template in 2014 dovetailed with changes to the national revenue redistribution structure. The 2011 Integrated Budget Law introduced the possibility of a more decentralised model of financial redistribution from the state budget to local administrations to take account of a growing sense of discontent around the terms of subnational 'revenue sovereignty' in the context of 'rapid economic growth' (Lkhagvadorj, 2012: 26), driven largely by the mining sector in rural areas. Article 59.4 of the 2011 Integrated Budget Law consequently stipulates that Local Development Funds in mining regions will be allocated up to ten percent more of the mineral royalties from the central General Local Development Fund than non-mining regions (18). The 2011 Budget Law, however, still maintained a significant degree of central control over the redistribution of mining licence fees and royalties. In response to the fact that 'the local government and local citizens don't like to support mining or geological activities' (author interview, Tax Officer, MRAM, November 2015), a further incentive of direct revenue sharing of royalties and mining licence fees was introduced in the 2014 mineral sector reform. As of January 2016, 50% of mining licence fees was allocated to provincial branches of local government in mining regions (with 25% going to district branches). Formerly, only 5% of mining royalties would be redistributed to local governments through the Local Development Fund (LDF). While the

5% distributed through the LDF has been maintained, additionally provincial governments in mining regions can expect to receive 20% of royalties and district governments to receive 10% through direct transfer. Thus, in conjunction with the introduction of CDAs, the financial incentives for local governments to approve mining licences and work closely with mining companies have greatly increased in recent years.

CDAs and executive power: democratic risks in the consolidation of an extractive development strategy

The current model of CDAs in Mongolia institutionally strengthens executive power and introduces private extractive interests into the fabric of local development planning and policy. Rather than providing a mechanism of meaningful participatory politics for rural communities in relation to mining projects, the CDA model imposes significant limits on the political space available to contest the terms of extractive development. It is highly problematic from a 'participatory' point of view that local governors are the designated 'representative' signing party on behalf of local communities, as they are the least representative office of local administrations. CDAs structurally encourage vertical stability for mining projects by incorporating district governors as the co-signatory, governors who are unlikely to challenge agreements which guarantee a flow of funds into the local budget. Recalling that the appointment of district governors is the prerogative of provincial governors, a provincial governor is unlikely to appoint a district governor who would challenge the terms of the CDA. The incorporation of the executive arm of local governments into the CDA to the exclusion of other bodies such as local *khurals* insulates mining companies from more 'demanding' parties; the structure of the agreements creates a strong incentive for governors to support the agreement. This anti-political structure certainly works in favour of mining companies by limiting the mandatory scope of stakeholder engagement. For example, in response to the question 'Is it better to work with the Governor or the local Parliament Chairman in relation to CDAs?', the CEO of a Mongolian mining company (author interview, November 2015) responded: 'The Governor. It's one person. The Chairman, with his cabinet, there are ten people, twelve people … but with just one governor, it's one person'. In this way, CDAs shift the constitutional balance towards state-management at the expense of self-government in practice, by privileging the appointed vs. elected position of governor in the agreement, as well as incentivising governors to support extractive development in rural territories through financial mechanisms.

Both CDAs and direct revenue-sharing mechanisms were portrayed by central state proponents as positive shifts towards decentralised and participatory governance, where local governments have a greater sense of administrative control around both their budget and local spending priorities. However, as the interview quotes indicate, these 'decentralised' legal mechanisms have been strategically deployed by pro-extractive central state institutions such as the Ministry of

Mining and the Mineral Resources Authority to curtail resistance to mining and get local governments 'on board' an extractive development strategy. As the Deputy Minister of Mining, E. Oyun, stated in a media interview (2014):

> There is a problem of miscommunication with local people, from the side of the government and from the side of the private industries ... We want more involvement of local governments and we want them to use the mining revenues to benefit their local communities ... This is a new approach that will help local people to see and feel the benefits of the mining industry ... It is also good for miners, because [there] will be no anti-mining activities.

Without overtly 'political' coercion, the central government has effectively created incentives for local elites (particularly governors) to support mining projects in rural areas which have been traditionally opposed to extractive development. The sense of local dependency upon mining was reinforced by the author's interviews with personnel from sub-national administrations, who seemed to occupy an increasingly circumscribed institutional and political space in mining development. According to the Director of the Development Policy Department of Selenge *aimag*, 80% of the *aimag's* income was derived from taxes from the mining sector (author interview, November 2015). Furthermore, a *soum* governor from Bayankhongor *aimag* emphasised the pressure he was under to balance local citizens' interests in protecting their land, on one hand, and to promote mining development on the other (author interview, October 2015). He observed that the central government was encouraging local governments to bolster local development funding through mining-related revenue (e.g. taxes and royalties), rather than increasing general redistribution through the national budget.

Thus, CDAs incentivise local governments to support the central state's extractive development strategy despite opposition from their local constituents. More significantly, CDAs undermine the democratisation of development in the long term. By securing local government support for national policies that promote global access to Mongolian minerals, CDAs are one piece of a larger picture where the preferences of global investment have been 'locked' into Mongolia's *national* system of law and policy-making (Gill, 1998). The new consensus in the central government to protect the minerals market from national sources of 'instability' following the FDI crisis (2012–14) means that fewer legal and policy issues are available for democratic contestation and review. This consensus is reinforced by national budgetary policies for local government which limit general budgetary provision, but allow local governments to receive more if they support mining licences and further enables them to generate capital independently of the central state through CDAs and local fee payments from mining companies.

However, these 'positive carrot' incentives come with sticks. For example, in the 2014 reforms to the Minerals Law, new time-linked financial pressure was imposed on local governments to compensate mining companies *within a year* should their decision to protect land conflict with mining licences. As the Head of the Mining Division of MRAM put it, local governments now need to have 'a good reason' to reject mining licences, based on objective factors (author interview, November 2015). While MRAM still requires local authorities' approval before issuing a mining licence, the basis for a legitimate refusal has been limited. As the Director of Strategic Policy and Planning at the Ministry of Mining (author interview, October 2015) explained:

> Before issuing a license, MRAM sends a letter to the local government to hear their opinion and local governments can agree or they can disagree. But in the case of disagreeing, they must provide legitimate foundations. Reasoning. … If they have any plans to protect an area for local protection, they must make a decision at the start, not afterwards.

The raised bar of legitimacy for refusal of mining licences counters the contentious local authority strategy of setting aside land for 'special needs' to legally block mining projects in their territories since the early 2000s (Endicott, 2012: 97). This new standard operates in conjunction with the predetermination of land for extractive development by the Ministry of Mining. The Ministry has designated 30% of national territory for exploration and mining licences.[9]

So far, I have argued that the centralising effect of CDAs is disguised by their 'decentralising' purpose as articulated in national policy, allegedly to provide a stronger institutional mechanism for local community engagement and direct distribution of social investment by companies. The central state absented itself from direct oversight of the process of CDA negotiation, apart from setting out a standardised template in accordance with the minerals legislation. However, the power of the central government was expressed through the force of law (i.e. the legislated, compulsory nature of CDAs) and the financial incentives they offer to the impoverished coffers of local administrations. Thus, CDAs do open up space for local administration-company negotiation of direct community benefits, but within a significantly tightened space of self-governing autonomy. In this way, the more fundamental question of 'do we want mining in our districts and regions?' in sub-national governance shifts to the more instrumental issue of 'how can we benefit the most from mining in our districts and regions?' By raising the requirements for legitimate restrictions on mining, the baseline moves from questions of 'if' to questions of 'how,' constituting a closure of political space as well as of the possibilities of alternative development pathways (Schneiderman, 2013; Anderson, 2005: 147).

9 This centralised determination of land was part of the 2014 reforms to the minerals law under the State Policy on the Minerals Sector 2014–2025.

Furthermore, the amelioration of local social conflict through CDAs has introduced a new 'social' frame to corporate–citizen relations that still operates along (political) lines of exclusion-inclusion even in the name of 'community participation'. For example, groups of residents impacted by mining projects become the 'affected community,' but the boundaries about who is included in 'the community' are determined on a case by case basis in the context of negotiations between companies and local representatives (Erdenebolor and Baigal, 2012). This process naturally depends upon political decisions about which level of local government to engage, which civil society organisations to include and which 'other' community groups to recognise as legitimate stakeholders (ibid.: x). Fundamentally, the substance of Mongolian citizenship for rural communities is in the balance, as corporate and state institutions and actors try to find collaborative solutions to the problem of local 'political risk' to mining projects. The ideal of multi-stakeholder negotiations is riven by local hierarchies around 'community' representation, not helped by the local perception of inequality in their treatment by different mining companies (ibid.: vi). As Crane, Matten and Moon (2008: 90) put it, 'The notion of a "stakeholder" is, on the surface, very simple, but at heart, deceptively complex'.

Despite being ubiquitous in corporate governance and management discourses, the process of determining 'what constitutes a legitimate stake, and how different stakes should be evaluated' (ibid.) is far from straightforward. As White (1996: 7) argues, there are two questions related to *who* participates and what *level* of participation a stake gives to its holder. This process-related complexity is particularly exacerbated when the concept is deployed beyond the boundaries of a corporate organisation, to include diverse groups of actors with *non-economic* stakes in the future of a mining project. Particularly when the coordinator or initiator of 'multi-stakeholder negotiations' is not local to the 'community,' there are serious risks that local complexities and hierarchies (e.g. gender, livelihood base, political affiliations, age) will not be recognised in the formulation of stakeholder groupings (see also Li, 2007: 192–229).

In this sense, the stakeholder concept is an *imposed* concept: it is not indigenous to local social or political institutions. The notion of 'stakeholding' has seeped into development policy and practice from its 'business-friendly' association with corporate norms, which infuse global governance standards. While the stakeholder framework may be appropriate for intra-organisational conflict in companies where employees are already *participants* in the organisation, it poses significant normative and practical problems when laid over pre-existing socio-political governance arrangements. For example, employee stakes in an organisation are mediated clearly by employment status and contractual relations with the employer. In contrast, the determination of stakeholder status for a project within a representative democratic system of national governance is a deeply ambivalent process. It is difficult to draw boundaries around the sphere of impact, particularly for large mining projects, and even when boundaries are decided upon, it is yet another ethical and practical question of how to engage stakeholders in a participatory process. Who is engaged? On what terms? Participation, as White

(1996: 7) argues, 'can take on multiple forms and serve many different interests'. Not only does the concept of stakeholder participation obscure the very *political* process of 'multi-stakeholder negotiations' in general, but more specifically displaces 'community' relations from their social context and into a new market-friendly arrangement. Despite the 'social' and 'community' discourse, these arrangements are a unique technique of governance for the purposes of protecting the mining economy from political risk. As Li (2007: 234) puts it, the emphasis on community in the governance of development projects belies a deeply political motivation, that of making 'collective existence intelligible and calculable' for the purposes of risk assessment.

Conclusion

CDAs have become prominent institutional mechanisms to address socio-political conflict produced by development projects. CDAs have been introduced in Mongolia by the central government to deal with the impacts of widespread mining on rural communities, and especially as a mandatory and limited form of redress in the wake of a crisis of foreign direct investment (2012–14). The timing is notable, considering that local communities had been overtly resistant to mining activities since the late 1990s and early 2000s, and vocal about their concerns regarding the socio-economic and environmental impacts from mining. Their demands for redress were not the ultimate impetus behind the introduction of CDAs. The central government's adoption of mandatory CDAs was part of a broader package of institutional reforms undertaken by the central government to resurrect investment confidence in the Mongolian mining sector in 2014 (see Lander 2019). CDAs were introduced by the national government in conjunction with the World Bank to respond to the concerns of *investors* about political risk at the project-level, allegedly caused by the resistant actions of rural residents and local governments. Reducing local-level political risk was a major component of the central government's plan to smooth processes of investment and extraction, as exemplified in the CDA model that has been instituted.

CDAs constitute a normative and institutional limit on the practice of citizenship in relation to the country's most political and contested economic sector. While CDAs do provide limited avenues for recourse and recognition in relation to development projects, they exacerbate the top-down structure of development by putting pressure on local elites and institutions to conform with investor and national-level interests. Consequently, they exemplify the depoliticising effects of community management strategies conceived by national governments and global financial institutions as they seek to secure stable conditions for extractive industry expansion. In the name of 'stakeholder engagement', and 'participatory governance', the material driver behind these initiatives remains conveniently veiled. CDAs present a stark reminder of the dangers of instrumental approaches to law and development which seek to use socio-political mechanisms to protect powerful market interests in the name of 'community.'

References

Amponsah, K. and Annor-Frempong, C., 2014. *Improving Public Expenditures in Agriculture: Empirical Evidence of the Effectiveness and Efficiency of Agricultural Public Expenditures in Mongolia*. World Bank Report for Mongolia's Ministry of Industry and Agriculture. Available online at: http://hdl.handle.net/10986/23359 (accessed 23 September 2019).

Anderson, G., 2005. *Constitutional Rights after Globalisation*. Hart Publishing.

Bawden, C.R. 1968/1989. *The Modern History of Mongolia*, 2nd edition. Kegan Paul International, Ltd.

Bebbington, A., 2011. *Social Conflict, Economic Development and Extractive Industry: Evidence from South America*. Routledge.

Bebbington, A., Hinojosa, L., Bebbington, D.H., Burneo, M.L. and Warnaars, X., 2008. Contention and Ambiguity: Mining and Possibilities of Development. *Development and Change*, *39* (*6*), 965–992.

Boikova, E., 1999. Aspects of Soviet-Mongolian Relations. In S. Kotkin and B. Elleman (eds), *Mongolia in the Twentieth Century: Landlocked Cosmopolitan*. Routledge, p. 107.

Buxton, A., 2012. MMSD+10: Reflecting on a Decade of Mining and Sustainable Development. Sustainable Markets Discussion Paper (June). International Institute for Environment and Development. Available online at: http://pubs.iied.org/pdfs/16041IIED.pdf (accessed 6 April 2017).

Byambajav, D., 2012. Mobilising Against Dispossession: Gold Mining and a Local Resistance Movement in Mongolia. *Journal of the Centre for Northern Humanities*, *5*, 13–32.

Byambajav, D., 2014. 'The River Movements' Struggle in Mongolia. *Social Movement Studies: Journal of Social, Cultural and Political Protest*, *14* (*1*), 92–97.

Byambajav, D., 2015. *Mining, 'Social License' and Local Level Agreements in Mongolia. Proceedings from the International Conference on Perspectives on the Development of Energy and Mineral Resources*. Hawai'i, Mongolia and Germany. 11–13 February 2015. Available online at: http://socialsciences.hawaii.edu/conference/demr2015/_papers/byambajav-dalaibuyan.pdf (accessed 6 August 2016).

Chatham House, 2013. *Revisiting Approaches to Community Relations in Extractive Industries: Old Problems, New Avenues?* Chatham House.

Combellick-Bidney, S., 2012. Mongolia's Mining Controversies and the Politics of Place. In J. Dierkes (ed.), *Change in Democratic Mongolia: Social Relations, Health, Mobile Pastoralism and Mining*. Brill.

Crane, A., Matten, D. and Moon, J., 2008. *Corporations and Citizenship*. Cambridge University Press.

Davis, R. and Franks, D., 2011. *The Costs of Conflict with Local Communities in the Extractive Industry*. Santiago, Chile, 19–21 October 2011. *Proceedings of the First International Seminar on Social Responsibility in Mining*.

Davis, R. and Franks, D., 2014. *Costs of Community–Company Conflict in the Extractive Sector*. Corporate Social Responsibility Initiative Report No. 66. Harvard Kennedy School.

Endicott, E., 2012. *A History of Land Use in Mongolia: The Thirteenth Century to the Present*. Palgrave Macmillan.

Enkhbaatar, C., Solongo, D., Amarjargal, P. and Ginsburg, T., 2015. The Role of the Constitution of Mongolia in Consolidating Democracy: An Analysis. United Nations Development Programme. Available online at: http://www.mn.undp.org/content/mongolia/en/home/library/democratic_governance/RoleoftheConstitutionofMongoliaInConsolidatingDemocracy.html (accessed 31 March 2017).

Equator Principles, 2017. The Equator Principles. Available online at: http://equator-principles.com (accessed 25 March 2017).

Erdenebolor, B. and Baigal, L., 2012. *Mining and Communities: Social Impacts and Stakeholder Interactions in Mining Areas of Mongolia.* Responsible Mining Initiative for Sustainable Development.

Fernandez-Gimenez, M., 2006. *Land Use and Land Tenure in Mongolia: A Brief History and Current Issues.* RMRS-P-39: 30–36. USDA Forest Service Proceedings.

Franks, D.M., Davis, R., Bebbington, A.J., Ali, S.H., Kemp, D. and Scurrah, M., 2014. Conflict Translates Environmental and Social Risk into Business Costs. *Proceedings of the National Academy of Sciences, 111 (21)*, 7576–7581.

Gill, S., 1998. New Constitutionalism, Democratisation and Global Political Economy. *Pacifica Review: Peace, Security and Global Change, 10 (1)*, 23–38.

Government of Mongolia, 1992. *Constitution of Mongolia.* ILO. Available online at: http://www.ilo.org/wcmsp5/groups/public/@ed_protect/@protrav/@ilo_aids/documents/legaldocument/wcms_117392.pdf (accessed 17 April 2017).

Government of Mongolia, 1994, 1997, 2006. Minerals Laws. In B. Ulziibayar and B. Tsetsenbileg (eds), *2010, Minerals Laws of Mongolia 1910–2010.* MBS Law Firm.

Government of Mongolia, 2013. *Investment Law.* Final Version, English translation published online by the Ministry of Foreign Affairs: https://www.mofa.gov.mn/new/images/banners/regulation/investmentlaw.pdf (accessed 26 April 2017).

Government of Mongolia, 2014. *State Policy on the Minerals Sector 2014–2025.* Appendix to Resolution No. 18, 2014 of the State Great Khural of Mongolia. English translation. Government of Mongolia.

Harvey, B. and Bice, S., 2014. Social Impact Assessment, Social Development Programmes and Social Licence to Operate: Tensions and Contradictions in Intent and Practice in the Extractive Sector. *Impact Assessment and Project Appraisal, 32 (4)*, 327–355.

Hatcher, P., 2014. *Regimes of Risk: The World Bank and the Transformation of Mining in Asia.* Palgrave Macmillan.

Hogan Lovells, 2014. Note on the Amendment to the Law of Mongolia on Minerals. Hogan Lovells. Available online at: https://www.hoganlovells.com/en/publications/note-on-the-amendment-to-the-law-of-mongolia-on-minerals-dated-1-july-2014 (accessed 25 April 2020).

Husband, C. and Songwe, V., 2004. *Mongolia Mining Sector: Managing the Future.* World Bank. Available online at: http://documents.worldbank.org/curated/en/867261468323101510/pdf/332480ENGLISH01ng1sector1report1ENG.pdf (accessed 30 March 2017).

ICMM (International Council of Mining and Metals), 2012. *Community Development Toolkit.* ICMM. Available online at: http://www.icmm.com/website/publications/pdfs/4080.pdf (accessed 15 March 2017).

IIED (International Institute for Environment and Development), 2002. *Breaking Ground: Mining, Minerals and Sustainable Development.* IIED. Available online at: http://pubs.iied.org/9084IIED (accessed 6 April 2017).

International Business Publications, 2013. *Mongolia: Mineral, Mining Sector Investment and Business Guide, Vol. 1 Strategic Information and Regulations.* International Business Publications.

Jackson, S.L., 2015. Imagining the Mineral Nation: Contested Nation-Building in Mongolia. *Nationalities Papers: The Journal of Nationalism and Ethnicity, 43* (*3*), 437–456.

Lander, J., 2014. A Critical Reflection on Oyu Tolgoi and the Risk of a Resource Trap in Mongolia: Troubling the 'Resource Nationalism' Frame. *Journal of Law, Social Justice & Global Development, 2013* (*2*). Available online at: https://warwick.ac.uk/fac/soc/law/elj/lgd/2013_2/2013_2_lander/lander_lgd_2013_2_pub02_2014-.pdf (accessed 25 April 2020).

Lander, J., 2017. The Law and Politics of Foreign Direct Investment, Democracy and Extractive Development in Mongolia: A Case Study of New Constitutionalism on the 'Final Frontier'. PhD Thesis. University of Warwick.

Lander, J., 2019. *Transnational Law and State Transformation: The Case of Extractive Development in Mongolia.* Routledge.

Li, T., 2007. *The Will to Improve: Governmentality, Development and the Practice of Politics.* Duke University Press.

Lkhagvadorj, A., 2010. Fiscal Federalism and Decentralisation in Mongolia. MPRA Paper 28758. University Library of Munich. Available online at: https://mpra.ub.uni-muenchen.de/28758/1/MPRA_paper_28758.pdf (accessed 4 April 2017).

Lkhagvadorj, A., 2012. An Analysis of the New Budget Law of Mongolia of 2011. MPRA Paper 38681. University Library of Munich. Available online at: https://mpra.ub.uni-muenchen.de/38681 (accessed 4 April 2017).

Mearns, R., 2004. Sustaining Livelihoods on Mongolia's Pastoral Commons: Insights from a Participatory Poverty Assessment. *Development and Change, 35* (*1*), 107–139.

Minter Ellison LLP, 2014. *High Level Overview: Amendments to the 2006 Minerals Law.* Minter Ellison LLP. Available online at: http://www.minterellison.com/files/uploads/documents/publications/articles/Pub_A_20142107_UB_Minteral_Law(2).pdf (accessed 31 March 2017).

O'Faircheallaigh, C., 2013. Community Development Agreements in the Mining Industry: An Emerging Global Phenomenon. *Community Development, 44* (*2*), 222–238.

Oyun, E., 2014. *Adding Value and Sharing the Wealth in Mongolia Mining.* The Worldfolio. Available at: http://www.worldfolio.co.uk/region/asia/mongolia/erdenebulgan-oyun-deputy-minister-of-mining-mongolia-n2639 (accessed 5 July 2015).

Reinert, E.S., 2000. Globalisation in the Periphery as a Morgenthau Plan; The Underdevelopment of Mongolia in the 1990s: Why Globalisation is One Man's Food and Another Man's Poison. In S. Lhagva (ed.), *Mongolian Development Strategy; Capacity Building.* Mongolian Development Research Centre.

Rossabi, M., 2005. *Mongolia: From Khans to Commissars to Capitalists.* University of California Press.

Schneiderman, D., 2013. *Resisting Economic Globalisation: Critical Theory and International Investment Law*. Palgrave Macmillan.

Sneath, D., 2003. Land-Use, the Environment and Development in Post-Socialist Mongolia. *Oxford Development Studies*, *31* (*4*), 441–459.

Suzuki, Y., 2013. Conflict Between Mining Development and Nomadism in Mongolia. In N. Yamamura, N. Fujita, and A. Maekawa (eds), *The Mongolian Eco-System Network: Environmental Issues Under Climate and Social Changes.* Springer, p. 269.

UNDP (United Nations Development Programme), 2007. *Employment and Poverty in Mongolia*. UNDP. Available online at: http://www.mn.undp.org/content/mongolia/en/home/library/National-Human-Development-Reports/mongolia-human-development-report-2007.html (accessed 11 November 2017).

Upton, C., 2012. Mining, Resistance and Pastoral Livelihoods in Contemporary Mongolia. In J. Dierkes (ed.), *Change in Democratic Mongolia: Social Relations, Health, Mobile Pastoralism and Mining*. Brill, p. 223.

White, Sarah, 1996. Depoliticising Development: The Uses and Abuses of Participation. *Development in Practice*, *6* (*1*), 6–15.

World Bank, 2017. *The World Bank in Mongolia: Overview*. World Bank. Available online at: http://www.worldbank.org/en/country/mongolia (accessed 11 November 2017).

Index

For Product Safety Concerns and Information please contact our EU representative GPSR@taylorandfrancis.com
Taylor & Francis Verlag GmbH, Kaufingerstraße 24, 80331 München, Germany

www.ingramcontent.com/pod-product-compliance
Ingram Content Group UK Ltd.
Pitfield, Milton Keynes, MK11 3LW, UK
UKHW022132190926
475702UK00013B/1773
9780367528003